Bernard McGinn—Associate Professor of Historical
Theology and History of Christianity, University of Chicago
Divinity School, Chicago, Ill.

John Meyendorff—Professor of Church History, Fordham
University, Bronx, N.Y., and Professor of Patristics and Church
History, St. Vladimir's Seminary, Tuckahoe, N.Y.

Seyyed Hossein Nasr—Professor of Islamics, Department of
Religion, Temple University, Philadelphia, Pa., and Visiting Professor,
Harvard University, Cambridge, Ma.

Heiko A. Oberman—Director, Insititue fuer
Spaetmittelalter and Reformation, Universitaet Tuebingen, West
Germany.

Alfonso Ortiz—Professor of Anthropology, University of
New Mexico, Albuquerque, N. Mex.; Fellow, The Center for
Advanced Study, Stanford, Calif.

Raimundo Panikkar—Professor, Department of Religious
Studies, University of California at Santa Barbara, Calif.

Jaroslav Pelikan—Sterling Professor of History and Religious
Studies, Yale University, New Haven, Conn.

Fazlar Rahman—Professor Islamic Thought, Department of Near
Eastern Languages and Civilization, University of
Chicago, Chicago, Ill.

Annemarie B. Schimmel—Professor of Hindu Muslim Culture,
Harvard University, Cambridge, Mass.

Sandra M. Schneiders—Assistant Professor of New
Testament Studies and Spirituality, Jesuit School of Theology,
Berkeley, Calif.

Huston Smith—Thomas J. Watson Professor of Religion,
Adjunct Professor of Philosophy, Syracuse University, Syracuse, N.Y.

John R. Sommerfeldt—Professor of History, University of
Dallas, Irving, Texas.

David Steindl-Rast—Monk of Mount Savior Monastery,
Pine City, N.Y.

William C. Sturtevant—General Editor, Handbook of North
American Indians, Smithsonian Institution, Washington, D.C.

David Tracy—Professor of Theology, University of Chicago
Divinity School, Chicago, Ill.

Victor Turner—William B. Kenan Professor in
Anthropology, The Center for Advanced Study, University of
Virginia, Charlottesville, Va.

Kallistos Ware—Fellow of Pembroke College, Oxford;
Spalding Lecturer in Eastern Orthodox Studies, Oxford
University, England.

Jacopone da Todi
The Lauds

TRANSLATED BY
SERGE AND ELIZABETH HUGHES

INTRODUCTION BY
SERGE HUGHES

PREFACE BY
ELÉMIRE ZOLLA

PAULIST PRESS
NEW YORK • RAMSEY • TORONTO

Cover Art:
The artist, LIAM ROBERTS, was born in Ireland and now lives in New York. After attending the National College of Art in Dublin for five years, he studied at the Academy of Fine Arts in Florence, at the Royal Academy of San Fernando in Madrid, and at the Academy of Fine Arts in Rome for one year each on scholarship.

Design: Barbini, Pesce & Noble, Inc.

Library of Congress
Catalog Card Number: 81-84069

ISBN: 0-8091-0323-0 (Cloth)
       0-8091-2375-4 (Paper)

Published by Paulist Press
545 Island Road, Ramsey, N.J. 07446

Printed and bound in the
United States of America

CONTENTS

For Bill Bryar,
parce que c'était lui, parce que c'était moi.

Our thanks are due to those who, in diverse tongues and ways, were of great help and comfort in the preparation of this manuscript, in particular: Theano Albert, G. L. J. Smerillo, Dom Charles Fitzsimons, Profs. Giuliano and Vittoria Bonfante, Prof. George Peck and Prof. Ignazio Baldelli.

Translators of this Volume

SERGE HUGHES, who has published extensively in modern Italian political-intellectual history (*The Fall and Rise of Modern Italy*, Macmillan, 1967) and contemporary Italian literary criticism, has long had an interest in Franciscana. He was responsible for the New American Library edition of *The Little Flowers of Saint Francis and Other Franciscan Writings*, a 1964 translation and study of those texts. He has also done work on Renaissance literature and religious thought (*The Essential Montaigne*, New American Library, 1970, as well as the more recent *Catherine of Genoa*, Classics of Western Spirituality, Paulist Press, 1979). He has been on the editorial board of the quarterly *Cross Currents* since the early 1950s. At present he is at work on a study of the theatre of Manzoni.

ELIZABETH HUGHES, in addition to collaborating extensively with her husband in his Italian studies over the past thirty years, has translated Jacques Maritain's *The Peasant of the Garonne* (Holt, Rinehart & Winston, 1960), *Man and Ethics* by Paul Bénichou (Doubleday, 1971) and Francis Jeanson's *Sartre dans sa vie* (Sheed, Andrews & McMeel, not yet published), as well as numerous articles of a philosophical-theological nature from both Italian and French. She is now working on a translation of Manzoni's *Conte di Carmagnola.*

Author of the Preface

ELÉMIRE ZOLLA was born in 1926 of mixed parentage, in Turin. He read law, wrote literary criticism, and worked for a period as a freelance writer. Later he taught American literature and Germanic philology at various Italian universities, finally becoming chairman of American literature at the University of Rome. Among other works in the academic field, he wrote on Anglo-Saxon runes and surveyed the literary images of the American Indian (*The Writer and the Shaman*, Harcourt Brace, 1973), the result of a journey through the Southwest.

He became well known in the 1950s for his works of fiction and social criticism (e.g., *The Eclipse of the Intellectual*, Funk & Wagnall, 1968), but the 1960s marked a change of direction for him. After a long retreat he devoted his efforts to the illustration of spiritual life, gathering the documentation for what developed into the most extensive available anthology of Western mysticism, comprising the Ethiopian and Syriac schools. The paperback seven-volume second edition, *I mistici dell' Occidente*, appeared from 1976 to 1980 (Rizzoli, Milan). Since 1969 he has edited the quarterly *Conoscenza religiosa* (La Nuova Italia, Florence), which has published through the years a group of spiritual masters, students, and poets from all countries who happen to share the idea of an ecumenical convergence of the paths, and who cherish metaphysical inspiration in the arts. Zolla has traveled through Taiwan, Bali, India, and Iran in search of living sources of wisdom, gathering material for his journal. He has researched particularly the alchemical tradition. His vast and important *Le meraviglie della natura* (Bompiani, 1976) is a general introduction to alchemy, giving an alchemical interpretation of passages in Petrarch and other Italian classics.

Since 1976 he has written mostly in English. Besides his crucial summation of metaphysics (*Archetypes*, Allen & Unwin, 1981; U.S. edition, Harcourt Brace Jovanovich, forthcoming) there have appeared two pamphlets with Golgonooza, the English press (*Language and Cosmogony*, 1973, and *The Uses of Imagination*, 1975), and an illustrated text, *The Androgyne* (Thames & Hudson, Crossroad 1981).

Preface

Even more than in the mainstream of Italian literature, Jacopone belongs with an insulated peasant subculture that became extinct only quite recently. Ten years ago in Italy Jacopone's like were still to be found—laymen or friars, mothers, "house nuns" or cloistered sisters, who had been blessed with vision and had acquired a knowledge of spiritual reality. A possible place to meet them would have been on one of the pilgrims' buses lumbering up and down the bends of the spiral that connects the holy spots of the Franciscan saga from Greccio to Gubbio. Their eight-centuries-old brand of piety is mostly unrecorded. Its literature of pathetic pamphlets (*Records of Graces Bestowed*), its village painting (*For Grace Received*) drifting clumsily back to the icon, all its quaint testimonials, have failed to amuse collectors. And yet this was the Italian version of what is known in India as *deśa prajña* ("village wisdom").

Jacopone was its prototype. Though he was certainly well read, he appeared indistinguishable from an intense peasant believer. He defined a rustic tone in piety that was to endure.

The various motifs that make up his story persisted through the centuries. He set a pattern. Padre Pio's protests about the Roman Curia are reminiscent of Jacopone's rebuffs. The chief point in Jacopone's writings with which theologians took issue, the possibility of a beatific vision in the technical sense, was still being debated well into the 1950s, in the case of the house nun Lucia Mangano.

The Jacoponean subculture has vanished, the simple souls and astute minds, the glaring gazes and the gruff voices are no longer available, and there is nothing living at which one may point to illustrate at least in part the human enigma that was Jacopone.

What appears so intriguing in him is the glaring contrast between the man and the mystic. The former is not only simple but even downright churlish. At times his pious ejaculations are shallow, and make dull reading. This shows all the more in this faithful modern English version, which peels off from the text its superimposed patina of noble bluntness—which is only the deceptive effect of Medieval Umbrian on a philologically untrained Italian ear. The wording and the sounds as such originally conveyed only homeliness, not the rough-hewn grandiosity that nowadays is read into them.

Not only is the reader put off by occasionally coarse singsong sermonizing or by ditties good for whipping up cheap feelings at Franciscan rallies; Jacopone's growling and snarling and scoffing can be more than we may wish to condone, especially when he starts on a bout of woman-baiting. He is then at his worst, boorish and shrill—even if the genre can be traced back to Tertullian and was considered ordinary stock padding for sermons. At the peak of his harangue, he strikes out into what may seem sheer lunacy, inveighing at the hussies who, prompted by vanity, pinch and tug into shape their baby daughters' crooked little noses. Or is he offering us a tidbit of Medieval burlesque, to top his grim invective with a quirk and a guffaw?

Jacopone must have been very effective, especially when he set out to make his listeners weep. He *was* all one with his public. He sensed the lurking national theatrical instinct, and improvised duets between the characters of the Passion; this was the beginning of the dramatic laud, the first step toward melodrama. It is praised by the ordinary historian as a highly meritorious deed. It can also be viewed in reverse perspective, as a departure from the omnicomprehensive, metaphysical art form of the liturgy, the stately pantomime, which is also a poem of sublime quotations and a plainsong rendition of purely spiritual notions. The laud itself can be seen as a fall from unction to sentimentality, from collectness to gush, from absorption to emotionalism. It was a demonstrative aside, a departure from hieratic restraint, a raw, brash appeal to feelings, a recoil from the complexities of meditation.

When all is said, there remains to be added that Jacopone was one of the world's great spiritual masters. The rustic with a flair for dramatization becomes, at the turn of a phrase, a smiling, enraptured saint whispering to us the highest, the boldest metaphysical truths. It just happens, the twist is unaccountable—suddenly he is lifted "to the third sky." Then we leaf on through the poems, and the seraph who has just given instruction in the art of achieving supreme quietude turns into a wrathful zealot breathing hot, unmistakable hatred at his political foe, Pope Boniface VIII. There is no transition between contradictory levels of consciousness. Mystical rapture and animal directness, sublime spiritual enlightenment and devotional trivia appear simply juxtaposed, black and white.

Leaving aside the psychological puzzle of his unfathomable inner split, the cumulative effect of Jacopone's lauds is that of Giotto's frescos, which departed from the holy composure and the fine shadings of the icon, turning painting into a matter of stark, huge bulks dented by downright shadows, of human features either solemn or laughing or turned awry with pain—a universe where nothing is graded, developed into nuance. One has to accept the same absence of shading in Jacopone, and leave him unexplained. To read him is like visiting certain villages of his Umbrian homeland, perched on a rock, their steep, winding passageways burrowing up and down in the damp dusk between towering stone-built houses. Then, at a corner, the lurid grimness changes to sweet peace and grace, as the outlying sunny slopes come into sight, gently rising and falling, checkered pastel greens and olive grays.

On his heavenly side, Jacopone was primarily a master of incantation. His cadences can swirl up into supracosmic bliss, and he shows us how this is done. One charged word is reiterated until it becomes more than a word, and as a mantra it triggers an upshooting spiral of rapture. This takes place in the laud "*O jubelo del core,*" with the word *jubelo* ("jubilation") so richly laden with reminiscences of the Psalms (Christopher Smart was to exploit its possibilities in *Jubilate Agno*).

Jacopone is suggesting that while we repeat incessantly *jubelo,* we fan up a sensation of warmth in the heart. As the warmth increases, the repetition should become an impassioned wail, till the heart is rocked by sweet exultation. Then one will discover himself shouting at the top of his voice, all shame forsaken and forgotten.

The various phases of the invocation, the stirring up of inner heat, the mounting swell and the final letting go that burns out our sense of shame, are not only described but also metrically imitated by shifts in rhythm. Only the English Medieval mystic Richard Rolle offers, in the West, a more detailed instruction in this peculiar technique, which links the increase of inner warmth to a vortical song.

It is not by chance that dervish methods come to one's mind. Jacopone's innovations in metrics have in fact been traced to Spanish Sufi songs.

PREFACE

The itinerant members of the sect of the Spirituals, to which Jacopone belonged, were haunting the parvises of churches in Italy, the Rhineland, and Flanders, while Sufi mendicants squatted in the porches of Spanish mosques. Spirituals and Sufis used common catchwords, and sang them to the very same beat. Both rejoiced in being despised, both insisted on intoxication. (One even surprises Jacopone using the Qur'anic disparagement of man as "issued from a fetid drop.")

Many Sufis dreamed of a supernatural Dame and it was probably they who passed the tradition on to Tuscan adepts. The otherworldly Bride is a feature of nearly all mystical experience. Among the Franciscans the betrothal was known and practiced in the modified version established by Francis's engagement to Dame Poverty. This is the crucial premise that underlies Jacopone's lauds, and is central to all early Franciscan mysticism.

Especially in central Italy, the Christian ideal of poverty appeared to be on the wane; the old austere, frugal way of life was threatened. New longings stirred people's hearts; one now relished the touch of soft silks, the varied flavors of spices; one hankered after festal parades and displays of striking dresses and ornaments. Glamour and lavishness seemed to be the gist of life; they called for money, as money was attracted to them. "Conspicuous consumption," caprice and taste, enhanced prestige, which fetched loans. Credit was a shorter cut to wealth than thrift and labor. This was the trend when Francis stripped in public to mark the recoil and publish his love of Poverty. The reel of history appeared as a backlash. Francis refused even to take shelter under a roof; he slashed his needs to a minimum.

He married Poverty. This was not a figure of speech. It meant a living experience on the level of active imagination, which is more than real, being reality-giving. Francis lived essentially, primarily on that level (he tripped lightly on stones, because they symbolized the stone the builders discarded, Christ the capstone). He truly wedded Poverty—in a reality-giving sense. Franciscan painters strove to represent what had taken place. Perhaps Sassetta was the most successful. In his *Betrothal to Dame Poverty* (at the Chantilly Condé Museum), robed Saint Francis is shown in the act of plunging forward to place a ring on Poverty's finger. In the scene, bodies are defined by arching lines and seem made of a weightless, swaying substance. The colors are pure, a range of ochers and soft browns, a long streak of coral, a long curve of pearl, which outlines Poverty herself.

PREFACE

The spiritual event of Francis's betrothal was a source of inspiration in all spheres. The cult of poverty provided a medicine for souls, a key to the Gospels, a program for commonwealths, instruction to magistrates, guidelines for householders, laws for the cloister, and advice to the Church. Itinerant preachers like Jacopone, in the name of Poverty, sped through the land, striking shame into the hearts of the spendthrift and vain.

It was a time when all claim to authority had to be founded in mystical visions. Their import, however, when drawn down to earth and put into practice, became unclear. Franciscanism often tied up with underground Messianic sects. Probably these infiltrated the Spirituals. Messianism shades off into antinomianism, which throws open here and now to adepts the gates of the Realm of the Free Spirit. The Inquisition suspected unspeakable evil all around and claimed to unearth what we may call Western versions of the left-hand path. In keeping with this climate of ideas, Jacopone swung from Messianic commitment and action to a jubilant celebration of the mystic's paradise on earth. The backdrop was always the cult of poverty. He explored its implications globally. Economic poverty was a symbol, a pledge, a pawn; its benefits were reaped in one's inner life, where Poverty scoured the mind, emptying it of all sensations, feelings, and ideals, making it so poor that it could finally identify with nothingness. On nothingness *(nichilitate)* Jacopone performs the same transmutations as on *jubelo,* using it as a mantra. Like Eckhart in Germany, Jacopone insisted that he who becomes poor in this sense attains to true freedom, willing nothing, knowing nothing, containing nothing, loving without affection, understanding without knowledge.

In another of Francis's followers, Egidio of Assisi, this meant standing beside his own body and observing it from the outside (Martin Buber selected the scene as the illustration of Franciscan mysticism in his anthology of ecstatic experiences). With Jacopone it meant that he saw the revolving world, laden with sin, rolling in space beneath him.

Poverty equals nothingness and nothingness equals quietude. Jacopone selects for rapt repetition the word *quietude* along with *jubilation* and *nothingness.* The quieted soul has nothing in common with the "stench" below—and even when it traverses ugliness, it remains blameless. From its spiritual coign of vantage, the restless psychic world or "subtle reality" appears like a revolving wheel in which pride kindles envy, which flames up in anger, which, once consumed, turns to cold sloth, which in the next round hardens once more into pride; and the drab old story starts all over again. It would be unthinkable for a liberated, quieted soul to ever come back to all this. Nor can it allow its body to revert like an automaton to the sullen ticktock of gluttony turning to lechery, of lechery stirring up gluttony. This last point brings out the enormous distance between Jacopone, his epoch and his subculture, and ourselves. What to him are sins of the body become in modern times essentially psychic conditionings, peculiar forms of mental restlessness. However, discounting the time lag, Jacopone's chart of the ordinary human condition is a masterpiece in the mystical tradition that insists on the realization of unawakened man's mechanical nature.

He added this superb variation on the theme: Man is a sea ravaged by winds blowing from the four quarters, the frosty north wind of fear, the hectic south wind of hope, the west wind of sorrows, and the east wind of glee. The liberated, emptied, quiet soul has no share in this wildly crashing or deceitfully slumbering sea, for it knows not fear of hell, it harbors no hope of heaven, and as it bewails not misfortune so it is not puffed up by success. Egidio of Assisi had boldly explained that the soul that sees God loses faith.

Jacopone was taking his risks when he dared to pen poems about ultimate liberation. In those years Marguerite de la Porée was tried and sentenced for stating that she had forsaken goodness for quietude. Jacopone went even further.

One is tempted to imagine that, while composing lauds "for the consolation and profit of novices," he was flashing out signals, hints to the few who might be turned into adepts.

The Virgin in the lauds would seem at first sight to be only the ideal figure of Compassion, both *the* compassionate and *the* compassion-deserving, but there is a line in which she is called the mother, the daughter, and also the wife of her son. As the arch-unifier of opposites, in which all human bounds are transcended, she becomes the mediator of liberation. Dante's and Petrarch's hymns to Mary will not dare to mention the divine marriage of Mother and Son.

At times Jacopone will toss into an ordinary context disclosures about the soul's formlessness or the possibility that it return to the "primal form," or that it rise and sit on God's throne. With God enthroned, it shall drink of God and be drunk by God "in transformation." What Jacopone means here is nothing less than a transforma-

PREFACE

tion into God, whereby the mystic becomes "both the woman and the lord"—androgyne as God in God, a rare doctrine, fraught with danger and highly suspect to the uncomprehending.

The betrothal to Poverty, the pivotal experience from which all of Franciscan mysticism flowed, was perceived by each devotee according to the peculiar mode of his calling. Jacopone insisted particularly on "enamored Poverty" leading to lordship, *signoria*. It conferred lordship over everything. His theme of the universe revolving below the liberated soul shades into that of Empire: "Mine are France and England," he declares, mentioning in succession all the names of lands, towns, and rivers that occur to him, inebriate with the endless list of his domains. He feels all-possessing, and as with Dante's universal emperor, owning everything, human greed can no longer enter his heart. All is his for his amusement, to make him jolly—a playful God to whom angels sing, since his will is God's own!

We reach the stage of the journey in which Oneness is achieved—the seventh, in Richard of Saint Victor's itinerary. Up here, Jacopone comments, God as love is that love with which the heart loves Him.

—Elémire Zolla

Foreword

The *Lauds* of Jacopone da Todi, the most powerful religious poetry in Italy before Dante's time, has until now, to the best of the translators' knowledge, appeared only in partial and dated translations; and it is not until recently that the corpus of the poetry as it appeared originally, without additions and counterfeit versions, has been available to us.

Their author is one of the more remarkable poets of the Middle Ages or indeed of any time. Lyrical, swashbuckling, togaed and flippant, coarsely blunt, learnedly simple, as passionate in his search for God and the true self as he is in his defense of holy poverty against the world, the papacy, and those members of the Franciscan Order who interpreted that teaching differently, Jacopone casts a violent and many-hued light on his inner world and that which surrounded him.

Born sometime between 1230 and 1236 in Todi of an aristocratic family at a time when Umbria, together with other parts of central and northern Italy, was experiencing a cultural-economic rebirth, the young Jacopone, after a period of studies in Bologna, married Vanna di Bernardino di Guidone and gave every sign of settling down to life as a *notaio*, a profession that combined elements of law and accounting. On the death of his wife, for reasons that are more or less plausibly conjectural, he turned his back on his previous existence and became a *bizzocone*, a ragged public penitent. This experience, similar in many respects to that of the Spirituals, those Franciscans who opposed the prevailing and more latitudinarian Conventual interpretation of the Rule, lasted for ten years. A good number of the penitential and meditative lauds are very probably of this period, and it is in these years that Jacopone won fame as a holy man, albeit a somewhat singular one. In 1278, at a time when the conflict between

xix

the Conventuals and the Spirituals was intense (four years after the death of Saint Bonaventure, who had done his utmost but failed to come to a universally acceptable resolution of the question of holy poverty), Jacopone became a Friar Minor. Increasingly appalled at the mounting corruption, Jacopone—principally through Francis and the mystical theology of Saint Bonaventure—deepened his Christocentric meditation.

The election of the holy hermit Pier da Morrone to the papacy in July 1294, after more than two years of wrangling among the cardinals, heartened many Spirituals but did not allay Jacopone's mounting fears. Though together with other Spirituals he appealed to the new pope, Celestine V, and was granted protection against the Conventuals, Jacopone's misgivings were not placated. He had intense doubts as to whether the new pope would find the strength to ward off the insidious corruption all about him. The dramatic and unexpected abdication of Celestine five months after his coronation heightened the poet's terrors, and when Cardinal Benedetto Gaetani ascended the throne of Peter in December 1294, Jacopone's obedience approached the breaking point. For his greed, nepotism, and arrogance the new pope appeared to the poet as the Antichrist.

The poems of this period range from lamentations on the state of the Church to visions of imminent apocalypse, from warnings to Celestine V to attacks on Boniface VIII, and include some of the "dark night of the soul" lauds. Here, too, though, as in the case of some of the exuberant lauds, it is impossible to date the poems precisely.

In affixing his signature to the Longhezza Manifesto of 1297, Jacopone and other Spirituals joined with the Cardinals Colonna in their rebellion against Boniface VIII, and in this challenge to the validity of his election the poet severed his traditional Franciscan ties of obedience to the papacy. The rebellion was short-lived. In less than two years Boniface routed the Colonnas, and Jacopone, captured, was condemned to life imprisonment in an underground cell in a monastery in Todi.

His pleas for a pardon ignored by Boniface VIII, Jacopone was released from his underground cell by Boniface's successor, Benedict XI, in 1303 and spent his last years with the friars attached to the Convent of San Lorenzo in Collazzone. He died in 1306, ten years after the death of Celestine and three after that of Boniface VIII.

The great mystical lauds of Jacopone, his highest utterance, belong to this last decade of his life, as do the intensely autobiographical lauds, which have few rivals in prison literature of that or any other time. It is in this last period, in his crushing defeat, that Jacopone's poetry rises to a Franciscan height and takes on an astounding variety of colors.

In the Introduction the author has chosen to limit himself to one very specific problem in his approach to the *Lauds*, the question of the relationship between poetry and the mystical-religious experience of the poet. This particular perspective may appear to some readers much too narrow and of very limited help. Others (the twenty-five readers of Manzoni!) may find it actually of some use. If as a result of leafing through this Introduction those readers gain some insight into the uniqueness, the intense individuality of Jacopone's utterance as well as its Everyman resonances, the work of the author of these notes will have been done. As the reader climbs his way up-country in this stony landscape, the discoveries that he makes of hollows and still deeper lights will be his own.

Introduction:
Toward a First
Reading of the *Lauds*

I   THE PROBLEMS

There is so much that we do not understand about poetry. No
other utterance, we know, gives more lasting dimensions to our be-
liefs than that spiraling intertwining of music, image, and conviction.
Yet we cannot see into the depths of that magical fusion, we do not
understand how it can transmute any subject matter into a presence.
To the last, the hold that poetry has on us remains something of a
mystery.

This dark aura that edges the center of poetical utterance be-
comes almost palpable when we seek to translate that light into terms
other than itself. It becomes all the more so when we try to share a
poetry to which we are very drawn with others who are less so. Then
we sense with a rush the inadequacies of all such translations and the
dilemma we find ourselves in as we redouble our efforts to that end.
For in singling out and isolating the elements of poetry so as to see
more deeply into it, we risk making its spirit more difficult to recog-
nize. And if we strive to counterbalance that tendency and give an
immediate response to that poetry in order to capture its spirit, we
run into other and no less deceitful successes. Like the man running
at full speed with a hang glider so as to be swept up in his leap and
borne aloft by the right air current, we run the risk that our flight
will be short-lived.

Our dreams may be Faustian, our reach is not; and in accepting
our allotted horizon, one for all its vastness, we pay poetry proper

1

INTRODUCTION

homage. For none of us responds with equal intensity to the many voices of poetry. We distinguish between the words we appreciate and those we stand in need of, and in so doing we define ourselves. In favoring the perspective from one particular window, though, we are not under any compulsion to pass by others with only a cursory glance. To deepen our love of the familiar and pause before the powerful denials of that which we hold most dear, to give ear to the utterance that reveals us to ourselves but not be deaf to other voices that force us to question ourselves anew, that is the need in us that makes of old men explorers. This openness of response, the attenuation of all that divides us one from the other, is the least we owe to poetry of some dimensions. We owe as much to the *Lauds* of Jacopone—and we have not consistently met that obligation.

Not that studies of Jacopone's work are scarce or of little value. In the last half of the nineteenth century and almost until the 1920s the problem of the locus of the poetry, its inner form, was very much discussed. In more recent times, from the early 1940s down to our day, the interest has shifted to the question of the elements of that utterance—its theological-political aspects as well as its more specifically literary dimensions—and the excellence of contemporary critical editions of the text attest to the value of this work.

And yet in spite of these contributions there is something quite recognizably askew in the prevailing appreciation of the *Lauds* in our day. Even among careful readers there is a tendency to take tools designed to facilitate our response to the spirit of this poetry and make them ends in themselves. This would be understandable if recent scholarship had turned the work into a testing ground for literary theories unconcerned with the question of the spirit of that poetry. This, however, is not the case. How, then, are we to account for the widespread current appreciation of the *Lauds* as a splendidly simple utterance, a poetry that makes limited demands on us? The question points to involved answers, but those complexities are traceable to one core difficulty. In our time, no less than in any time past, it is difficult to concentrate on the highest moments of the poetry of Jacopone, a violent quest for the kingdom of God, mottled and radiant in its diverse moments. The poetical-spiritual center of the *Lauds* makes prodigious demands on us. It is hard enough with respect to a poetry of the past that sings of forgotten gods to work out a balance between our convictions and that temporary act of faith which makes that poetry our own; what, then, of the poetry of a belief that is distant and close, that belongs to a past and also to the present, an enduring sign of contradiction? This difficulty, a stumbling block of considerable size, can be circumvented and indeed often is. Some do so by claiming that when all is said and done only the reader in whom aesthetic considerations are supplanted by religious ones can respond to the poetry of Jacopone. This solution, however, almost necessarily brings with it second thoughts. For merely to allow for the chance that among those who respond to the *Lauds* there might be some whose aesthetic sensibilities match their religious is to completely undo the argument. And is it so difficult, after all, for readers with religious sensibilities to distinguish between doctrinal truths and poetry, to grasp the difference between religious fervor and poetical utterance? Do readers of the *Lauds* with some sympathy for their tonality have to make very strenuous efforts to recognize and admit that as poetry the utterance of Jacopone occasionally leaves something to be desired?

In fact, such readers have no trouble in agreeing that misgivings are indeed called for. Were Jacopone a poet in the highest sense of the word, turning the pages of the *Lauds* would be quite a different experience for all readers. The work, however, is what it is—a rough-textured coat of many colors, with nothing in it of the ideal of seamless beauty. The poems as a whole, manifestly, do not cast a spell over us. Their beauty is not that of incantation, that luxuriant intertwining of music and image that almost drowns the word. There are lauds that soar, but their flight has a different arch.

Indeed Jacopone, whose meter and rhyme are that of the craftsman, has an erratic sense of pitch, tone, and musical line. Nothing is more alien to the lauds than *"de la musique avant toute chose."* We do not recite those lines out loud to ourselves for the echoes they evoke in us—and particularly in the first part of the collection, where rhyme and meter, more often than not, trot along slowly. As we move further on, admittedly, the rhythms become quicker and more varied. Colors glow. Rhyme and meter acquire a cutting edge, a sharpness we do not forget. Toward the close, in the last great mystical odes, that music in its alternation of the hushed and the rhapsodic, turns into a melodious presence. Yet in spite of this ascending scale, for all of the magnificence of its high point, the place of music in the *Lauds* as a whole is that of a humble handmaiden.

The images in the *Lauds*, for their part, are not more compelling.

INTRODUCTION

Jacopone is not the poet to "set the lake on fire." Studies in shades of black, the poems of the first part have cumulative power but individually they tend to fall into the monotonous. Here too, though, the lines become progressively more animated, sinuous; and at certain points, as in the laments over the corruption in the Church, they gash. In the mystical lauds, the striving to voice the inexpressible gives rise to forcefully contrasting images, some splendidly carnal, others tenuous, luminously evanescent. As in the case of musical line, however, in spite of these glowing moments the role of image remains subordinate.

Thus, we continue to turn to this work after seven centuries above all because of the mottled word of Jacopone, his multifaceted meanings, the twists and turns of his descent into the self, his wrestling with God. And we have trouble understanding the drama of this poetry because it unfolds within a strikingly individualistic experience of Christ, one set in a complicated Franciscan world of the Middle Ages with all of its poetical and doctrinal ambiguities. Given the nature of this craggy terrain, one would wish at times that among the rewards for first seeking the Kingdom of God Jacopone had received more of a pied piper's gift for music. Alas, this is not the case.

Yet if it is the word, the meaning, that so utterly dominates in the *Lauds* and is the very grain of the wood, does this not bring us full circle back to the point where we were tempted to conclude that only those in strong sympathy with the spirituality of Jacopone could wholeheartedly respond to his utterance? It does, but this is something of an optical illusion. With respect to the notion of a *wholehearted* response, those who can give the fullness of consent, doctrinal and aesthetic, are obviously in a privileged position; but there is on aesthetic grounds alone ample justification for a common response from very divergent points of view.

There are degrees of unbelief, and though a response to the poetry of the *Lauds* in this spirit remains to the last something of a mystery, it is possible to distinguish between those paths that lead to an understanding of that poetry and those that lead away from it, provided we seek in Jacopone's work what we seek in any authentic poetry—insights of such authority that they challenge us to deepen or revise or modify basic beliefs. In a reading of a number of lauds, and particularly those that dig into the self with bruised, raw hands to bring to light all that which is counterfeit and hollow within, such a

4

INTRODUCTION

response will be effortless. In a similar way, the tumultuous moral passion of Jacopone, its defiance of brute power and hypocrisy, whatever our ultimate conclusions on the meaning of the various moments of that struggle, is bound to evoke long reverberations within us. And even though the explorations of Jacopone in the realm of faith, by comparison, make for great difficulties, their culminating moments, the mystical love songs, cannot but give us pause. The ring of authentic experience is not to be denied.

To recognize these positive approaches is, of course, also to realize how confusing other directions can be. Jacopone's utterance, so reminiscent of the horse and rider sculptures of Marino Marini in their struggle and precarious serenity, cannot, for example, be put to decorative use. Nor can we get far by considering the poetry of the *Lauds* as indissolubly linked to a stage of knowledge long since superseded. The work has been read in this key, of course, but the results are not brilliant. An alternative approach, more truly and humbly agnostic in its refusal to assign a fixed place to the religious or literary experience, is far more perceptive—and this, too, has been documented. By itself this refusal to draw the map of knowledge in a once-and-for-all spirit constitutes a solid common ground; and if readers do not preclude the possibility that the horse may be as real, palpable, and mysterious as the rider—if they allow that the *Lauds*, in short, *may* be the account of a struggle and a triumph that is not an unconscious self-deception—then in truth they will come to a common ground though they come from the ends of the earth.

Too all-inclusive for some and excessively narrow for others, this convergence of approaches will, of course, exasperate the apologist of common sense. Should this Introduction fall into his hands, accordingly, he should quickly put it aside. These pages will be of limited interest to him, and their basic premise that the revelation of Christ and the probings of literature go far beyond the established boundaries of common sense will merely bolster his conviction that in this instance, too, as in so many others, the notion of any possible agreement, or even collaboration, between those with such divergent views is utter nonsense.

In fact, however—*pace* the apologists of common sense—there have been more than a few signs for some time now of a common, indeed chivalric, reading of Jacopone's text. Sympathy for this poetry has not kept religiously oriented readers from acknowledging very specific flaws. The *Lauds* (and who could deny it?) often sag under an excess of argumentation. With some frequency allegory and doctrinal concerns stifle Jacopone's imagination. On some occasions the poet diminishes poetry and piety by having rhyme and meter substitute for both. A genuine flair for dialogue and monologue again and again peters out with the close of a laud because of either heavy-handed moralism or a *deus ex machina* solution. Even a number of the mystical lauds, entangled in theological constructs and labyrinthian symbolism, remain earthbound.

All very true, fair-minded nonbelievers have pointed out, but not the whole truth. A number of the dramatic monologues bring to mind Browning; and certain of the dialogues have been rightfully recognized as precursors of religious drama. The tendency to allegorize and philosophize, no doubt, has drawbacks, but that is the unavoidable risk involved in bracing vision with something stronger than passion. Jacopone's gift for the sculptured word, after all, is connected to his habit of thought. And though, admittedly, rhymed theology is unfelicitous, as are some attempts at philosophical translations of the mystical experience, there is much high rhetoric in the *Lauds*, and the greater number of the mystical lauds soar.

Counterbalancing criticism of this sort does much to clear the way for a proper understanding of the poetry. It does not, however, do away with one central problem, and unless one comes to terms with it any reading of Jacopone will inevitably be off-center.

In a Christian a certain tension between the act of faith and the response to a literature that has its own values and that openly or covertly makes rival demands on life is inevitable in any epoch, and particularly when a literature is coherently and forcefully non- or anti-Christian. The believer lives with that tension, susceptible of many gradations; he cannot entirely do away with it. The challenge can be met by sallying forth, seeking to put the best of that rival culture to good Christian use; or, sensing a real and present danger, the believer may raise the drawbridge. These are the extremes of the two possible responses. As to the superiority of one over the other, that is not a question that can be answered in terms of categorical absolutes. In practice, each of the two attitudes is usually tempered with elements of the other, but even in that instance when one or the other approach clearly dominates, it behooves the Christian not to dogmatize about the superiority of his preferred stance. The individual solution, in the last analysis, is a highly personal equation. There are instances in which the refusal to acknowledge the existence of another world is sectarianism or worse. Equally true, for certain temperaments, regardless of the tendencies of their times, anything short of the most intense concentration on and absorption with that religious center is distraction and threat.

This predicament may be of little interest to some nonbelievers. A number of Christians may also be troubled by the narrow intensity of that approach to God, so austerely vertical; yet unless the reader, whatever his orientation, is willing to allow that a content of this vertical intensity *is* transformable into poetry, the animating spirit of the greatest lauds will appear in a twisted light.

For Jacopone intensely mistrusts a literature with a multitude of horizontal interests. The stuff of life that poetry glories in—youth, the love of man and woman, grief over loss, the idle curiosity in things and persons that leads to splendidly nonidle truths—all these lines and colors and dimensions are absent in the *Lauds*. They are not condemned; they are passed over in silence, skirted as a distraction. Any poetry with wide-ranging sensitivities, for Jacopone, took on the appearance of a threat, so that for him almost to the end no poetry, no beauty was beyond suspicion. Augustine's fear that in responding to Ambrosian chant he was succumbing to an incantation of sorts, the dread that Jerome expressed for the hold a Ciceronian style had on him, are misgivings of which Jacopone may or may not have known but to which he responded with his whole heart. Unjust to those of his time who sought to put that culture and literature to Christian use, he heightened his narrow and magnificent isolation, moreover, by castigating the literature of his time, which took into account the cultural disparities of its readers, adamant in his insistence that only a God-permeated poetry that spoke to simple and learned alike was of value.

Of the many obstacles that block the way to an understanding of the *Lauds*, none has been harder to overcome than the antipathy for this fierce, one-sided intensity. By itself alone this repugnance does much to explain why for a long time the *Lauds*, denied recognition as poetry, was relegated to that dubious category, pious literature—a catch-all that offends piety as much as literature. And in fifteenth- and sixteenth-century Italy, when the struggle between a Christian-inspired literature and that of hostile contemporary paganism was in-

INTRODUCTION

tense, the *Lauds* was indeed very popular among readers with a fervent religious sensitivity. The fact is undeniable. Its implications, though, particularly with respect to the literary qualities of the *Lauds*, are not at all univocal.

The thirteenth-century Franciscans who first collected and edited the poems were not simple pious souls. They were readers of taste and discernment with an appreciation of literature. Bernardino of Siena and Giovanni da Capestrano, among those who first meditated the text, were more than ordinary popular preachers. Francesco Bonaccorsi, the Florentine religious humanist responsible for the 1490 edition, had a fine feeling for the literature of his own time as well as that of the Middle Ages and had a good ear for distinguishing between the apocryphal and the authentic. In the sixteenth century the circle of Catherine Adorno of Genoa and the saint herself, whose *Spiritual Dialogues* point to an awareness of the depth of the probings of the *Lauds*, did not turn their backs on the culture of their day. Saint Philip Neri, who incarnated the best of the religious ideals of the Catholic Reformation in Italy and for whom the *Lauds* was a *vademecum*, as his well-annotated copy indicates (it was at his urging that G. B. Modio produced the second edition in 1558 and that a number of the poems were first put to music in the Oratory in Rome—the beginnings of the oratorio), had no want of interest in contemporary authors. Nor is there any reason to assume that the many anonymous readers who continue to turn those pages slowly today are wanting in literary or, for that matter, theological sophistication—unless one posits an unbridgeable divide between the world of poetry and that of mysticism and religion.

Very well, the reader may impatiently interject at this point, an injustice was apparently done to the literary sensibilities of religiously oriented readers of the fifteenth and sixteenth centuries; but what is the point now of these discussions of the *Lauds* as literature and poetry, the limits of its appeal and the problem of Jacopone's intense verticalism? Today Jacopone has a very visible place in the fresco of Italian medieval literature. In the background, of course, for he is no Dante, nor is his mysticism that of Francis. Nevertheless, in those schools where literature still has a place Italian students are to know his dates and one or two representative lauds. As a subject for a thesis the credentials of Jacopone are beyond criticism. Newspapers with some cultural tone from time to time devote a column to his life or his work. In some quarters one can even come across discussions of the

INTRODUCTION

realism of the *Lauds* and its proletarian, antielitist and antibourgeois implications. During the tourist season the poems are recited by professional actors in exquisite medieval surroundings.

Confronted with a success of this scale one can only say, together with the peasant whose prayers to Saint Anthony were granted to excess, *"Troppa grazia, Sant'Antonio!"* For what does this institutionalized chrism, reminiscent of the appreciation that turns medieval manuscripts into lampshades, say for a proper response to the spirit of the *Lauds?* No more facile solution could be given to the problem of the center of that poetry and the extent to which readers with different sensibilities and outlook can converge on a common response than this mélange of public relations, folk poetry, and staged religiosity.

It is also true, however, that on an altogether different plane, on the level of university scholarship, the study that in modern times marked the beginning of a fresh interest in the *Lauds*, F. Ozanam's *Les Poètes francescains au XIII siècle* (Paris, 1882), offered disappointingly little toward a solution of the problem of the true spirit of the *Lauds*. Its main concern was to place this poetry in a Franciscan corpus and it did so in a very convincing manner, underscoring the neglected medieval cosmopolitanism of the work. At the same time, however, the response to the gentle, joyous aspects of the *Lauds* was excessive, and so were the misgivings over an alleged quietistic mysticism in Jacopone and the violence of the poet's attacks on Boniface VIII. Francis is not consistently the Francis we find in the pages of the *Fioretti* and Jacopone is much more than one of the more notable (though dubiously orthodox) Franciscan poets of his time.

One might suppose, though, that in this period among his own, in scholarly circles in Italy, where it would be easier to respond to his language if not to his spirit, the appreciation of Jacopone's poetry would have been more perceptive; that the measure of his poetical achievement would have been quickly recognized. The expectation points to a naive notion of Italy in the mid-nineteenth century and even in more recent times. The discovery of the dimensions of that poetry and the wide arch of its appeal was slow and gradual. Before today's reader could make his way to the clearing in which the *Lauds* stand out in all their Romanesque presence and strength the road would twist and turn and on more than one occasion head in the wrong direction.

INTRODUCTION

II PROPOSED SOLUTIONS

For Francesco De Sanctis, the critic who first introduced the *Lauds* to a wide literary public in his *History of Italian Literature* of 1860, the Middle Ages appeared somewhat as they do to some contemporary anthropologists—a society and a culture apart, a prehistory of sorts. In his view, however, that distance, infinitely greater than the chronological, did not make a case for cultural relativism. The period, which extended from its vague origins in the ninth or tenth century to the fourteenth, brought to a close the adolescence of modern man; and for all of its achievements, its literature, like its culture in general, reflected the limitations of that phase. Much like Burckhardt, De Sanctis viewed the Middle Ages as that time in which, as the author of *The Civilization of the Renaissance in Italy* writes, "both sides of human consciousness . . . lay dreaming or half-awake beneath a common veil. The veil was woven of faith, illusion and childish prepossession, through which the world and history were clad in strange hues." Quite unlike the Swiss thinker, though, De Sanctis had no doubts, much less apprehensions, as to the onward march of history. It was the glory of the Italian Renaissance culture of the fifteenth and sixteenth centuries, he fervently believed, that it enabled man to contemplate reality directly, without a veil. In politics, in art, in literature, from the time of Boccaccio to that of Machiavelli, man asserted his dominion, the only being who shaped history and gave it meaning; and this confident proclamation was the foundation of progress as Europe had come to know and experience it in the following centuries. Temporarily arrested by the Counter-Reformation of the seventeenth century, the role of Italian culture in this ascending spiral once again acquired new force and momentum in the nineteenth century. *The History of Italian Literature* was itself a documentation of that resurgence, that revitalization. It was also in effect the denial of the historical pessimism, the devaluation of politics and philosophy voiced by two of the most eloquent and contrasting poets of nineteenth-century Italy, Manzoni and Leopardi.

As an approach to literature or poetry, this theory of historical progress, the theme of a number of variations from Vico to Hegel, has some palpable drawbacks. In strict coherence, in its implicit stress on content, the progress of dialectic thought, it consigns any poetry or literature with a religious content to the graveyard of long since superseded religious notions. The literary sensitivities of De Sanctis,

10

INTRODUCTION

however, were stronger than his philosophical bent; and in his response to and stress on image, music and passion—the elements of "form"—he sought to infuse a "dead" religious content with new vitality. No doubt the compromise-solution satisfied him; but it cannot do as much for more rigorous systematic thinkers or those for whom religious experience or religious poetry is sustained but not fully accounted for by image, music and passion. In effect, his Solomon-like division of poetry into this particular variant of a traditional notion of content and form, taken to be the whole of that mystery, for all of its good intent, leaves matters unchanged. The quality of a poem still depended on the place its content had in De Sanctis's scale of progress; and the rigor and unbending zeal with which the critic applied this principle is amply documented by his approach to Dante's masterpiece. *The Divine Comedy*, he acknowledged, was indeed unsurpassable in music and image. Its content, however, shared in all the weaknesses of the culture of its time. In the primitiveness of its beliefs, in its fundamental outlook on life and understanding of man, that poetry had only scattered insights to offer the modern reader.

His approach to Jacopone, quite consistently, followed along similar lines. Almost cavalier in its self-assurance, that account appears almost as persuasive today to readers with little or no knowledge of that poetry as it did when it first appeared.

The robust tonality of the *Lauds*, more than any other trait of that poetry, strongly appealed to the critic. He rejoiced in its simplicity, the absence of that rhetoric of love which cheapened so much of the religious poetry of the age. And Jacopone's "realism," the quality that offended an eighteenth-century sensibility so proud of its refinement, was very much to his taste. That coarseness was bracing, refreshing. Though "Gothic" (the term was pejorative), that poetry, according to De Sanctis, had much to recommend it; it merely—as Chesterton once put it—"called a dirty thing by a dirty name." The shortcomings of the *Lauds*, therefore, "natural poetry, not spiritualized by art, raw stuff at odds with itself that results in some beautiful sketches but nothing finished or harmonious," did not distress De Sanctis. That unevenness of expression was part of the charm of its simplicity, characteristic of the expression of "a religious sentiment as it appears in uncultured classes without the clouds of theology and Scholasticism." In keeping with this alleged lack of sophistication, De Sanctis quoted at length from proverbs attributed to the poet (all of which were later proven to be apocryphal), underlining their homey

11

wisdom and felicitous turn of phrase. These insights were part of a Franciscan folk wisdom of sorts. Very much a presence in the *Lauds* according to De Sanctis, Francis and the fragrance of his sanctity lingered in the pages of Jacopone.

A very sympathetic portrait and in part a likeness, this response to the *Lauds* is still quite popular, especially among those who, with little time to read that poetry, admire it. That very excess of benevolence, by the same token, will put some readers on guard. There is more than a little in that appraisal of Milton's patronizing bow to Shakespeare, the poet "warbling his native woodnotes wild." What does it mean—and the question cannot be sidestepped, and indeed will be insisted on by anyone who has found himself nodding over the more involuted and unrelenting rhymed theological passages of the *Lauds*—to assert that Jacopone knew nothing "of the clouds of theology and Scholasticism"? How can the mystical lauds, with the demands they make on the reader, be considered the simple words of a simple poet? And how can one explain the total and baffling omission of pivotal experiences of Jacopone that must be taken into account in even the most summary version of his life and work? De Sanctis, for example, does not make one reference to the central experience that draws together so many of the different strands in that poetry: the meditation on Francis and holy poverty. Nor is there one allusion in his sketch to the crisis in Jacopone's life that led him to the defiance of Boniface VIII and his subsequent imprisonment, or to the lauds of his final period. And to make these omissions all the more perplexing, Jacopone's rebellion, as well as his role in the conflict between Spiritual and Conventual Franciscans, were facts that were well known at the time of De Sanctis. They are not discoveries of modern scholarship.

Whatever the explanation of these odd lacunae, they are evidently not traceable to ignorance. De Sanctis could not but have been aware of those central facts. In organizing and editing his material, most probably he simply concluded that they were expendable. In the great fresco of the Middle Ages as the critic conceived it, the principal grouping, the dominant dramatic contrast (a device of which De Sanctis was particularly fond) was represented on one side by Dante, a Christian poet of prodigious complexity, and on the other by Francis of Assisi, no less awesome in his simplicity. The question, then, was to determine the place to be assigned to Jacopone along the coordinate defined by these two figures, and the answer appeared self-

INTRODUCTION

evident. The poetry of the lauds, it seemed manifest to the critic, was infinitely closer to that of *Il Poverello*, whom De Sanctis saw more as the founder of a medieval version of The Society for the Prevention of Cruelty to Animals than as the gaunt mystic of La Verna. Jacopone was a Franciscan, and simplicity was therefore necessarily the hallmark of his poetry. Consequently, to have elaborated at any length those aspects of his poetry and life that distracted from or clashed with that dominant trait as De Sanctis saw it would simply have weakened the plausibility of his portrait. This is the most likely explanation of the utterly blank parts of that canvas, those puzzling omissions. A remarkably one-sided notion of Jacopone and the *Lauds*, this particular approach, nonetheless, set a pattern of interpretation that was to be followed for some time. Though of greater and lesser sophistication at different points, the confusion it initiated was to have a long resonance.

Echoes of it are clearly discernible in Alessandro D'Ancona's full-length study of Jacopone and his poetry, *Jacopone da Todi—Guillare di Dio* [Jacopone da Todi, The Fool of God], a work that appeared some twenty years later in an intellectual climate that had changed in many ways. The belief in the *sorti progressive dell'umanità*, the almost inevitable progress of human affairs, had waned somewhat, and the history of Italian literature in particular no longer appeared a ringing confirmation of a general and constant advance. The sweep and breadth with which De Sanctis, for all his simplifications, endowed history and literature now became suspect. A division of labor appeared more reputable and the ambitions of literary criticism were scaled down substantially. The modest monograph replaced the long essay; the concentration was on the literary text itself more than on the relationship of literature to philosophy, politics, or the *Zeitgeist*; and in any case those relationships were looked on more as a matter of common sense than of dialectical metaphysics. In this new climate D'Ancona gave more than adequate witness to the Positivist cause. The dean of the literary critics of his time, he prided himself on his mistrust of aesthetics and philosophies of history and, with good reason, considered his forte to be a scrupulous respect for facts and for commonsense empiricism. In him thoroughness was a virtue that made any bewildering omissions of factual data inconceivable. No reader of D'Ancona's work can ask himself, as he could with respect to De Sanctis, who the critic's Jacopone is and what relation he bears to the real poet. The facts are accurate, well organized. Not one rele-

INTRODUCTION

vant item in the scholarship of his time escaped D'Ancona. Taking
into account the biographies written some two centuries after the po-
et's death and making a good case for the caution with which they
should be used, D'Ancona offered a life of Jacopone, from the time of
his wife's death when he was some forty years of age to his death in
1306, that covered every decisive phase—his conversion, the ten years
(1268–1278) of penance as a *bizzocone*, a public penitent, his entry into
the Friars Minor in 1278, the espousal of the cause of the Spirituals in
the Order and the culminating moment in that struggle, the defiance
of Boniface VIII in 1297, as well as Jacopone's subsequent imprison-
ment and his death in 1306, three years after his pardon by Boniface's
successor, Pope Benedict XI. As for the text itself, D'Ancona stressed
the need for "a critical edition which would restore the primitive
Umbrian Italian language of the lauds and resolutely exclude the
apocryphal poems."

In terms of factual data D'Ancona's work is still very useful. The
indefatigable scholar was plodding and uninspired compared with De
Sanctis, but his thoroughness and precision had distinct advantages.
They shielded him from the excesses of dramatic historical contrasts.
From this point of view his study is exemplary. The question of his
insight into Jacopone's poetry, though, is another matter. Wary as he
was of metaphysics of any kind, and in particular of Hegelian-in-
spired philosophies of history, the measuring rod that D'Ancona used
had problems of its own. Common sense, on which he relied strongly,
is a notoriously mutable notion, and today the faith he had in the bio-
logical-psychological sciences of his time appears more than a bit na-
ive. There are, of course, biologists and psychologists today quite
disposed to agree with some of the conclusions of their predecessors
in D'Ancona's generation, but they do so as individuals, as members
of a scientific community that is generally agnostic in its outlook. Not
many biologists or psychologists of our day would feel confident that
they had provided D'Ancona with the necessary scientific basis for
dismissing as he did the better part of the mystical lauds as the work
of *"uno stato di coscienza alterata"*—a pathologically disturbed state of
mind. Kinder to the less ecstatic or exuberant poems, D'Ancona con-
tended that a good part of the work was a Franciscan version of *poesia
giullaresca*, the poetry of wandering minstrels of the time, as well as
poesia popolare, unpretentious, spontaneous folk poetry. Since, howev-
er, this judgment, too, appears as romantically naive as De Sanctis's
notion of Jacopone the "simple" poet, the better part of D'Ancona's

14

interpretation of the *Lauds* stands or falls with his ideas on a scientific criterion that can properly gauge religious and mystical phenomena. And with respect to these ideas the stance of D'Ancona is reminiscent of the answer of the technically superb violinist to the question of the exasperated conductor as to how he could play a particularly throbbing passage with such correctness and total lack of passion—"Maestro, I never did like music."

Thus, for all of the differences between the approach of De Sanctis and the commonsense empiricism of D'Ancona, their conclusions on the literary and religious merits of the *Lauds* were substantially the same. If anything, the discomfort with the religious dimension had increased. De Sanctis, in following a line of nineteenth-century thought with very distant and distinguished precedents, felt that the best of the Christian experience could be salvaged by incorporating it into philosophy. D'Ancona, with his mistrust of philosophy and his devotion to the cult of the natural sciences, would have none of that. Common sense told him that those noble ruins had outlived their season, that if the *Lauds* were literature they were such *in spite* of their religious dimensions.

The turn of the century, when Positivism was dominant in Italy and in general throughout Europe, was, however, also the moment in which the presence of Benedetto Croce first asserted itself. By 1900, the impact of his critique of that ideological stance (for Positivism was a general outlook more than a clearly articulated philosophy) was already noticeable; and with the founding of his cultural review, *La Critica*, in that year, Croce assured the long-lasting influence of his systematic thought on the whole of Italian culture, an influence that reached a high point shortly before the advent of Fascism. In literary criticism, Croce argued, a philosophy of history or an aesthetic could not substitute for a certain literary sensibility; but that sensibility, in turn, could not be exempt from further probing, and if in some instances it led full circle back to more abstract philosophical insights, so be it. With this basic notion, illustrated in countless ways in works that sought to do equal justice to the here-and-now concreteness of historical research and the abstract demands of metaphysics and esthetics, Croce rehabilitated philosophy in Italian intellectual circles and not only restored to literary criticism the range with which De Sanctis had endowed it but indeed gave it a far greater one.

Yet though its horizons were immeasurably broader, literary criticism as Croce conceived it owed very much to De Sanctis. At a time when it was fashionable to minimize, even dismiss the works of the Risorgimento critic, Croce lost no occasion to defend them; and willing to concede that as a philosopher the author of *The History of Italian Literature* had at best very approximative ideas on Hegel, the Idealist philosopher nonetheless saw in the literary criticism of De Sanctis a confirmation—in terms of an extraordinary literary sensitivity and a superb historical sense—of Hegelian insights. The antithesis Middle Ages–Renaissance was crude, no doubt, but not altogether wrong. And for all of the simplicity of certain elements in De Sanctis's theory of progress, Croce shared that vision of history. Most important, he had virtually no reservations regarding De Sanctis's theory of content and form; that concrete literary criticism, he acknowledged with some frequency, had been of more help to him in understanding literature than any number of abstract treatises on aesthetics.

With respect to Christianity, too, Croce's stance was basically that of De Sanctis, for all the subtle shadings that the Neapolitan philosopher gave to his appreciation of certain of its manifestations. The mellow wisdom with which Croce argued the case for an appreciation of the relativity of all our knowledge ought not to be misunderstood: On the basic question of transcendence and immanence he allowed for no reality other than human. On this basic conviction he was unyielding. When late in life, in the essay, "Why We Cannot But Be Christians," he paid the well-known homage to Christianity, the tribute did not involve any reconsideration of this fundamental stance. It simply expressed gratitude for the Christian ethic, which had survived the gradual dismemberment of the Christian creed. For Croce to the last, the Kingdom of God was not among us but in us and of our making; and once due allowance was made for the relativity of all truth, he argued, a good case could be made for progress in human affairs, a progress that in philosophy was marked in negative terms by the increasing recognition of the inadequacies and basic incoherence of any notion of transcendence. Therefore, in all coherence, a literature that sang of man as creator was the highest poetry. With this conclusion, for all of its suppleness and range, Croce's thought, like the literary criticism of De Sanctis, found itself enmeshed in a by now traditional ambiguity. The stress on the primacy of form, with a concomitant attenuation of the importance of content, was deceptive. In practice the insistence that it was possible for any content to be translated or transformed into poetry was consistently accompanied by a clear preference for certain content. All contents were equal, but some were more equal than others.

The most unswerving confirmation of this approach, a cubing of De Sanctis's notion of content, appears in Croce's famous essay *La poesia di Dante* [The Poetry of Dante], his most extended work on a poetry that has more in common with that of Jacopone than is generally appreciated. Structure (in effect, content) and form in this analysis were divided into virtually watertight compartments. The whole of the core convictions of Dante, and not merely those parts that showed the wear and tear of seven centuries, were for Croce historical curiosities with little or no relevance for a contemporary reader. The view of revelation, in which the convergence of pagan and Jewish-Christian elements was one of the more striking aspects, the insights into human nature that were indissolubly tied to a Christian notion of sin and beatitude, the analysis of the many forms of love, were placed on the same level as Dante's thought on the empire and the Church or his views of Rome's historical mission in the world: All were expendable. So was the philosophical structure that braced that vision. Unconcerned with the niceties of its dominant traits, whether it owed more to Aristotle and Aquinas or Averroës or in some instances Augustine, that pseudophilosophic thought (for it was no more than that in Croce's eyes) was part of an old dispensation that no longer had much meaning for contemporaries who realized that philosophy, for all practical purposes, began with Kant and found its master road with Hegel.

What, then, remained of the *Divine Comedy?* Its poetry, Croce insisted—the unsurpassed evocations of the beauty of the world, the magical conciseness of image and thought, an exquisite moral sensitivity, a music that once heard could not be forgotten. Such was the "form" of the *Divine Comedy,* its authentic poetry; and it had no ties with the structure. Like magical water lilies anchored in their own beauty, a beauty in no need of roots, that poetry glowed in its own light.

The truth was that Croce responded to religious poetry—but that of Goethe, of Carducci, a poetry that was superior to any faith, as he wrote in *Poesia popolare e poesia d'arte,* a poetry that was "skeptical of all faiths . . . because it is fixed, victorious and serene, in the drama of the soul, in the suffering and joyful life of the cosmos with which it is one."

In the light of this response to the greatest poet of the Middle

INTRODUCTION

Ages, Croce's reading of Jacopone was predictable. He did not need to express himself at length on the subject; the cursory reference in *Poesia popolare e poesia d'arte* in praise of the touchingly human grief and bereavement of Jacopone's Madonna is sufficient.

The tone was more judicious but the conclusions were indistinguishable in substance from those of De Sanctis and D'Ancona; and even in instances where there was an increase of sympathy for that utterance it was accompanied by an equally remarkable misreading. Thus, the transformation that Croce's work helped bring about in the cultural climate of these years contributed little to the question of the relation between the religious-mystical experience of Jacopone and his poetry.

This is evident in one of the finest works of these years, conceived in a very Crocean spirit, Natalino Sapegno's *Fra Jacopone* (1926). Sapegno, whose understanding and appreciation of the culture of the Italian Middle Ages was incomparably superior to that of D'Ancona and De Sanctis, responded to the *Lauds* in a forthright fashion. More drawn to the poetry of that age than Croce, he found the drama of Jacopone's life and work absorbing. He understood that the *Lauds* was not of one piece, realized the importance of the Christian roots of that utterance, and in distinguishing between the poetical value of one laud and another often made a remarkably good case for his particular reading. The most impressive sign of his insights and independence of judgment, however, was his appraisal of the mystical lauds. He spoke eloquently of Laud 91 in particular, "Self-Annihilation and Charity"; Laud 77, "Silent Love"; and Laud 66, "The Lament of the Soul for Grace in Hiding." Though refashioned in a much more sophisticated way by Croce, D'Ancona's dictum, "We firmly believe that mystical doctrines are not fitting material for poetry, since poetry demands the concrete," mattered as little to Sapegno as that other forceful injunction of the Positivist scholar to quickly pass over the lauds that dealt with *alta nichilitate*. Ignoring these admonitions was no mean accomplishment for a scholar out to distinguish between poetry and nonpoetry in terms of a basically Crocean outlook.

That favorable response to the *Lauds*, however, had its limits. The primacy of the word, in particular its moral-religious passion, which is the deepest font of that poetry, disturbed Sapegno. Unaware that the blackest hues of that utterance, its most repugnant aspects,

18

were there to document the horror of a Godless world unredeemable by human beauty or strength or power, in his summing up the critic argued that

> the sentiment which inspires this poetry could not but be hatred and contempt; the disgust that is born of the contemplation of the corrupt and the diabolical, of perversity, frivolity and guilt, of gloomy, tormented anguish ... all this accounts for those pedantic arguments, preachy moralism and hate-filled invectives.

The final act of incomprehension in a series of readings that began with De Sanctis, this last variant of an inadequate theory of content and form brought the period to a close. The *Lauds* had been granted standing, official recognition—but only at the price of having its central experience of God changed into one that was either accepted because of its "simplicity" or rejected because of its alleged fanatical condemnation of the world.

Even before Sapegno's work appeared, though, the wind had begun to shift direction. All along, the *Lauds* had continued to find silent readers among Christians with some poetical sensitivity; and in 1920 Mario Casella, in two long articles that appeared in the *Archivum Romanicum* (Volume IV), with scholarly thoroughness and a fine feeling for poetry and mysticism made a case for a reading in a completely different key.

The gist of Casella's argument was that it was not necessary to first resolve the question of immanence and transcendence in strictly philosophical terms in order to properly respond to the poetry of the *Lauds*. A degree of agnosticism was an offense to no man. There were more things between heaven and earth, probably, than were dreamed of in any system of philosophy, even Idealist metaphysics. It was also possible—while at the same time expressing reservations on the faith of Jacopone—to consider Christianity as more than the precipitate of morality that had survived a centuries-long critique. Moreover, mysticism, an intense manifestation of an order of love above and beyond man, while an essential element in Christianity, was not its exclusive prerogative. That experience, whatever doctrinal problems it presented, had an ontological and metaphorical value. Moreover, if the expe-

INTRODUCTION

rience of God in Jacopone's "inner travail that vibrates continually in the struggle between the old man and the new" was, as Casella urged, the center of that poetry, then the deepest experience of that travail, Jacopone's mysticism, his living and singing and meditating on that love, was anything but an irredeemable content. In mystical poetry, indeed, the poetical experience and the experience of God reached as far as words could reach. Not consistently recognized (and least of all by the authors of the *legenda* of Jacopone, who understood the "folly" of the poet in a heavy-handed literal fashion and thereby reduced him to the level of Brother Juniper in *The Little Flowers of Saint Francis*), the spirituality of Jacopone, which culminated in the doctrines of *alta nichilitate* and *follia*, was a magnificent variant of Paul's "stumbling block to the Jews and an absurdity to the Gentiles," a grandiose recurring Christian theme. It was precisely Jacopone's dread that this fiery incomprehensible truth was being lost sight of, dealt with as one truth among others in a listless creed, that explained the violent tone of his poetry, its assault on and excessive denigration of a literature that, dwelling on the world, did not see beyond it. In no other way did Jacopone know how to voice "the folly of God that is wiser than men and his weakness that is stronger than the strength of men."

With Casella's work, for the first time the way was cleared to an understanding of the *Lauds* that avoided the deadend to which the prevailing notion of content and form had consistently led. It may seem curious that this valid alternative asserted itself so late; but to adequately account for this phenomenon would require a very long digression on the fortunes (and misfortunes) of the cultural level of Italian Catholicism in this period, and that in turn would be to venture very far afield indeed. Suffice it to say that in this context the delayed recognition was quite understandable. It was for good reason that the work that preceded Casella's study and pointed in the same direction, Evelyn Underhill's study, *Jacopone da Todi, A Spiritual Biography* (1919), appeared not in Italy but in England. That study has its small blemishes: The Victorian sensibility of the author precluded the discussion of lauds that may be shocking but are certainly not in dubious taste, and that excess of sensitivity in turn led to the omission of key lauds in the very limited number of poems translated to accompany the study. Underhill's knowledge of the Italian of the *Lauds*, moreover, was little more than adequate, and on all questions relating to textual matters she had to rely on a judgment other than her own,

INTRODUCTION

specifically that of Giovanni Ferri in his 1910 edition of Bonaccorsi's text. As a student of mysticism (and she came to the *Lauds* primarily from that experience, not out of literary interests) she also unduly stressed the sources of Jacopone, and in underlining the elements that he shared with other mystics of his and other times neglected some of his more intensely individualistic traits. These are minor flaws, however, in a very perceptive study. In vastly enlarging the horizons of the *Lauds* by comparing them with those of medieval and Renaissance English mystics, by placing the poems in the plenitude of their spiritual setting, Underhill uncovered those dimensions of the poetry and mysticism of Jacopone that had been consistently minimized, if not ignored in literary and philosophical discussions in nineteenth- and twentieth-century Italy. And though not primarily interested in the relation between that religious-mystical experience and poetry, her implicit conclusions on that score are remarkably sane.

Much the same holds true for a very recent work, *The Fool of God* by George T. Peck (Alabama University Press, 1980). There is nothing in Italian or English that can compare to it in the scope of its ambitions. To an unparalleled degree—for some readers at times to a fault—Professor Peck paints a vast detailed fresco of the world of Jacopone in its political, economic, and social dimensions. Utilizing to the full the finest and most recent scholarship, he offers a *sitzen im leben* of the *Lauds* of Jacopone that is not only generally persuasive but does a great deal to clarify some of the more obscure references. At no time, though, does the erudition become an end in itself, lose sight of the central all-determining conviction that "the true meaning of Jacopone's holy madness lies much deeper than what D'Ancona and other critics took it to be . . . it lies in the recognition that Jacopone denied human reason, that he stilled the mind in order to let in the flood of God's love."

As a confirmation of the insights offered by the interpretation of Casella and Underhill, Peck's work adds much to the persuasiveness of this more recent trend. The approach leaves open, of course, the question of the limits of the assent that may be given to the *Lauds*, the warp and woof of Jacopone's utterance, and it does well to do so. At a certain depth we can no more distinguish between our aesthetic and religious responses than we can hear our accent as we speak. Closer to the surface, though, at a point that varies in each one of us, it is well that we make called-for distinctions, as these works suggest, when those distinctions imply no violence to our beliefs or those of the poet.

III   THE CRITICAL EDITIONS

The first critical edition of the *Lauds*, that of Franca Ageno, appeared in 1953, nearly a century after De Sanctis's time and some thirty years after the alternative interpretation of Casella and Underhill. The absence of a definitive text, apparently, had not impeded critics in their expression of contrasting views. At one point or another, they must have felt, research into the tangled question of manuscripts would solve the problem of dubious lauds and identify the linguistic strata of the various collections, but in the meantime there was work to do. Does this suggest that for all its value the work of Ageno will probably do no more than confirm today's reader in his particular response to that poetry? In most instances this will probably be the case. Whatever the implications of that critical edition and the equally fine one of Franco Mancini, which appeared in 1974 (a remarkable feat of philological research that reconstructs the text of the first collections of the lauds some twenty to thirty years after the death of Jacopone), they are not likely to modify the reader's basic stance with respect to the utterance of Jacopone. Had a critical text been available at the time, De Sanctis would have done better than to include twelve apocryphal lauds in the fourteen he chose to illustrate his points, and just as certainly he would have discarded the apocryphal proverbs he used to document the case he made for Jacopone's penchant for folksy wisdom. But that, most likely, would have been the extent of his revisions, and much the same probably holds true for later critics. D'Ancona, for his part, would have been particularly appreciative of the rigor of the philological analysis that led Ageno to deny the authenticity of Laud 86, "The Soul Asks for Forgiveness of Sins and the Taste of Love," an exclusion accepted by contemporary scholarship, and he would have savored the remarkable philological reconstruction of Mancini, but this appreciation would have brought with it no change in basic views. Similarly, Underhill would no doubt have profited by these critical editions and offered quite a different selection of the lauds for a first introduction to English-speaking people: Seven apocryphal lauds out of thirty-four leaves room for improvement. Yet in her case, as in the others, the correction would have involved no major modifications of perspective.

The importance of the exclusion of the apocryphal lauds, moreover, was very much attenuated by the fact that with the exception of Laud 86 all were already considered dubious by Bonaccorsi in the fifteenth century. Though disclaiming to speak with finality ("This is not to say, however, that Jacopone might not have written other lauds not included here, or that all those contained are his, for there is no certainty on this score . . ."), the Florentine editor, in the preface to that collection, had expressed serious reservations about Lauds 94 through102. They did not appear authentic to him, and that spoke very well for his sense of the poetry of Jacopone. For those lauds— ranging from the dull and lifeless "The Dispute between Honor and Shame" (Laud 94) and "A Teaching for the Sinner Seeking to be Reconciled with God" (Laud 97) to the fragrantly mystical "To Love in Truth Is Not to Be Idle" (Laud 101) and "Jesus, the Deepest Joy" (Laud 102)—at their best and worst do have something Jacoponian about them; a lesser critic would have endorsed them as authentic. Consequently, to accept Bonaccorsi's estimate of these lauds—as virtually all readers of Jacopone did after 1910, the year in which G. Ferri's edition of the Bonaccorsi text appeared (we do not know what edition of the *Lauds* De Sanctis used)—was in effect to anticipate the conclusions of modern scholarship on the question of the apocryphal lauds. The works of Ageno and Mancini in this respect, for all of their excellence, merely confirmed the judgment of Bonaccorsi.

Are the recent critical editions, then, of very little use? Hardly. For the Italian reader, and especially the nonspecialist, they are indispensable. To read those poems without philosophical-theological notes in some instances is not to understand them (a problem solved in part in this translation by clarifying the difficulty within the text) and for this reason alone a new edition of the Ageno work, now out of print, is very much called for. The Mancini work is equally invaluable; since the text he offers is no longer the predominantly Tuscan one of Bonaccorsi's edition, the glossary is an indispensable aid for an understanding of the variety of linguistic strata, in particular the Umbrian.

Essential to Italian nonspecialists, the editions of Ageno and Mancini, moreover, are no less so to the reader of the present edition who has some knowledge of Italian and of that old Italian proverb

INTRODUCTION

"traduttore, traditore." These are the texts that the reader should consult when in doubt about some parts of this translation; and, ideally, it is to them that he should turn once this translation has served its purpose of introducing him to this poetry or deepening his insights into it.

IV JACOPONE, PERSONA AND POET

Compared with the progress made toward the reconstruction of the original text of the *Lauds,* modern discoveries of new facts with respect to the life of Jacopone are few and of limited importance. We do not know much more today than did D'Ancona or, for that matter, Bonaccorsi. It would be well, then, for us to take to heart the admonition of the Florentine editor:

> With respect to the life of the Blessed Jacopone it appears that we have no certain knowledge thereof; but from his writings we can gather a good deal with respect to his perfection and his transformation in the love of God, as well as the times in which he lived and wrote.

Those writings, with few exceptions, suggest very little as to dates of composition. Some, such as Laud 17, "The Late Brother Rinaldo," or Laud 63, "Letter of Consolation to Brother John of Fermo," can be corroborated by outside evidence; most cannot. Born of an aristocratic family sometime between 1230 and 1236 in Todi, one of the two sons of Iacobello Benedetti, Jacopone practiced the profession of *notaio*—one that combined the skills of a lawyer with those of an accountant—and sometime between 1265 and 1267 married Vanna di Bernardino di Guidone. These facts, in sum, constitute all that can be confirmed by outside sources on his early years. From 1278 on we can document far more—his entry into the Friars Minor, his passionate support of the Spiritual Franciscans in their struggle against the Conventuals, his successful appeal, together with other Spirituals, to Celestine V in 1294 for autonomy and protection from persecution by their adversaries within the Order. After the abdication of Celestine V, whose pontificate lasted five months, we have documentation of Jacopone's defiance of Boniface VIII. On making common cause with the Cardinals Colonna, the leaders of the revolt, and with other Spirituals, he affixed his name to the Longhezza Manifesto of May 10, 1297, which denounced the election of Boniface and called for the convening of a council to choose a new pope. We also have certain knowledge that on his imprisonment after the defeat of the Colonnas the following year Jacopone appealed at least once to Boniface VIII for a pardon. Freed by Boniface's successor, Benedict XI, after the death of his old enemy, Jacopone died some three years later, in 1306.

Not many facts and dates are needed, however, for a *grosso modo* chronology of the *Lauds*. Leaving aside the two lauds to Our Lady, which Bonaccorsi acknowledged he placed at the beginning and end of the collection in keeping with a Petrarchian sense of the poetically and religiously fitting, the sequence of poems in the 1490 edition corresponds rather well to the major stages in Jacopone's life as indicated by those dates. Before the poet-mystic came to the point of dreading his reputation for sanctity, earned in his ten years' penitence as a *bizzocone*, he had to have acquired that reputation. The defense of holy poverty, its proper observance, became more vehement, most probably, after his entry into the Order. And similarly, the laments over corruption in the Church no doubt paralleled the escalation of those polemics, just as his pleas to Boniface VIII for a pardon manifestly followed his imprisonment.

This general linking up of given lauds with certain periods, though, leaves a number of gray areas. The sorrow for one's sins—and it is voiced in numerous lauds—is not a characteristic of any one period. The laments over corruption in the Church, though more intense after his entry into the Order, probably also preceded it. The same uncertainty holds true for the dark anguish of the absence of God: How can we be sure whether the poems treating of that anguish reflect a period after his imprisonment or even long before? And since the mystical experience was not limited to one period of Jacopone's life, we have no way of precisely locating a number of the mystical lauds. Some clearly precede the apocalyptic terrors of Jacopone and others follow. There are, of course, some distinct autobiographical allusions to certain moments in his life, such as that in Laud 55 on the ten years as a *bizzocone*, but they are extremely rare.

Yet these gray areas as well as the scarcity of historical documentation for the first part of Jacopone's life constitute no insurmountable difficulty. Many lauds have value in and of themselves. They do not need to be inserted into moments of that life to be fully appreciated.

INTRODUCTION

But what of those poems that have everything to gain by being inserted in an overall design? Is it at all possible to connect moments of that life and poetry with the historical data at hand, to have a sense of the interconnection of life and poetry? It is, provided we recognize that in the construction of the overall design in which the individual chips of mosaic take their proper place we must go far beyond facts and dates. We may have greater or lesser reservations as to the general framework in which Underhill views the *Lauds*—the traditional mystical pattern of purgation, illumination, peace—but clearly some such framework is indispensable; and in that completed sketch chronology will be the least of our problems. It will be our powers of empathy, our notion of history and progress, our ideas on man and poetry and mysticism, that will account for the design of the mosaic. The resultant likeness, needless to say, will not be a model of scientific inquiry. It will, however, allow for degrees of persuasiveness, and the reader who is willing to accept the limitation of the medium and asks no more precision than the subject matter can provide will be well disposed to this work. Though there is, of course, a degree of guesswork involved, that—as Manzoni once drily observed—is precisely the sort of thing historians are accustomed to.

But in this search for the authentic features of Jacopone, can we distinguish between the autobiographical "I" and the "I" of the literary persona? And how can we be sure of differentiating between those two categories and an additional one, also present, that of Everyman? It is easy enough to fall into the pitfall of considering the gripping realism of Jacopone as an undoubted autobiographical clue; yet that verisimilitude is no more than a *trompe l'oeil* technique, a sign of literary skills, not of confessional exactness.

On a certain level, misinterpretations of this sort do limited harm. Yet more than once an extended fundamentalist understanding of Jacopone's words has led to a very confused portrait of the author of the *Lauds*. To cite but one example, even today there are readers who are inclined to accept Laud 24, "The Pain of Living," as a more or less factual account of Jacopone's life, particularly his youth, and who read the lines

> I wanted a wife, and I dreamed of a beautiful
> woman, no shrew,
> Healthy, of my own people, deferential,
> eager to please,

26

INTRODUCTION

> With a handsome dowry, gracious, well-mannered
> and composed:
> Visions of this sort rarely leave heaven

as an explicit reference to his marriage. If such readers, though, are at all open to a reconsideration of the text, they might dwell on the conclusion of that laud. In strict coherence that would have them accept a Jacopone whose old age is one long bitterness, and for whom neither wife nor children nor the whole of life has anything to offer. As for God, in that laud He is absent to the last.

We commit a worse blunder yet when, dissatisfied with Jacopone's reserve, his reluctance to dwell on certain pivotal moments of his inner life, we ignore his silence, devise an explanation of our own, and then use that arbitrary conjecture as a key to an understanding of possibly autobiographical references in other lauds. And in proceeding in just such a manner with respect to Jacopone's conversion, that crucial moment which divides the whole of his existence into a before and an after, we are not only guilty of spiritual voyeurism but we assure our radical incomprehension of the depth of that experience. This is the blunder that those pious fifteenth-century Franciscan biographers made when they provided the explanation of the turning point in Jacopone's life that he himself does not care to reveal. Jacopone's change of heart, we are told in *La Franceschina*, a fifteenth-century Franciscan *legenda*, was the dramatic consequence of the sudden death of his wife. In this account the conversion occurred at the moment when, disrobing her lifeless body (she had been killed in an accident at a wedding feast), he discovered that beneath her rich attire she wore a hairshirt. The story, one known to many readers with none but the vaguest ideas on Jacopone, is undeniably dramatic. It speaks very well for the view of women held by the biographer. But this does not alter the hard fact that the tale is made of whole cloth, that there is not one thing we know of Vanna di Bernardino di Guidone, her character or her death. Indeed, we know nothing of the marriage itself.

If the poet is unwilling to speak in recognizably autobiographical terms of the most decisive moments of the first part of his life, does it follow that there are few if any traces of the young Jacopone in the *Lauds?* Can we make out any of those lineaments? It would be ill advised, in any case, to consider those lauds that speak of the loathing for oneself—lauds that are especially offensive to those for whom the

INTRODUCTION

notion of man made in the image of God is a self-congratulatory truth—as mirror images. These references may be autobiographical, but could just as easily be depictions of Everyman. We are not in a position to distinguish with any certainty; and this limitation alone ought to caution us against too summary identifications. More important, that not knowing ought to alert us to the glibness of a psychological explanation of that conversion in terms of one extreme answering another. To judge from the sins of which the "I" accuses himself in a good number of lauds, in fact—sins that are not of the blackest kind—it would be well if our assumptions moved in a contrary direction. Jacopone's conversion was quite probably brought about not by the blackness of his sins but by the blandness of his virtues. The answer of God to that "Have mercy on me, for I am the worst of sinners" was quite likely, as the Victorian poet suggests, an undocumentable "Nonsense, my little man, you're nothing of the kind." And this strong likelihood is borne out by a laud that as a rule is completely overlooked for its possible autobiographical allusions—Laud 39, "How the Life of Jesus Is the Mirror of the Soul." The contrition avowed therein is not for avarice, lust, sloth, gluttony, sins writ large. The grief is for the hollowness, the sham of the love of God:

> I saw my faith—it was diffidence,
> My hope was presumption, full of vanity.
>
> I saw my charity,
> Love half-spoiled.

The terms are those of the Pauline triad, one of the many signs of the central place Scripture has in Jacopone, but here they do not appear as elements of a theological discourse. In this instance they become a variant of Peter's "Depart from me, O Lord, for I am a sinner"—the overwhelming sense of the holy and the concomitant awareness of the abyss that separates the creature from its source of life. In Jacopone, however, that realization took a particular form, the adamant conviction of the evil of all halfway measures, the blasphemy of the measured tribute to and acknowledgement of God, of approximative, halfhearted devotion, the semblance of judicious love. It was the awareness of the counterfeit nature of his love, in brief, that brought Jacopone to his knees. This is the experience that marks his conversion, his *vita nova*, and whether it occurred of a sudden or was gradu-

INTRODUCTION

al and cumulative is not of crucial importance. At one point the perception, no matter how astigmatic or fuzzy, of the depth and intensity of God's love redimensioned the world as Jacopone knew it.

In its most visible form, that transformation was given witness to with a literal practice of poverty that must have verged on eccentric sanctity. With his radical mistrust of compromise, Jacopone could not have lived poverty as a spiritual metaphor. Poverty meant spiritual riches, yes, but also want and willful deprivation. For Jacopone, in sum, poverty meant to walk in the steps of Francis—to strip oneself naked as the saint of Assisi had done before his father, in defiance of the world and its standards. His contempt for possessions, though, was not all of one piece. There were times when it appeared to be the whole of that conversion and other times when it was one dimension among others of varying importance in visions of God and of a godless world. In their bleak estimate of human nature, particularly repugnant to some who consider the same evaluation in Machiavelli an unflinching acceptance of a grim reality, a number of lauds, such as Laud 19, anticipate (and in a far more graphic way) Pascal's *"Misère de l'homme sans Dieu."* Beauty, age, strength, power—none survived the cutting edge of that acid evocation, so much in keeping with Jacopone's tendency to feel and visualize in terms of extremes. Yet paralleling that condemnation there are also hosannas—the exultant Laud 76, "On the Heart's Jubilation," and the hushed Laud 77, "Silent Love." The pounding tempo and the stunning climax of "The Ills and Evils Frate Jacopone Called Down on Himself in an Excess of Charity" (Laud 48) has its counterpart in the Handelian largo of Laud 49, "On Conscience at Rest," the softly meditative "On the Difference between True and Counterfeit Love" (Laud 34) and the psalmlike introspection of Laud 11, "Contrition for Having Offended God."

These are the extreme contraries in Jacopone, the wide and at times wild swings of the pendulum. Together with them there were other moments that evidenced the complete control of passionate imagination—the monologues and dialogues such as that of the hypocritical friar in Laud 29 or that of the nun in Laud 16, too late aware of her sham spirituality. And alongside these lauds there are others, such as Laud 37, "On Chastity and Its Need to Be Accompanied by Other Virtues," that show a gift for still meditation, the poetry of layered silences.

The very range of these lauds, the better part of which may well

INTRODUCTION

have been composed before Jacopone's entry into the Friars Minor, gives some sense of the depth and height of his world as a *bizzocone*. A singular penitent, he was neither fanatical nor simpleminded—no more, certainly (and the comparison comes naturally to mind) than Francis of Assisi. It was altogether in keeping with his temperament as Christian and poet, consequently, that in 1278 Jacopone brought those ten years of penance to an end and joined the Friars Minor. It is equally true, however, that the poet could have continued on in his way, a disciple of Francis in effect but not a member of the Order. Why, then, did he not do so? Friendships, above all, accounted for that decision—attachment to the Franciscan Spirituals, particularly that group in the region of the Marches who remained steadfastly loyal to the spirit and teachings of John of Parma and Pier Giovanni Ulivi, and in a particular way his friendship with the saintly John of La Verna, one of the most revered Spirituals of his time. Where could the poet of the *Lauds* have found an imitation of Christ more in tune with his own temperament than that of the Spirituals, which with some reason they claimed to be that of Francis himself? Those who sought to adapt the spirit of the founder of the Order to the times, whether they did so discreetly or with complete unconcern for the wishes of *Il Poverello*, were anathema to the poet of the *Lauds;* for better or for worse they embodied compromise, and compromise had no place in Jacopone's lexicon. And who but the Spirituals had the right to condemn a world in which commerce and the utilitarian ethics of the marketplace were ultimate values, a world in which the higher clergy was indistinguishable from those they preached at? The question, consequently, was not why he joined the Order at this time but why he delayed so long in doing so. Hardly the man who sought to keep the turbulent world at bay so as not to have it disturb his meditation, Jacopone certainly was not seeking a sanctuary from the escalating conflict between Spirituals and Conventuals. In fact, the contrary appears much more likely. In all probability he joined the Order at this time precisely *because* of the accelerating tempo of the persecution of the Spirituals, out of a need to give witness to their cause. It was enough for him to know the end to which a group of Spirituals had come during the generalate of Ganfredi. Initially the group had emigrated to Armenia to escape from fanatical Conventuals Ganfredi could not control; but those Conventuals, intent on their prey, denounced the group to the Armenian authorities, accused them of heresy, and had them extradited. Adhering selectively to

30

INTRODUCTION

Francis's disconcerting injunctions on how to deal with those who betrayed the Rule, those Conventuals then had them cast into an underground monastic dungeon for life. In the Second Rule Francis had admonished his followers "to be affectionate with one another and confidently tell one another of their needs, since as a mother nourishes and feeds her son, how much more one ought to love and nourish one's spiritual brother," and this is how the admonition was sometimes understood and practiced. Confronted with such interpretations it was small wonder that Jacopone felt the time had come for a common front, for taking his place at the side of his persecuted friends.

But rallying to the cause was not necessarily the only consideration that led the poet to join the Order. Since the community he joined was one of moderate Conventuals, it is altogether probable that Jacopone also strongly felt the weight of solitude and a particular need to increase humility. In this connection there is a group of lauds— principally "The Five Senses," "On Being on Guard against the Five Senses," "On the Dangerous Charms of Women," "How Grace Transforms the Hell of Sin into Bliss," "On the Contemplation of Death and the Burning Away of Pride"—that will tempt more than one reader to an explanation that, while not verifiable, appears very plausible. Simplistic, heavy-handed, depressingly hortatory, these flat rhetorical exercises have nothing in common with poetry. They could be explained away as moments of fatigue, the perseverance in writing down words even when we know they will leave us with lasting dissatisfaction, for Jacopone did at times capitulate to this tiredness. It is just as possible, though, that those works were written some time after joining the Order as exercises in humility. This would not have been out of character for Jacopone. The head of a Franciscan house, moreover, could very well have been tempted to get some practical use out of a poet; and what more useful assignment to give him than that of using his gift for rhyme and meter to instill some basic religious notions into the heads of novices who for all their good intentions were not always clear-eyed with respect to doctrine and deportment? Laud 43, "On Mercy and Justice and How Man Was Made Whole," and Laud 44, "The Petitions in the Our Father," two lauds relentless in their elaboration of the obvious and in their thoroughness, may also have been composed for similar reasons.

Be that as it may, whether or not at this stage in his life Jacopone's humility assumed this particular form, to judge from all the

31

references to holy poverty there can be no doubt but that he joined the Order to give witness from within the community to an austere and heroic spiritual interpretation of the Rule. To do so in 1278, four years after the death of Saint Bonaventure—who, together with John of Parma, of all the leaders of the Order had come closest to the solution of the conflict between the extreme wings of the Spirituals and Conventuals and yet had failed—was a singularly bold gesture. It was to lead Jacopone to a glorious and confused defense of holy poverty that was without equal in the Order and in his time.

V   THE GROWING CONFRONTATION

By the time Jacopone became a Friar Minor in 1278 the three changes that had gradually metamorphosed the Order—its transformation from a group of lay friars into one with priests, the modification of the notion of holy poverty, and the increasingly central place given to learning—gave every sign of having become irreversible. Those modifications and the Order's prodigious increase in numbers had taken their toll, and the measure of those unresolved and mounting tensions was aptly conveyed by the failure of Bonaventure, whose compromise solutions for all of their good sense (and to some extent because of it) remained abhorrent to many Spirituals, and certainly to Jacopone. On the central question of holy poverty the poet of the *Lauds*, together with his comrades, would continue to do battle.

With respect to learning, however, the one aspect of the conflict that appeared to be waning in intensity, the stance of Jacopone showed how very much he was his own man. There were many Spirituals who denounced those in the Order who studied at the Sorbonne and, worse, taught there—theologians who because of partisan learning, university politics, and occasionally dubious orthodoxy more than once came into conflict with the secular clergy and the bishop of Paris. But there were also Spirituals who were conscious of the anomaly of condemning a learning of which they themselves made abundant use. Moreover, whatever reservations some might have as to the thought of Bonaventure and his followers, that theology had undeniably far more in common with the spirituality of *Il Poverello* than did the new theological currents. Even an extreme Spiritual would find more to his taste in Bonaventure's *The Soul's Journey into God* and *The Tree of Life* than in the *Summa Theologica* of Thomas Aquinas.

INTRODUCTION

These shadings of approval and disapproval, however, did not much interest Jacopone. As a Friar Minor his concern was to deepen his spiritual life through a meditation on Francis and that remarkable revitalization of Augustinian thought that was the glory of Bonaventure. Impetuous and insulting in his more polemical moments, Jacopone was not of the stuff of those Spirituals who in their hatred of Bonaventure made no distinction between the saint's teaching on holy poverty and his mystical theology. The poet of the *Lauds* read the Franciscan doctor's work with great care. He pondered *The Soul's Journey into God* and even more *The Tree of Life;* so much so, in fact, that in "The Tree of a Hierarchy Similar to That of the Angels Based on Faith, Hope, and Charity" (Laud 69) he made abundant use of that imagery to describe the stages of his own journey into God—though not quite to the advantage of his art. Of some value as spiritual autobiography, that laborious construct has little to do with poetry, and even as a personal document its obscure imagery virtually assures ambiguities. Still, as a tribute to the great theologian of the Order, vilified with some frequency by his Franciscan brethren (one thinks of the portrait of him in the *Fioretti,* in which he is seen pursuing John of Parma and seeking to claw at him with iron fingernails, desisting only after the intervention of Saint Francis himself, sent down from Heaven by Christ) this laud is more than worthy of note.

It seems all the more so in the light of a common misinterpretation of certain lauds that present Jacopone as the advocate of a glib and wearying anti-intellectualism. Those poems—Laud 17, "The Late Brother Rinaldo," and Laud 31, "How Ambition and Idle Knowledge Destroy the Purity of the Rule" (Order or Rule is the proper translation here of the Italian *religione*)—are not at all instances of anti-intellectualism, an undeniable characteristic of the more extreme of the Spirituals. A Franciscan at any time has a particular obligation to humility, and that is precisely the point of Jacopone's question-accusation in the first of the two lauds:

You earned your doctorate in Paris, Brother;
Great was the honor and great the expense.
Now that you're dead and buried the real test begins.

Tell me now, did you truly feel
That the greatest of all honors lay
In being a poor and despised *fraticello?*

INTRODUCTION

Even the knowledge of non-Franciscans, it would seem, gains in being scented with humility; certainly there was nothing improper, much less anti-intellectual, in reminding Frate Rinaldo of that lost fragrance.

The point made in Laud 31 is quite similar. The furious sorrow is not over theology. It is over the dedication of all energies and concerns to theological disputes to the point of the virtual disappearance of the animating spirit of Saint Francis—and what is anti-intellectual in this reproach to members of the Order?

> That's the way it is—not a shred left of the spirit
>   of the Rule!
> In sorrow and grief I see Paris demolish Assisi,
>   stone by stone.
> With all their theology they've led the Order
>   down a crooked path.

In the same way, the other famous lines of Jacopone on this subject, also from Laud 31,

> See how these theologians love one another!
> One, like a young mule, watches and waits
> For the right moment to kick the other in the chest

—a comment applicable to some theologians of all periods—are directed to Young Turks in the Order exulting to excess in their intellectual prowess, not to any one theologian in particular, and certainly not to Bonaventure.

With a limited interest in the particulars of theological system (it was above all the mystical theology of Saint Bonaventure that fascinated Jacopone), the poet was even less drawn to the grandiose attempt of the time to clearly distinguish the domain of philosophy from that of theology. Neither the work of Aquinas nor that of the Aristotelian Averroists disposed to let reason have the last word on matters of faith as well interested him. That world seemed as remote and as meaningless to him as did Anselm's *Cur Deus Homo;* for in the eyes of Jacopone the Incarnation was not an event that could be best understood through the analogy of categories of Roman jurisprudence—a mystery, it could elicit only wonder and awe. In this connection the title of Laud 82, "How the Soul through the Senses Finds

34

INTRODUCTION

God in All Creatures," is quite misleading. The poem has nothing to do with the debates on this particular philosophical issue, so popular at the time. It is an exercise in the joy of creation, not rhymed philosophical apologetics. An expression of joy in the spirit of Saint Francis, it is a rendition in a minor key of the exuberant Laud 84, "To Be Considered Mad Because of the Love of Christ Is the Highest Wisdom."

This sense of wonder, not any philosophical or theological conviction, was the center Jacopone deepened in his years in the Order; joy in the world as a sacrament, a world that would become, as holy poverty taught, all the more attractive the more it was renounced. For then, Jacopone sang in his most swashbuckling way,

> Lakes, rivers, and oceans teeming with fish,
> Air, winds, birds—all pay me joyful homage.
> Moon and sun, sky and stars are but minor treasures:
> The treasures that make me burst into song
> Lie beyond the sky that you can see.
>
> Since my will is centered in God, who possesses all,
> I wing with ease from earth to heaven.
> Since I gave my will to God
> All things are mine and I am one with them
> In love, in ardent charity.
>
> (Laud 59)

Basic convictions did not change—Jacopone never completely put aside his mistrust for words and experiences that did not lead directly to God—but now they acquired a new softness. Just as Bach made good use of secular music for religious ends, so Jacopone, in Laud 80, airily imitated the rhythms and tone of the love poetry of the time:

> Do you know of the Love that has swept me up
> And continues to hold my heart,
> That keeps me imprisoned in its sweetness—
> The Love that would have me die in pain?

The reply is much in the same melodious vein:

> The love about which you inquire
> We know in many forms;

35

INTRODUCTION

> Yet if you do not speak of your beloved
> We know not how to answer you.

That love, Jacopone sang, was free and unending, and contained within it (the reference could not have been lost on the reader familiar with the lengthy discussions of the many forms of love so prevalent at the time) all other loves—it was the love of God. This was the mystery of the Incarnation, a paradigm of Christian poverty:

> Why did You leave the golden throne resplendent with gems,
> Why did You put aside the dazzling crown?
> Why did You leave the order of cherubim,
> The seraphim, that joyous court of ardent love,
> The honored servants and courtiers You loved as brothers—
> Why did You leave them all, O Lord?
>
> (Laud 65)

Still, the renunciation of this Byzantine world of gold, gems, and dazzling crown was as nothing compared to the culmination of divine madness, the cross:

> For love of man You seem to have gone mad!
> And think what You will receive in return—
> For joy, reproaches; for riches, niggardly recompense.
> Is it not folly, in the name of love, to surrender mind and will?
>
> —*(Ibid.)*

For Jacopone this "divine madness" was more than poetical phrasing. In a singular meditation on the cross that has scandalized some critics who in their unbelief consider such sentiments hardly Christian, Jacopone slashed to ribbons all the rhetoric in which the cross is often swaddled. In "Two Different Modes of Contemplating the Cross" (Laud 75), the one speaker alludes to the cross in the tired rhetoric of the day—the delight of the cross, the cross in flower, the light- and life-giving cross. The other, Jacopone, speaks a different language. He flees the consuming fires. They blind him and strike him dumb. Their assaults bring him close to death:

> Brother, you have barely sipped,
> But I have drunk of this new wine,

36

INTRODUCTION

And no iron bands could contain this pressure,
Which threatens to split me stave from stave.

Was it any wonder that a Christian who so responded to the mystery
of the cross should have responded so overwhelmingly to the saint of
the stigmata?

The burning love of Christ, whose depths are lost to sight,
Enfolded Francis, softened his heart like wax,
And there pressed its seal, leaving the marks
Of the One to whom he was united.

I have no words for this dark mystery;
How can I understand or explain
The superabundance of riches,
The disproportionate love of a heart on fire?

(Laud 61)

And just as understandably he was at times to experience the sudden
sickening sense of emptiness, a trial common to so many mystics:

I seek out Your nativity, Lord,
Seek out Your suffering;
There is no joy in the quest,
For love has gone cold . . .

Contemplating my own grief I weep,
The dry tears of a heart in ruins.
That precious, inaccessible sweetness—
Where has it gone?

(Laud 66)

Such were the colors and lines of the Franciscan world of Jaco-
pone in this period. By contrast, the other world, that which turned
its back on Francis and holy poverty—the world of buying and sell-
ing, of power and pleasure—appeared more and more to the poet as a
whirlpool swirling on itself with ever-increasing speed, reducing all
to flotsam. Everywhere an obsession with things, property, gold, and
benefices, litigations, the buying and selling of ecclesiastical offices.
Before Dante thundered his denunciations Jacopone railed against
the clergy for dwelling not on Holy Scripture but on decretals, and

37

INTRODUCTION

against the Curia for embodying the spirit of profit and loss, of spiritual bookkeeping. He loathed that bureaucracy, which survived all popes and, he was sure, manipulated them. At their very best the members of that group represented the triumph of legalism over the spirit of Christ, and at their worst the abomination of desolation.

Were these charges actually an excess of indignation on the part of a champion of holy poverty for whom even modest creature comforts seemed a vile contamination? No doubt some colors did appear darker to Jacopone than they actually were. Yet his was not a voice crying in the wilderness. There were other such voices, and not all of them Franciscan Spirituals. Clearly those lamentations and accusations were prompted by more than an excess of idealistic indignation. Even though corruption cannot be weighed and measured, there certainly was more than enough of it to justify Jacopone's anguish over those whose "one concern is for ecclesiastical office" (Laud 53) or his trembling in wrath because

> A faithless clergy has slain and destroyed Me,
> Laid waste My work and spoiled its fruit.
>
> (Laud 52)

The Church, Jacopone lamented, was dressed in mourning:

> Guided by other popes and cardinals it once illumined the
> night,
> Now that radiance is blotted black . . .
>
> (Laud 50)

The harshest indictment, though, was for his own, for those who had betrayed the Rule of Francis, Franciscans now indistinguishable from the most corrupt clergy:

> . . . Bastard sons [who] have made many enemies
> By letting gold and silver back in their lives
> And setting their opulent tables;
> They have lost all virtues and all respect.
>
> (Laud 53)

Hypocritical, unctuous friars now exercised power, and like wolves in sheep's clothing (Laud 32), those Conventuals went about seeking to win over to their ways the simple and innocent.

38

INTRODUCTION

Charges such as these led many Spirituals to a steady contemplation and proclamation of the coming of the Apocalypse; in their certainty of the imminence of that day they sought through prayer and resignation to do the will of God, to prepare for that trial. Jacopone in these years was of their company. In one of the most revealing poems, Laud 38, "The Difficulties of Attaining to the Virtuous Mean," though, he showed how painfully conscious he was of a tension he could barely sustain:

> Love compels me to love the lovable;
> The hatred of evil is a part of love.
> Love and hatred, that is to say,
> Are locked in unending struggle
> In the selfsame heart . . .

> Offenses against God make me want to avenge His honor;
> The love of neighbor inclines me to forgiveness.

What to do?

> I am caught between the two blades of the scissors,
> Each of the blades cutting into me.

The love of holy poverty made absolute demands, but how were they to be reconciled with the hatred, indeed the horror, of a corruption in head and members? The popes of his time as well as the higher clergy were, if not the whole of the putrefaction, a good part of it—was obedience to them to be unconditional? And the most agonizing question of all, in these fears and terrors that beset Jacopone, was that of the Order of Francis. When each day brought with it an increasing distance from those early ideals that had aroused exuberant hopes for a world made Christian, how could he love those brothers in Christ?

The anguish of these questionings was only intensified by Jacopone's irresolution, the paralysis that made the needed decisive gesture impossible. The dilemma would be resolved, of course; but to resolve it, at this turning point of his life as in previous crises, Jacopone would need to cling desperately to the example of Francis—but not the Francis who wildly gloried in holy poverty or the saint who

39

unflinchingly faced all that is most repugnant in life, as he mentions in the beginning of the Testament:

> The Lord God gave me, Francis, this way of doing penance. I was a sinner and found it hard to look at lepers, and the Lord God led me among them. As I left them, what had previously seemed bitter turned into sweetness of body and soul.

The Francis on whom Jacopone centered all his being in this time of trial was the founder of the Order, the lawgiver who sought to give permanent form to holy poverty; and as a brief excursus will show, that attempt reflected more than a little of the drama and suffering of Jacopone.

VI IN IMITATION OF FRANCIS

For some observers of the time, the report that a bedraggled group and its leader had appeared before Pope Innocent III in 1210 and asked for and been granted approval of their Rule seemed altogether incomprehensible. That small band—virtually all laymen—did not appear in any way noteworthy. Its members exercised no recognizable power. And, all the more bizarre, that request was made to a pontiff who, for all of his austere piety, was a legend in his own time for his absorption in and mastery of political struggles. That small community and its leader could very well have gone on with their work of prayer and assistance to the poor, and just as the pope paid scant attention to other such groups dotting the religious landscape of the day, so Francis and his followers, too, would have passed by unnoticed.

There are today many very drawn to the figure of Francis who share that perplexity. What was the point of his insistence on papal approval? Or of his determination to found an order—a work that anyone knows calls for gifts and skills not usually associated with poets and mystics? As long as the Rule consisted of a few evangelical precepts on poverty (as was the case with the first Rule, subsequently lost), all well and good; but even a minimal success, foreseeably, would make for problems.

And indeed at first sight there *is* something baffling about that

INTRODUCTION

determination to obtain papal approval, to found an order and give it rules; but rhetorical questions do not solve much. Our chances of finding plausible answers, moreover, are not increased by confusing two distinct problems, that of papal approval and that of Francis as head of an order and its lawgiver.

With respect to the request for papal approval, some have argued that the saint's stance toward the priesthood and the papacy was no more than deferential, that in effect he was seeking to ward off an inevitable conflict with "organized religion." Nothing could be further from the truth. At no time in his life did Francis consider his overwhelming experience of God, that awesome realization of his love, in any way a substitute for a sacramental Church. For him the sacraments, and above all the Holy Eucharist, were living water. He looked with reverence on the priest who administered them. The priesthood and its hierarchy in his eyes were part of a divine dispensation, a treasure; and in this apostolic Church, the traditional teaching on the popes as the successors of Peter had a central place for Francis. The temporal power that the higher clergy and the papacy had come to exercise in his day did not stand in the way of Francis's recognition that the spiritual authority of the papacy mattered. The notion of an inevitable conflict between priesthood, papacy, and believer, thus, would have appeared to him nonsensical if not blasphemous. Indeed, one of the reasons, though not the dominant one, that led him to approach Innocent III was the concern to distinguish himself and his followers from other groups of the day that did not give the fullness of their assent to orthodox doctrinal Christianity.

This acceptance of creed and ecclesiastical structure is the more submerged part of the core conviction of Francis. It is inseparable, though, from its complementary aspect, the ringing condemnation of the new society of the times where "all is seared with trade; bleared, smeared with toil"—with its indifference or patronizing condescension toward the poor, those whose lack of means made them unrecognizable as brothers in Christ. This perversion and loss in the eyes of the saint drowned out the period's grandiose achievements in poetry, stone, and thought. The condemnation was blunt; at the very time that a new capitalist world (capitalism as an outlook on life, not in the narrower Marxist connotation of the term) was vigorously asserting itself, the call of Francis went out to Christians to renounce that world completely. This was the meaning of the insistence on holy poverty, the radical, uncompromising renunciation of things, of pos-

sessions. Extreme danger called for extreme solutions, and only a lit-
eral living of the Sermon on the Mount, Francis passionately urged,
could rescue Christendom from an inert doctrinal orthodoxy or per-
verted notions of individual salvation.

But what of those traits of the papacy—one can well interject at
this point—that were not at all reminiscent of the reasons for which
Peter was given the primacy? And even good popes, the best of them,
in their attempts to transform the world used means that were notori-
ously at odds with the spirit that moved Francis. Was not the saint's
life an obvious condemnation of such papal policies?

The condemnation, of course, is unmistakable. The very act of
founding the Order, the call for a very special kind of brotherhood,
certainly attests to Francis's passionate conviction that those other
means had failed, that politics were bankrupt in terms of power as
well as in terms of justice. In the saint's eyes even Innocent III, that
remarkable pontiff who had demanded of politics more than justice,
who had viewed it as a means for the establishment of a Christian
commonwealth that would adumbrate the Kingdom of God on earth,
had failed. Not consistently capable of distinguishing between his
will and God's—a particular danger for all religiously oriented lead-
ers bent on the political implementation of their visions—that mighty
pontiff had merely accumulated political power. In terms of the imi-
tation of Christ, though, did it mean much to be the virtual king of
Rome and of the papal states as well as arbiter of the fate of English
and French monarchies and the Holy Roman Empire? Had this con-
summately skillful maneuvering done much to bring about the one
needed transformation of man that had nothing to do with power and
rank—that indeed proclaimed the hollowness of those triumphs?

Francis's condemnation of the most highly motivated of the pa-
pal policies of his day, thus, was unambiguous; but as in the case of
the recognition of the popes as successors to Peter, it pointed to an-
other essential aspect of the saint, and a no less important one, the
willingness to bide his time. *Il Poverello* was not guilty of incoherence,
much less failure of nerve, for not having made explicit a message
that was immediately and joyfully recognized by the multitudes. If
we do not drown out the voice of Francis (that is, his actions—for
they were his strongest words) with our own, the logic of his stance
toward that papal policy becomes evident. There were prudent rea-
sons for the absence of any such explicit condemnation of that papal
view of politics, and others of a far higher order. In Francis's vision of

a reformed Christendom, quite simply, the papacy played a central role. He believed in the primacy of Peter and his successors; and like many good men of his time and indeed far more intensely, he believed that the day would come when the papacy too would experience something of the freedom of holy poverty, divest itself of a power that hindered it in its mission, and run fleet of foot to the Kingdom of God. In brief, the firm hope, immoderate and magnificent, was that the papacy—again, in God's good time—would be reformed with the help of the example of a corporate living of the Sermon on the Mount. Viewed in this light Francis's condemnation of the political policies of the papacy in his times appears in its true configuration, and the partial truth in otherwise rhetorical questions assumes its just proportions.

There is, however, in Francis one central tangled problem that is not as easily done away with by making the necessary distinctions. We would be wrong in insisting on a notion of Francis the poet and mystic to the exclusion of Francis the founder and administrator of an Order, but we would be just as obtuse if we assumed that his talents for each of those very disparate vocations were equal. We give away the smallness of our dreams and visions, moreover, when we argue in a commonsense way that from the very beginning Francis should have realized the difficulties that he was bound to crash into as he went about translating his heroic reality of holy poverty into rules for an order. The truth is that Francis throughout his life sought to achieve a goal that was beyond any administrative reach.

Here again, however, one more caveat is called for. The story of those contrasting interpretations of holy poverty is *not* best understood in terms of an inevitable struggle with the papacy. There was such a struggle, of course, and it was decisive. But to dwell on that aspect exclusively (one thinks of Ignazio Silone's *The Story of a Poor Christian*) and see the papacy as the institutional moment that transforms all values into notches in a finely calibrated scale of the more or less useful and sees Francis, implicitly, as the symbol of an admirable and glorious religious naiveté is to view the problem with astigmatic lenses. In effect, to reduce it to these dimensions is to present it as Machiavelli presents problems in *The Prince*, in terms of alternatives (strength or fortune, chance or skill) that are absurd in their mutual exclusiveness. The precise locus of that conflict is elsewhere. It lies in Francis himself. Once the saint concentrated to excess on the renunciation of all possessions (an essential element in holy poverty but not the whole of it), his virtually unsolvable dilemma assumed its true dimensions; and in recognizing that complexity we see into the drama of his quandary and the marvel of its resolution.

There were few complications, needless to say, in the beginning when the literal adherence to a few Gospel texts on poverty had sustained Francis and his followers and made them luminous. But from the time the saint appeared before Innocent III until the close of his life, when in the Testament he took particular care to reiterate his teaching on the true observance of holy poverty, the changes were prodigious. As the Order grew in number, two problems with respect to holy poverty became more and more difficult: Was it possible to continue to make a hard-and-fast distinction between what was indispensable and what was superfluous? And did not the stress on the renunciation of possessions carry with it an attendant danger of losing sight of inner poverty? ("If I give everything I have to feed the poor," Paul admonishes, "but have not love, I gain nothing.") As long as Francis and his followers were the small group who worked and prayed and slept together in the dilapidated church of the Porziuncola these problems did not arise. The saint made prodigious demands on himself, and his disciples followed suit. By 1221, though, at a general chapter of the Order, the number of Franciscans was estimated at five thousand. The figure may have been exaggerated, but it is unlikely that there were fewer than three thousand, a community bearing little resemblance to the original circle of friends and followers the saint had worked with daily, the members of his "family." In the enlarged Order there were those who, when they became sick or old and feeble, did not find in themselves the strength of Francis, and sought some degree of comfort to alleviate their sufferings—a bed, shelter from the cold—and they found brothers within the Order willing to provide them with such help. According to the letter of the law that aid was good, provided that the shelter did not belong to the Order and provided that the brothers did not have to handle money. Again, as the Order grew in numbers friars sought to live together in one place, no longer in huts; and not surprisingly they sought to pray together in one church. Was that change in keeping with holy poverty? It was, as Francis wrote in the Second Rule, if the friars obeyed the injunction "not to receive money or its equivalents under any circumstances for themselves or through an intermediary." And to allow of no possibility of ambiguity the saint added, "The brothers are to own nothing, neither place, nor house, nor anything at all; but as

INTRODUCTION

'strangers and pilgrims' in this world, serving God in poverty and humility, they are to go out begging for alms without shame, because for us our Lord Jesus Christ took the form of a poor man in this world."

The authoritative tone, though, could not dispel one basic dilemma. Requests for modification of the rules on holy poverty could be rejected on grounds that bordered on fanatical fundamentalism or granted with a consequent attenuation of the rigor of the original demands. And since Francis could not steadfastly continue to demand of others an adherence to his own strict standards and at the same time respond to those compelling needs, he accepted the prevailing pragmatic solution: the *usus pauper*, which made a distinction between use and possession:

> For the necessities of sick brothers or others in need, or for clothing, let the ministers alone and with them the guardians through spiritual friends solicitously assist them (according to the place, time and cold of the season) doing what they believe necessity requires—provided, as has been mentioned, they do not accept money or its equivalents.

The sick or those in need received the necessary help, the friars did not touch money, and not even the ministers or guardians were contaminated by it since a solution had been found for this problem: They turned to "spiritual friends," who handled that unpalatable and dangerous work. The solution was ideal—but only in appearance. It was a transparently legalistic remedy for a problem that Francis knew could not be solved on a legalistic plane. The proviso that not even the guardians or ministers "accept money or its equivalents," moreover, brought out, and in a very garish light, one more particularly troublesome aspect of Francis's view of holy poverty. In his horror of *la gente nova e i subiti guadagni*, the new rich and their quick profits, as Dante described them, consciously or not Francis came very close to making money itself a fetish. The story of his ordering a friar who had handled coins to take them, hold them with his lips and insert them into dung is all too convincing; at one point his concern did become almost obsessive. To see money almost exclusively as a power for evil, in effect, was to put any possible balance between the rights of common sense and the heroism of holy poverty even further out of reach.

Nor did the distinction between use and ownership eliminate the

45

danger of losing sight of that inner disposition of charity which alone can imbue poverty with an evangelical spirit; indeed, in some ways it heightened the risk.

It was probably the awareness of this dilemma and its dangers that led Francis in the close of that Second Rule, a document that was remarkable in so many ways, to come to a startling solution of the problem, the ratification of the role that Cardinal Ugolino had for some years now come to play in the major decisions that confronted the Order:

> Again, in the name of obedience, I order the Ministers to ask the Pope to designate one of the Cardinals of the Holy Roman Church to act as governor, protector and corrector of this Order so that, always subject to and at the feet of this holy Church, and confirmed in our Catholic faith, we may observe the poverty and humility of the holy gospel of our Lord Jesus Christ, as we firmly promised to.

Henceforth, the ultimate responsibility was no longer that of the head of the Order. In the increasingly baffling business of deciding what fell within and what fell outside the orbit of authentic holy poverty the cardinal protector, like the pope, was to have a decisive say.

A Draconian solution, this answer to the problem still did not provide a final and definitive resolution of those vexing difficulties. In the five years left to him, doubts and misgivings continued to anguish the saint, and in his Testament Francis reiterated his teaching on the proper observation of holy poverty in three admonitions. In the first he urged the brothers not to receive "on any account, churches and houses made for them, *if these are not in keeping with holy poverty*—in accordance with what we promised in the Rule—and let them always adhere to these injunctions and live in this world like strangers and pilgrims." The original ban was modified but the admonition was no less intense.

In the second warning, against accepting papal assistance in any form, there was no weakening of the structures. Ever since Francis had discovered to his fury and consternation that papal privileges had been forced on the Poor Clares against their will, and persuaded Ugolino, his friend and later cardinal protector of the Order, to have them withdrawn, he saw offers of papal help as a most insidious temptation and threat to holy poverty. That aid could bribe the Order, sap it of its strength, make it lose its salt. "Let none of them dare to ask for any letter from the Roman court—to ask themselves or through intermediaries—for any church, for any place, for preaching, or even for protection from persecution."

And because Francis had long observed how his words could lose their original meaning and acquire new ones, he summed up all of his misgivings and anguish and strength in one final command:

> And let the Minister General and all the other ministers and custodians, out of holy obedience, neither add nor take away from my words. Let them always in all future chapters to be held, read this Testament together with the Rule.

> I firmly command all my brothers, lay and clerics, out of holy obedience, to put no gloss on the Rule or on these words in any way by saying, "This is how it is to be understood."

*　　*　　*

Over the years, and particularly in the period that followed Jacopone's entry into the Order, this battle cry, "No gloss, no gloss," the sign of a glorious and enduring contradiction in Francis, had given heart to the poet in his polemics and anguished meditations. Far less willing than Francis to recognize that certain problems justified modifications in the Rule on grounds of the Order's increase in size, intransigent in his demand for obedience to the letter of the law, Jacopone gloried in the accelerated tempo of the persecution of the Spirituals. His sufferings and those of his comrades, Jacopone *knew*, were a sharing in the Calvary of Francis. He was keeping the faith, fighting the good fight; and for the longest time he at best sensed obscurely that he was not altogether incarnating the spirit of Francis.

For Francis had not simply reluctantly acquiesced in the growing modifications of holy poverty—in an almost incomprehensible way he had embraced them. This has scandalized historians of the saint and the Order from the time of Paul Sabatier down to our day. That submission (and one might well marvel at the cost of it) can be read as an *avant la lettre* Franciscan version of *ac perinde cadaver*. In effect it had enabled Francis to make a distinction of which Jacopone was to be incapable until the final decade of his life—a distinction between those followers who made a travesty of holy poverty and those who in modifying it did not crush its fragrance. For all of its contra-

47

INTRODUCTION

dictions this solution, this Michelangelesque act of humility, had been in character. Obedience was central to the Rule; and the saint who toward the end of his life ordered one of the friars to lead him, sick and naked, with a rope around his neck through the streets of Assisi denouncing him for his hypocrisy would not be beyond wanting others to consider him virtually servile and cowardly in his obedience. For nearly the whole of his time as leader of the Order (he resigned in 1220) he had seen holy poverty as the key to humility; at the very end he found that humility in obedience.

As a follower of Francis, Jacopone could hardly avoid the problem of obedience, but as the conflict with the Conventuals became increasingly sharp he found it hard to follow in Francis's footsteps in this respect. Understandably so. With each passing year the poet's dread increased that holy poverty was being utterly ground into the dust by those who were pledged to give witness to it. More terrifying yet, it seemed undeniable that the papacy to which Francis had turned, toward the end of his life as in his youth, was giving aid and comfort to those apostates.

Viewed from the perspective of these fears, the actions of the papacy from the death of Francis in 1226 to that of Pope Nicholas IV in 1292 did indeed appear, and quite coherently so, as a gradual rending apart of that wild virtue which the saint held most dear. Again and again the popes had intervened in the struggles within the Order, and each time the spirit of holy poverty as Francis had lived it had been betrayed, or at least weakened. The papal deposition of Brother Elias in 1239 because of his flagrant disregard of holy poverty—the scandal that more than any other accounted for the fury of the Spirituals' indignation—in the judgment of most Spirituals had not gone far enough. Gregory IX, for all of his undoubted closeness to Francis and admiration of him, had not made the most of the occasion; the compromising Conventuals had continued in power. In 1230, but four years after the death of Francis, that pontiff had declared the saint's Testament null and void as a binding rule. Nor had Innocent IV done much to allay growing fears. In 1243, serenely oblivious of Franciscan sensitivities, that pontiff had deposited the papal treasures in the Sacro Convento in Assisi. He had also authorized friars to accept money and offerings of ornaments of great price for the construction and embellishment of the papal basilica in Assisi. In 1245, with a gesture that no Spiritual could forget, he had decreed that friars could turn to their spiritual friends not simply for basic necessities but for what they considered useful.

The papal policy had not changed substantially in Jacopone's own time. The major modifications of holy poverty had already been carried out; and though from the time of the election of Nicholas III in 1277, one year before Jacopone joined the Friars Minor, to the death of Nicholas IV in 1292 there were no new affronts to Franciscan sensitivities, the papacy in those years contributed little to the splendor of the Church and still less to its spiritual might. Compared with the preceding papal interference, Jacopone may have felt, the brazen nepotism of pontiffs such as Nicholas IV was preferable—but that was meager consolation. Recurring vacancies in the Holy See in this period, too, added little to the moral stature of the college of cardinals. After the death of Honorius IV in 1287 almost a year passed before a new pope was chosen, and on the death of his successor, Nicholas IV, in 1292 the throne of Peter was vacant for two years and three months.

This apostasy in the Order and the papacy—it was no less for Jacopone—now made it impossible for him not to acknowledge his agonizing dilemma. Was he to obey the pope or the founder of the Order in an apocalyptic time, in a world that in swirling down to its destruction remained deaf and blind to the teachings of Francis?

> The cracks in the world grow wider and wider
> And ruin hovers over the chasms.
> The world is like a man gone mad,
> And doctors despair of medicine and incantations;
> We can sense the approach of the death agony.
>
> (Laud 50)

"The members of the Antichrist call themselves Your Church," Jacopone screamed in his nightmare vision. "No longer, Lord, let this be so" (Laud 51).

It was precisely in these years of Jacopone's wailing despair, though, that a stillness came over Christendom, and an event occurred that gave even Jacopone pause in his quandary. After that last long stalemate, the result of power struggles among rival factions of cardinals, the princes of the Church on July 7, 1294, elected as pope Pier da Morrone, a seventy-year-old monk, abbot of an order of hermits and friend of many Spirituals. The reasons for that election are no clearer now than they were then. A sense of shame and desperation had some part in it, and just as probably more mundane considerations, such as the advantages of a holy man as a stopgap measure, played a key role. We shall never know the precise extent to which each of those considerations was a factor before they merged and became one. But the fact of that election appeared almost unbelievable. The new pope had no ambitions. The extent to which the papacy was a power did not interest him. He knew very little of canon law. The teachings of Gregory VII and Innocent III on political power and the papacy in all probability were completely unknown to him. Simply and unbelievably so, he was, in Ignazio Silone's famous phrase, a *povero cristiano*, a humble Christian. And when Charles II of Naples, holding the bridle of the new pope's ass, led him to his coronation in Aquila it seemed to many, afraid to hope, that the sign could no longer be denied: This was the day of the true followers of Francis, this was the fulfillment of the hopes for a papacy refashioned in the Franciscan image.

In all this elation, the unbounded joy of many of the Spirituals, Jacopone stood somewhat apart. When a number of his comrades, ignoring the admonition of Francis not to seek from popes even protection from persecution, asked Celestine to defend them—a request that was granted by incorporating them into the Poor Hermits of Celestine—Jacopone joined them. Still, that papal gesture did not dispel his doubts and fears. The poet remained guarded in his expectations. Did he have reasons for his dread that Pier da Morrone might not resist the blandishments of the Curia or those of the King of Naples? He may have. We know no more of the basis of that mistrust than we know of the character of Celestine V. There is no certainty that those lineaments, as sketched out by a few friends and opponents, are truly his. The best known presumed reference, Dante's *"colui che fece il gran rifiuto,"* is a case in point. It strains credibility to think that the poet of the *Divine Comedy*, whose Spiritual sympathies are clear and unmistakable, would have branded Pier da Morrone a coward; in any case to specifically identify anyone in that circle of the *Inferno* is to misread entirely the punishment that Dante metes out to the *ignavi*, the cowardly. The point of that punishment is that those who so sinned are *not* to be identifed; they are to remain anonymous.

Be that as it may, and whatever the reason for Jacopone's mistrust and the extent to which Celestine V may have justified it, there were no ambiguities in the tone of Laud 54:

What now, Pier da Morrone?
This is the test.

And the reference was very pointedly personal:

Now we'll see what comes
Of all those meditations in your hermit's cell.

Could Pier da Morrone defend himself against the snares of office, the insidious traps that were all about?

This is the test: we'll see if you're gold, iron, or copper,
Whether your yarn be coarse wool or fine.

This was followed by a threat, all the more menacing in its spelled-out consequences:

Disappoint those who have placed their hopes in you
And they'll rain curses on your head. . . .

Should you take delight in your power,
That would be the worst, the most infectious of ills.

Within a very short time, as Jacopone had warned, Celestine V was indeed tested. Not long after, so was Jacopone—and in no less wrenching a manner.

VII   APOCALYPSE AND TRIUMPHANT DEFEAT

"Moved by lawful considerations," Celestine V solemnly announced to the gathered cardinals on December 13, 1294, "namely by humility, the desire for a better life and tranquil conscience and likewise because of weakness of body and want of knowledge, the malice of people and the infirmity of my person," he, Pier da Morrone, was resigning from his high office. In a way such as few could have foreseen, that pontificate had come to a sudden end. Without precedent, the resignation stunned Christendom. In terms of politics and corrupt practices, some aspects of that brief tenure, no doubt, had been all too traditional. The King of Naples, forcing the pontiff to reside in his capital, had made the most of the move (the number of Neapolitan cardinals rose conspicuously) and the Curia had not lagged far behind in putting to its own use Celestine's simplicity and ignorance of bureaucratic practices. But that very exploitation had merely increased the growing admiration for the hermit-pope; as for favoritism toward any one group, it was well known that the aid and assistance the pontiff gave members of his own community was modest. The utter absence of self-interest was more unique than remarkable; so much so that in a very short time that goodness, piety, and poverty had earned Celestine the reputation of an angel-pope. At the news of his abdication crowds of poor people rushed to the royal palace, where the pontiff lived in a monastic cell, and on their knees pleaded with him not to abandon them. That demonstration may have been encouraged by the King of Naples but many of the supplicants had undoubtedly come of their own volition out of a sense of genuine grief and despair.

Even those who allowed a large place for political power in their view of the papacy sensed, if they did not acknowledge, the ominous implications of that abdication. A Christian, a good man, albeit without experience in administration and politics, had not succeeded in shouldering the responsibilities of the chair of Peter. He had failed, that is, in an assignment in which a number of his immediate predecessors, in no manner distinguished in doctrine, sanctity, or force of character, had somehow muddled through. The point did not need belaboring. For the first time, perhaps, in the whole of the Middle Ages the distance between the reality of the papacy and what good, simple Christians asked of it had appeared nearly bridged, and of a sudden the bridge had collapsed. Among Celestine's predecessors there had been popes who were admirable for many virtues; none of them, however, had reflected as he did the qualities for which Peter had been given a special place among the apostles. A small flame had illumined the night and shortly after had been extinguished, leaving Jacopone burning with shame for his taunting mistrust.

That shocked grief, however, did not overwhelm the princes of the Church. Nine days after that resignation a new consistory met and soon thereafter announced the election of a new pope. Once

again in the designation of the head of the Church political consider-
ations and strength of resolve were the major considerations. Anxious
to reassert the power and independence of the papacy, which they
considered to have been debased by Celestine, intent on preparing for
a confrontation with ever stronger monarchies, particularly the
French, the cardinals elected Cardinal Benedetto Gaetani.

The new pontiff, Boniface VIII, who acceded to the papal throne
on December 24, 1294, did not disappoint those expectations.The
leader of those cardinals who restrained Charles II in the uses he
sought to make of Celestine, Boniface, with his experience of diplo-
macy and his friendships in the highest aristocratic circles in Rome,
had distinguished credentials for the task, which he eagerly under-
took. An authority on canon law, imbued with the spirit if not the
suppleness of Innocent III, from the very beginnings of his pontifi-
cate the new pope meant to reassert the plenitude of papal power, and
particularly in its political form.

As a notification to all that a new regime was now in charge, five
days after his election Boniface VIII abrogated a large number of the
acts of his predecessor. The move had little to do with internal ad-
ministrative matters. Included among the abrogated acts, however,
was the authorization of Celestine that had rescued the Spirituals
from the harassment and persecution of the more extreme Conven-
tuals. Though not at all a sign of renewed papal hostility, it appeared
to some Spirituals, and Jacopone among them, that the new pope in-
tended to waste no time in disposing of them as with guile and craft
he had, according to rumor, disposed of Celestine V.

It was not the guile of the new pope or the reach of his political
ambitions, however, that outraged Jacopone. Boniface VIII, in the po-
et's eyes, embodied the vilest of moral heresies. An utterly false Chris-
tian, he was distinguishable from most such only in his power and the
arch of his greed. How, the poet of the *Lauds* asked in hatred and
fury, could a man who devoted the better part of his energies and
skills to the acquisition and accumulation of riches be pope? How did
he have the impudence to claim that he was a friend of the Order
when his life up to that point—and the prospects for the future in
this connection seemed even less promising—expressed contempt not
only for the fragrance of holy poverty but for Christian virtues?

This outburst, needless to say, was not a clearheaded analysis of
very tangled problems, but on one issue Jacopone was quite justified.
Boniface VIII was indeed greedy. While not yet a cleric the young

INTRODUCTION

Gaetani had managed to obtain the revenues of a handsome benefice
in Todi. As a cardinal he had spent considerable time and energy us-
ing his good offices to expand the land holdings of his family, espe-
cially those of his brother Roffredo. In his eagerness to obtain
territories of the Aldobrandeschi near Orvieto, not long before the
conclave that elected him pope, he had proposed to the commune an
exchange of territories the day he would be elected pontiff. And with-
in a short time after his coronation, following established custom, he
named a number of close relatives cardinals, and spent more than five
hundred thousand florins in land acquisitions that made a good part
of central Italy a virtual family fief.

There was also, for all of its almost uncontrollable passion, a hard
kernel of truth in the charge that Boniface despised holy poverty. The
pope did indeed on occasion speak well of the spirituality of the Fran-
ciscans, going so far at one point as to praise some of the Spirituals. In
all fairness, Boniface could claim that it was only when the Spirituals
attacked him and denounced the validity of his election that he moved
to defend himself and the papacy. The fact remained, though, that
even at his best, taking him at his word in his contention that he was
fighting for the political vision of the great Innocent III, Boniface
made it transparently clear that any admiration he felt for Franciscan
virtues and holy poverty was of an aesthetic, not a religious, order. A
leader completely immersed in political struggles, he most likely
viewed the Franciscan ideal as Montaigne at times (it was by no
means his final say on the matter) saw faith—a pillow for a weary
head.

In sum, then, though it was true that there were tangible
grounds for Jacopone's outrage—

Body and soul, sweeping aside all sense of shame,
You've given yourself to advancing your family's fortunes. . . .

O vile greed, thirst that grows and grows,
With all you drink you are never sated!
Have you ever thought, you wretch, that those for whom you
        steal
Have stolen from you something you were not aware of?

(Laud 58)

—it was equally true that on some other essential aspects of Boniface VIII Jacopone's passion blurred his vision. Like any inflamed partisan of a cause, moreover, he had no trouble discerning the workings of God where it most suited him:

> On the day of your enthronement
> (There was no want of witnesses)
> Forty men were killed as they were leaving the palace,
> A clear sign of God's displeasure.
>
> *(Ibid.)*

For two years, through 1295 and 1296, Jacopone wrestled with the demons of his fury, unable to come to terms with the meaning of that papal election, uncertain as to what he should do. Determined not to go into exile, as did some Spirituals, but to stand his ground in spite of the papal command to the Spirituals on April 8, 1295, to return to the control of the Order (in effect the control of the Conventuals), Jacopone now took a stand on the problem of obedience. Francis himself, he concluded, in these circumstances would have defied

> ... a new Lucifer on the papal throne,
> Poisoning the world with his blasphemies!
>
> (Laud 58)

After those two years, possibly spent in hiding, his hatred of Boniface VIII turned into overt defiance. Like Lodovico in Manzoni's *The Betrothed*, the poet "in the name of justice allied himself with thugs." He made common cause, that is, with the rebellious Cardinals Colonna, enemies of the pope whose moral stature was not visibly higher. On May 10, 1297, together with other Spirituals, Jacopone affixed his name to the Longhezza Manifesto, which denounced the conclave that elected Boniface VIII and called for the convening of a new council.

The answer of Boniface, in this case as in so many others weighing political considerations, hardly pure, with more strictly religious ones, was immediate. Within two weeks he excommunicated the Cardinals Colonna as well as the other signatories and called for a crusade against the "heretics," who had taken refuge in the Colonna fortress in Palestrina. The besieged forces held out for a year and a half. Shortly thereafter Palestrina was overrun, razed to the ground, and the central parts of the city were covered with salt. The captives were condemned to life imprisonment and Jacopone, among them, was stripped of his Franciscan habit and incarcerated in an underground cell in the monastery of San Fortunato in Todi.

Some sixty exhausted years old, cut off from all contact with the outside world, with no idea of the fate of his closest friends, more than once in these years Jacopone must have regretted not having met his death in Palestrina. His work done, he would have gone to his rest. Not the Christian to prize poetry or eloquence more than the imitation of Christ, he would have left behind him nonetheless a living legacy; and in his intransigence and defiance—that magnificent rarity, the anger of an old man—in hurling his stone against what he took to be the abomination of desolation, his life would have come to a good end. Rumor had it that Boniface had persuaded his predecessor (who had consulted him on the juridical propriety of resignation) to abdicate, speaking through a tube hidden in the wall of the room where Celestine slept and claiming to be an angel. For the poet, to die in combat against such a man would have been a good death.

And alternating with such regrets was the equally probable frenzied need to forget all, to push aside those tenaciously held convictions on holy poverty, to become numb, unfeeling in a

> . . . prison, underground, [that] opens on a latrine
> Whose odor is not quite the fragrance of musk.
> No one is allowed to speak to me, except for one attendant.
> And he has to report every word that I utter.
>
> (Laud 55)

"Take my hand," he besought Boniface from the depths of that cell,

> . . . give me back to St. Francis,
> Who will set me down at a table again,
> Where I may take my humble meal.
>
> The members of my Order weep for me
> As I stand on the brink of Hell;
> Let me hear a mighty voice proclaim,
> "Old man, arise, let your lament be turned into song."
>
> (Laud 57)

INTRODUCTION

These were the supplications and anguished silences of the prison years. In that turmoil, though, and strong from the very beginning, a new poetry asserted itself, an utterance that, rooted in the past, was altogether new. The years of horrid solitude did not break Jacopone. The convictions that had sustained him for a lifetime continued to do so. Now, though, they were heightened, transformed. The anguish and terrors over the betrayal of the Order, the nightmare fears of the Antichrist, the despair over a world oblivious of Saint Francis, all disappeared, exorcised.

With the exception of a few instances there is no sure way in which we can date the lauds of this period and determine which were composed in captivity and which belong to the last few years after he was granted his freedom. That does not matter much. It is the transformation, not the particulars of its chronology, that counts—that change which imparts a new depth, height, and breadth to the *Lauds*.

In prison poems that are without rival in the literature of his time for their mocking self-scrutiny, an astounding variant of Franciscan humility, Jacopone marked the beginning of a *vita nova* and a new poetry:

> I am fettered like a falcon,
> And my chains clank as I move about—
> The attendant outside my lodgings
> Can hear me practicing my new dance steps. . . .
>
> With all my talk, all my asslicking around the Roman Court,
> I've gotten myself thrown into prison.
> Wallow, wallow in this pigsty, while they fatten you up—
> Come Christmas, there'll not be enough lard on me to cut off a
>   slice.

(Laud 55)

The temptation to take refuge in martyrdom, all the more subtle for want of an audience, was dealt with as effectively:

> My good name,
> I entrust you to a braying ass.
> Let your place be behind the ass's tail;
> That will be your reward.

(*Ibid.*)

INTRODUCTION

The sarcasm that only a short time before had cut into Celestine V was now turned on himself:

> What now, Fra Jacopone?
> Now you're put to the test . . .
>
> *(Ibid.)*

And here in his prison-latrine, as in the past, it was holy poverty that sustained him, a living and close presence:

> As for my bill, I say eight Our Fathers
> For each penny I owe the Divine Innkeeper;
> That's the only kind of currency I have
> To settle my account.
>
> If the friars who go to the papal court
> And come back home mitre-cuckolded
> Had laid away more of this kind of treasure,
> They'd be better off.
>
> *(Ibid.)*

The strength that sustained him, he knew and gloried in the knowledge, was not his own:

> . . . I am accustomed to evil days;
> And this champion of mine will prevail against pain.
> He is armed, and self-hatred is his shield;
> As long as that protects him he cannot be wounded.
>
> *(Ibid.)*

The self-hatred was hatred of the weak self, the vain self, the self unredeemed:

> O admirable self-hatred that masters all suffering,
> Nothing can injure you, for to shame you is to exalt you.
> You have no enemies; all are your friends.
>
> *(Ibid.)*

INTRODUCTION

And the enemy whom Jacopone denounced as he danced triumphantly on these heights was not Boniface VIII:

> I am the only enemy that stands between me and salvation.
>
> (*Ibid.*)

The servant of the servants of God, who did not once deign to answer the poet's pleas for forgiveness, who ignored the prisoner's requests to speak to him through an intermediary, was not beyond the reach of the effects of his other shield:

> The shield on the right is of ruby;
> It blazes like fire, flames leaping high:
> It is made of ardent love of neighbor.

"Step closer," Jacopone urged the pope,

> ... and you'll feel its heat with a rush.
> Do what you will, this love will overcome you.
>
> (Laud 56)

The hatred that feeds on politics and apocalyptic fears and glows so fiercely in the pages of the *Inferno* was well known to Jacopone. But rarely in his or any other time have those who succumbed to it ever succeeded, as he did, in ripping it out root and branch.

In this spirit, Jacopone faced with serenity the dreadful emptiness that must have assaulted him again and again in these years. In one of the most moving pages of the *Lauds*, in a letter to John of La Verna, how to endure that fast when He imposes it, Jacopone wrote:

> I have always held, and still do, that it is a great thing to be filled with God. Why? Because humility is then wedded to reverence. But I have also always thought, and still do, that to know how to suffer His absence is even greater. Why? Because faith is then attested to without witnesses, hope without expectation of reward, charity without signs of benevolence.
>
> (Laud 63)

Among the last lauds, though, we find a still higher transformation of the theme:

> . . . if He embraces you,
> Return His embrace, but do not feel wronged
> When He absents Himself. Give no thought to yourself;
> If you love as you should, you will be filled with joy,
> Because that love in itself
> Glows with a light that does not fail.
>
> (Laud 91)

In the discoveries of a new and immeasurable world, the deepening insight into the love of God, those issues that had until then appeared pivotal assumed new dimensions. The question of why God allowed unworthy Christians to be successors of Peter, as far as we can determine, was not resolved. It merely receded further and further and disappeared. Clearly, had Jacopone been convinced to the last that the papacy had become the lair of the Antichrist, and for all time, the last lauds would have a different ring. But whether his silence on that score suggests that toward the very end he made his own that heroic obedience of Francis, or whether he turned from a problem that he could not solve to a love that he experienced as never before, we do not know—and it does not matter much.

It also appears quite evident that after a lifetime of struggle in defending a precise notion of holy poverty that brooked no compromise, the total absence of any such references in the last lauds suggests some change of heart. Here again Francis comes to mind. Though we have no way of documenting the probability, it does seem that in the cessation of all polemics, in asking to be given back to the family of Francis, Jacopone had made his peace with the Order. While the poet was faithful to his strict Franciscan ideal to his dying breath, the absence of all stinging references to friars who modified those austere demands suggests that the chapter had come to a close.

And just as the silence on popes and the papacy was extended to the clamorous events of those years—the humiliation of Boniface at Anagni at the hands of the thugs of the French monarchy and his pathetic death—in the same way that silence now appeared as a cautionary sign (as Francis had insisted) "not to have contempt for nor to judge those whom they [the friars] see dressed in rich and colorful attire, who are accustomed to fine food and beverages." Jacopone had come to his own version of Dame Julian's "and all will be well, and every kind of thing will be well."

And the joy, like Brother Fire in Francis's hymn, was jubilant and playful:

O jubilant joy and somersaults of happiness,
Pray, learn to be prudent;
Sensible people with sensible smiles
Cannot understand the wildness of your ecstasy!

Learn to conceal the bliss
Throbbing thickly beneath the surface;
There is meaning all unknown to sensible people
In the joyous gyrations of the wounded heart.

(Laud 76)

Now in his last meditation on total self-surrender, the experience that in proto-baroque language he called self-annihilation, the charity of Jacopone opened like rose petals when the sun is high. When man lost all, all things became his; in disowning all things he shared in their possession. In such moments the images and music that had previously played such a modest part in the lauds flowered, and Jacopone sang of "stone [that] will liquefy before Love lets me go," and of the transformation of the soul:

Just as a red-hot iron
Or forms touched by burning colors of dawn
Lose their original contours,
So does the soul immersed in You, O Love.

(Laud 90)

The soul, Jacopone wrote, ". . . ventures forth/Onto a sea without a shore/And gazes on Beauty without color or hue" (Laud 91). Once indifferent to the world of nature, the poet now sang of "the tree [that] harbors in its branches/Birds that announce the winter's end/With piercing sweetness . . ." (Laud 88).

In Laud 91, which begins:

Love beyond all telling,
Goodness beyond imagining,

61

INTRODUCTION

> Light of infinite intensity
> Glows in my heart . . .

Jacopone saw

> The doors open wide, and entering within
> The soul becomes one with God,
> Possesses what He possesses . . .
>
> Because it has renounced all
> That is not divine,
> It now holds in its grasp
> The unimaginable Good
> In all its abundance. . . .

In its plenitude, peace brings striving and contradiction to a close:

> The cycle of the seasons is no longer,
> The heavens are immobile, they spin no more.
> Their harmonies are stilled, and the profound silence
> Makes me cry out, "O unsoundable sea,
> I am engulfed by your depths
> And shall drown in the abyss!"

(Laud 92)

The sea that had quietly emerged in the close of Laud 39, "How the Life of Jesus Is the Mirror of the Soul,"

> Overwhelmed by the Infinite glory of my sweet Lord,
> I settle into the sands at the bottom of the sea.

reappears after so many years to the poet immersed in the greenness of rocky Umbria and crests to a height:

> What happens to the drop of wine
> That you pour into the sea?
> Does it remain itself, unchanged?
> It is as if it never existed.
> So it is with the soul: Love drinks it in . . .

(Laud 91)

INTRODUCTION

The language of metaphor is not that of precise theological analysis, and this image may disturb some readers who, like Ozanam, are particularly apprehensive of the dangers of pantheism. In Jacopone's ascent to God, though, that metaphor involved no greater theological danger than did certain visions of Joachim of Flora whom he, like Dante, considered *"di spirito profetico dotato,"* endowed with prophetic spirit. A sign of a cosmic flowering and convergence, that image expressed the certainty voiced in the last great mystical lauds, the high ecstatic certainty that

> God does not dwell in a heart that's confined,
> And a heart is only as big as the love it holds . . .
>
> (Laud 59)

Here, in this last flaming plunge into God, Jacopone came to his peace.

He died in 1306, three years after his pardon, granted almost immediately after Boniface VIII's death, and ten years after the death of the virtually imprisoned Celestine, kept in custody by Boniface as a precautionary measure.

According to tradition he died on Christmas Day after John of La Verna had brought him the Holy Eucharist. The exact date and the story of John of La Verna are matters of scholarly dispute. There is no questioning, though, their appropriateness. In what they suggest of the parabola of that life and utterance they are small masterpieces of medieval midrash.

VIII NOTES ON THE TRANSLATION

This translation is based on the text of Franco Mancini, the most recent scholarly edition of the *Lauds*. In all instances in which the text is at best dubiously authentic (the passages are indicated by brackets in Mancini's text) it has been omitted in the translation. Such indecipherable readings or interpolations and additions are rare.

The numbering of the lauds, however, follows the traditional one of Bonaccorsi, first used in his fifteenth-century edition. The same sequence is kept in the 1953 critical edition of Franca Ageno, and since that numeration, *grosso modo*, points to a plausible chronological sequence and conveniently groups together lauds with a common theme the arrangement has been retained. Reading an edition that ad-hered to Mancini's plausible reconstruction of the original numera-tion would have proven to be a very discouraging experience for those who came to the poems for the first time. For somewhat similar reasons the titles Bonaccorsi gave the poems, though often admittedly ponderous, have been kept as useful traditional labels.

Faithfulness to the text has been the primary but not the exclu-sive consideration of the translation. There are advantages in know-ing the precise meaning of Jacopone's words (that meaning, as Ageno's notes and Mancini's glossary amply document, is not always obvious), but that is only half the job. Had we but world enough and time, we first thought, it would be tempting to meet Jacopone on his own ground and offer a translation very close to the original in meter and rhyme. But after many a thought, and especially after repeated readings of the valiant attempt made by Mrs. Theodore Beck to do just that with the poems selected for inclusion in Evelyn Underhill's work (*Jacopone da Todi, a Spiritual Biography*, London: J. M. Dent and Sons, 1919), the translators thought it best to use another approach. The *Lauds* are not well served by making rhyme and meter the prima-ry considerations. Indeed, all too often in the original those consider-ations become the tail that wags the dog. A translation that concen-trates on the strength of Jacopone, by contrast, the mottled word, can bring out the muscular texture of that utterance.

As to the extent to which this effort has succeeded, that is not for us to judge. Not so modest as to be more sensitive to failures than suc-cesses, we are aware that one man's translation is another man's yawn and discomfort. We are particularly disappointed, moreover, in not having been able to do justice to Jacopone's relish for word play and punning (the word for hook, for example, *amo*, used on more than one occasion, also means "I love") and in one instance rather than discard the pun we have taken slight liberties with the text.

The language of the *Lauds* has an exceptional range, and includes vivid examples of what some call Anglo-Saxon bluntness. This trait is apparently not the monopoly of Anglo-Saxons and the translation, when the occasion demands, reflects that characteristic. Moreover, though one occasionally feels nostalgic these days for a pinch of Vic-torian reserve, that yearning was not such as to make the translators share Evelyn Underhill's distress with "the crudest and most auda-cious physical parallels" that characterize the "daring and detailed de-scription of the 'Spiritual Marriage'" in Laud 81, a laud that

INTRODUCTION

according to Underhill, "could hardly be offered to the modern reader."

In addition, since this translation is principally an introduction to the *Lauds*, it has not been weighed down with a detailed commentary. Even though Jacopone is not Dante, he is hardly devoid of theological learning and wide-ranging interests; so anyone familiar with the usual modern Italian edition of the *Divine Comedy*, with one-quarter of the page text and the rest commentary, will appreciate the reasons for this decision. Happily, the *Lauds*, as a whole, are not hermetic; and in those instances that demand some knowledge of the historical background—above all the conflict between Spirituals and Conventuals and Jacopone's defiance of Boniface VIII—the reader will find in the Introduction the indispensable minimum notions to put those lauds in context. For those who wish to deepen a knowledge of that and related areas, the bibliography will be of use.

The omission of the *Stabat Mater*, will no doubt come as a surprise to a number of readers. It has been excluded because the translators share the common judgment of most modern scholars, including Ageno and Mancini, that the composition is not the work of Jacopone. There are many reasons adduced to deny him this pearl of medieval poetry, and they are not of equal weight. At least one of them, a presumed ignorance of Latin on his part, is pure nonsense. (Laud 63, as the title indicates, contains a prose part that Jacopone composed in Latin.) But the fact that the *Stabat Mater* was not attributed to him until some hundred years after his death, and even more decisive intrinsic stylistic considerations (rhyme and meter point to a much earlier date of composition) persuade us to omit it in an edition limited to lauds known to be authentic.

The Lauds

1 THE SINNER AND THE BLESSED VIRGIN MOTHER

O gracious Queen, heal, I beg of you, my wounded heart.
Despairing, I come to you, confiding in you alone.
Without your help I am ashes.
My wound is past telling, my Lady, it festers.
Hasten, help me. This suffering unravels me;
The pain swells to a height, wails.

Prostrated humility is all I have to lay at your feet.
A new covenant I beg of you;
Redeem me in my servitude!
Lady, the price has been paid: He to whom you gave suck.
In the name of that filial love, turn to me.
Hasten, lily fragrant, hasten.

Son, I hear your cry,
And gladly will I come to your side.
First, though, you must submit to healing art,
And control the appetite of the senses.
Only then will crippled nature
Run no further risk.

Take the tonic of the fear of dying
(You are young, but death will come soon enough);
Put an end to your vanities
And their long dominion.
Drink of the fear of hell;
From that dungeon, remember, none escape.

Then the abscess in you will burst,
And the poison will ooze out.
All this do in the presence of my priest,
Called to this ministration.
God will cancel the debt, and in your strength
You will ward off the blows of the Enemy.

JACOPONE DA TODI

2 THE BLESSED VIRGIN MARY

Hail, Virgin, more than woman, holy, blessed Mary!
More than woman, I say: For humankind,
As Scripture teaches us, is born in sin;
In you, holiness preceded birth.
Womb-hidden, a mighty presence enfolded you
And shielded you from all contagion.

The sin that Adam sowed did not take root in you;
No sin, great or small, has place in you.
High above all others is your virginity and your consecration.
Your secret virgin vow leads you,
All unaware of charity's intent,
To a wedding feast, to your spouse.

The high-born messenger's annunciation strikes fear in your heart:
"If you accept the counsel I bring, you will conceive a son without
    peer."
"O Virgin, assent, assent!" the multitude cries out,
"If aid does not come quickly, we shall hurtle to our doom."
You consented, and so conceived the loving Christ,
And gave Him to those who had lost their way.

Conception by a word stuns wordly wisdom—
To conceive without corruption, untouched, intact!
Reason and experience know nothing of such a possibility;
Never was woman made pregnant without seed. You alone,
Mary Immaculate, you alone; in you the Word, *creans omnia*,
Residing in majesty, becomes flesh, God Incarnate.

You carry God within you, God and man,
And the weight does not crush you.
Unheard-of birth, the child issuing from the sealed womb!
The infant joyously leaving the castle, through locked gates,
For it would not be fitting for God to do violence
To the womb that sheltered Him.

O Mary, what did you feel when you first saw Him?
Did love nearly destroy you?

70

JACOPONE DA TODI

As you gazed upon Him, how could you sustain such love?
When you gave Him suck, how could you bear such excess of joy?
When He turned to you and called you Mother,
How could you bear being called the Mother of God?

O Lady, I am struck mute
When I think of how you looked on Him,
As you fondled Him and ministered to His needs.
What did you feel then
When you held Him at your breast?
The love that bound you makes me weep!

O salamander-heart, living in flame,
How is it that love did not consume you utterly?
Fortitude sustained you, and steadied the burning heart.
Yet the humility of the child dwarfed yours:
With your acceptance you ascended in glory;
He, instead, abased Himself, descended to wretched state.

Compared to His humility in becoming man,
All other humility is nothing but pride.
Come one and all, come running!
Come see Eternal Life in swaddling clothes!
Take Him in your arms, He cannot run away;
He has come to redeem those who have lost all hope.

3 THE ARGUMENT BETWEEN BODY AND SOUL

Listen to this argument between body and soul.
A bitter exchange, until almost the very end.

*   *   *

Let us do penance together. In this way
We can escape a harsh judgment
And come to a shared joy and glory.
Isn't that well worth a bit of suffering?

71

JACOPONE DA TODI

The idea upsets me. You know me—
I'm fond of my pleasures and comforts.
Besides, rigors of that kind would make me—
Weak and vulnerable as I am—lose my balance,
And quickly. That's enough of such talk!

Filthy, evil body, lustful master of gluttony!
Is this your answer in my hour of need?
Here, feel the lashes of this knotted cord!
They may sound like jarring rhythms to you,
But you will have to master them
And learn to dance to this music!

    Help, help! The soul is killing me!
    He's gone completely mad,
    He attackes me without cause!
    All bloodied, I call out for help.
    Oh, will my sufferings never come to an end,
    Will I never know joy again? Help, Help!

You are not going to die a quick death.
First, you have to take part in an experiment.
I'm going to see to it now
That your senses stop giving you pleasure.
You'll know what it feels like to lose all taste
For one satisfaction or another.

    Do that and you'll see me turn swollen
    And sullen, wracked with pain. What's more,
    I'll make sure that some of your joy is diminished.
    Think on it before you act rashly.

Take off your shirt. Here, put this one on—it's a hairshirt.
(There's not much room in penance for pleasure.)
Anyway, this is a sumptuous garment if you compare it
To the skin of the sow I first thought of giving you.

    Where did you find it, in Hell?
    The Devil must have woven it out of porcupine quills.

JACOPONE DA TODI

Each and every hair stings like a bee.
It's so stiff I can hardly bear it.

Come, here is your bed—
Lie down on this mat woven of reeds;
Note the pillow, a handful of straw.
You can use your cloak as a blanket—
If a donkey can keep warm, so can you.
Keep in mind that this is pure pleasure
Compared to what I have in store for you.

A fine featherbed—round stones from the quarry!
No matter how I turn I feel my ribs crack.
I'm black and blue—how can I get any rest?

Come, Body, get up! They're sounding matins—
Wake up! It's time for the divine office.
A new law summons you; come, set out on this path.

How can I get up when I haven't slept a wink?
This strenuous life, you know,
Is particularly bad for the digestion—
In fact, I haven't digested at all.
And the cold! It's given me rheumatism.
We have time, though—first let me rest a bit.

Where did you get your ideas on medicine?
Be stubborn and you'll face the consequences.
At any rate, I'm going to heal you once and for all—
And we'll start by doing away with all hot meals.

Now here's a lavish spread! O the scent
Of that bread—black, unleavened and hard.
A dog wouldn't want to gnaw on it.
I can't swallow it, it tastes so bad;
If you want me to survive,
Give me something else to eat.

JACOPONE DA TODI

You do go on and on, don't you?
Now I think we'll do without wine
And have no hot meals for lunch or dinner.
Keep complaining and things will get worse;
And believe me, I'll keep my promise.

> Suddenly I find myself thinking
> Of a woman I used to know—soft,
> Rosy-hued, elegant, a model of grace.
> I feel sick with longing for her;
> I wish I could speak to her.

Let me reward you for that mad fantasy:
For the whole winter now you'll go
Without a cape and without shoes.
And then we'll scourge you
Until the flesh comes off in strips.

> That water you gave me to drink is bad;
> I feel I'm getting the dropsy.
> Give me a little wine, please!
> It will be to your advantage—keep me healthy
> And I'll stay on the right path.
> Once I fall sick, you're the one
> Who will have to take care of me.

Since water makes you sick
And wine is a risk for my chastity,
We'll compromise: we'll do without both.
This will be for our common good.

> Too much, too much! You've won, I'll complain no more.
> Besides, what good has it done me? From now on,
> All I'll ask is not to transgress God's law.

Good! Keep your word and I'll see to it
That you'll not suffer any more.
Now to our common joy we'll both be saved!

* * *

Enough of that. Reflect on this struggle within man.
There are other aspects I have not mentioned,
And those I dealt with I shortened, so as not to bore you.

4   ON PENITENCE

Lofty penitence, suffering endured for love's sake,
You are precious indeed, for through you heaven is won.
Not imposed from without, but embraced by my will,
I forge you into joy. To the well-ordered soul
The only real suffering is sin;
All other pain is joy in potency.

The damned know nothing of this—
Fleeing suffering, they find joy in sin.
O admirable self-hatred, master of all suffering,
You do not take offense, so you do not need to pardon;
Loving all men, you recognize one enemy only
Worthy of hatred: the sin in yourself.

Self-love, at the opposite pole—you hold no man dear.
Quick to take umbrage, slow to forgive,
Your enemies are legion; in you hell has already begun.
O lofty Penitence, rooted in self-hatred, free gift of love,
Put to rout, I pray you, Self-love and all his cohorts,
Who darken the light of the soul.

Penitence is threefold: Contrition first wins forgiveness;
Confession then makes the soul once more pleasing to God;
And satisfaction cancels the debt due.
Similarly, sin inflicts three types of wounds:
It offends God, destroys our likeness to Him,
And delivers us into the hands of the Evil One.

Contrition brings with it three remedies
To heal these wounds—stabbing pain,
Burning shame, and terror of the Enemy.
Fear drives back the evil brood,

JACOPONE DA TODI

Shame restores the likeness to God,
And suffering wins forgiveness.

Confession, by drawing hidden evil
Out into the light of day,
And satisfaction for sins,
Justice in action, free man for sanctity.
The fruit of death felled the tree,
The fruit of grace makes it green again.

To acquire wisdom
Hearing sits at the feet of the teacher;
To atone for sins of sight,
The eyes weep;
To learn moderation, taste learns to fast;
And scent acknowledges her frailty.

Casting off soft garments,
The sense of touch renounces pleasure
And puts on a prickly robe.
The soul adorns itself with chastity
And in a fresh awareness gives itself,
An acceptable gift, to God.

5   THE FIVE SENSES

Each of the five senses argues heatedly
That his is the most short-lived joy,
That his delights fade fastest away.

The first to speak is Hearing.
"The contest is over," he announces.
"The sound I just heard is no more—
It touched the ear and vanished.
You can't deny that."

"Hold on," argues Sight, "I am the winner.
When I closed my eyes just now

JACOPONE DA TODI

I blotted out all shapes and colors.
How short-lived the vision!
Can there be any doubt who has won this contest?"

Taste is the next to dissent,
Arguing that he has bested all rivals.
"Who can doubt how fleeting is my moment of joy?
My mouth barely opens and already
The pleasures it gives fade away like a dream."

The sense of Smell does not hesitate
To come forward and press its claims:
"Rare essences are sent to me from overseas
To give me pleasure, at great cost and great risk,
And what is left of them is clear for all to see!"

But lustful Touch says nothing;
It is ashamed to come forth
And speak of its foul-smelling delights.
Now consider the advantages
Of this unmentionable, unbearable stench!

Suffering is not short-lived;
Unremitting pain is not a fading mood.
Consider the risks of the game carefully:
For the one move you're intent on making,
You appear willing to give up your soul.

My soul, eternity lies in you,
And eternal are the joys you seek;
The senses and their delights do not last.
Climb up to God: in happiness that knows no end,
In infinite joy, He will give you fulfillment.

6 ON BEING ON GUARD AGAINST THE SENSES

Careful not to trip, my friend,
                    take care!

JACOPONE DA TODI

On guard against the Enemy,
Who masks himself as a friend;
Do not believe his lies,
                    take care!

Shield your eyes from what you see:
It can wound the heart,
And healing is slow and painful,
                        take care!

Close your ears to vanities
That cling to you
And ensnare you,
                take care!

Keep watch over the joys of taste
And their poisonous excesses,
Cesspool of lust,
                take care!

On guard against the disorderly appetite
Of the sense of smell,
Ever eager for new scent,
                    take care!

On guard against the sense of touch
Not acceptable to God,
Your body's doom,
                take care!

On guard against family ties
That bind you tight
And lead to woes,
                take care!

On guard against a multitude of friends
Like armies of ants
That dry up your roots in God,
                    take care!

JACOPONE DA TODI

On guard against evil thoughts
That wound the mind
And make the soul sick unto death,

                take care!

7   ON THE DANGER OF NOT GUARDING ONESELF AGAINST SIGHT AND THE OTHER SENSES

If you would once more be made whole, Brother,
Do not trust the sense of sight;
It often wounds the soul mortally.
Sight is the Devil's pimp, a master of the art.
On spying your sins, it denounces you
Before his court, anxious to hand you over.
Outside the court, Flesh waits impatiently,
Straining to hear what is being discussed.
She then declares war on Reason,
Unyielding in purpose and fierce in desire.

If she finds the soul without defenses
She wins it over to her side.
"Sin," objects Conscience, "offends God
And leads man to his damnation."
Flesh's answer, by now a habit, comes quickly:
"God, the All-Merciful, will forgive me."
"That's a specious argument," Truth interjects;
"God forgives only those who repent.
You are not truly repentant;
You don't have it in you to repent."

"But I am burning with desire," Flesh retorts,
"I can no longer endure it.
Let me satisfy myself just once,
And then I will submit to your rule,
Be as pure and chaste as you want me to be."
"If you act that way," says Reason,
"You will become an object of contempt.
People will point you out,

'There she goes, the shameless hussy,
Bringing dishonor on her whole family.' "

The Devil then speaks up:
"Now what if you sin in secret, just this once?
Enough of this wrestling with your conscience:
You must sin and sin quickly,
Or you'll go out of your mind."
This is the whirlwind of fleshly desire.
When Reason yields to it, it turns bestial,
Becomes false to itself.
And once it has succumbed,
Flesh feels the bite of Conscience.

Sea tempests and howling winds will calm,
But not the fury of Conscience,
Uprooting joy—trunk and branches.
Peace and happiness are gone forever.
Flesh, in her misery, feels
That there is not one person
Who is not aware of her shame;
Wherever groups huddle together she suspects
They are staring at her, whispering about her;
And whatever they might suggest, she will not heed.

All her joy, laughter, and playfulness are gone.
People continue to murmur among themselves,
Relatives hear and begin to complain—
It's more than enough to make one think of suicide!
This is the right moment for the Devil:
"And what will you do now,
Now that all the world despises you:
Is there anything, anyone you can hold onto?
It makes you think, doesn't it,
Of putting an end to things?"

Pay no attention to him!
He only compounds evil.
There is a way out:

JACOPONE DA TODI

Regain control of yourself
And in tears confess your sins;
Then you will be healed.
See how great sins grow
From little ones,
And end in murder
And the downfall of families!

Be alert,
Keep the fire away
From the city gates!
Once it burns within the walls
You'll not be able to put it out.
Now see the fruit of false delights—
Body and soul subjected
To searing torments!
Remember, Brother, be on guard:
The good watchman does not nod.

8 ON THE DANGEROUS CHARMS OF WOMEN

Women, you know how to inflict a mortal wound!
There is poison in your sidelong glances.

The gaze of the basilisk is fatal;
Your glances are no less so
To the souls redeemed by Christ.
The basilisk hides and does not show itself;
Unless we happen upon it by chance, it hurts no one.
You, the greater threat, move about openly,
Poisoning with a glance.

Do you know, women, that you destroy souls?
And with nothing more than burning desire?
You steal from Christ, wound Him mortally;
Handmaids of the Devil,
You wait solicitously upon your master,
And your knowing ways assure him a plentiful harvest.

81

JACOPONE DA TODI

You say you paint your face for your husband,
Who takes delight in you.
You lie:
He takes no joy in your vanity,
Suspecting that you might be making yourself up
For something much less to his taste.

Howling with rage,
Burning with jealousy,
He will strike you and beat you,
Insisting you tell him
With whom you went out, and where.
Excuses will not help.

Yet I must admit
You are clever, very clever!
You've made an art of deception.
With high heels and thick soles
You transform your small self
Into an elegant and stately lady.

A woman with a pale complexion becomes rosy-hued,
And without much effort a dark head turns fair.
Does the wretch adorn herself with intertwining braids,
Tresses that make a rich halo around her head?
She does it with a hairpiece made of vile-smelling fibers.
Fools are taken in by this.

Should her husband unexpectedly come to her
While her hair is still undone,
She'll grab a pile of braids
And quick as a flash, with devilish skill,
Wrap them around her head so expertly
You would think the hair was her own.

And what will she do, the wretch,
To make her face smooth and soft?
She'll make use of a cream
That's good for old scuffed leather,

And that will rejuvenate her.
Fools are taken in by this.

And when she gives birth to a baby girl,
If the baby's nose should appear misshapen,
She'll push and tug and pull at it,
So utterly reshape it,
That the girl will have no trouble
Competing with her sisters.

Then there are others instead
Who care less about attracting men,
But delight in high elegance among themselves.
They do not realize the dangers
Of their stupid vanity,
The risk to their souls.

You women lack the strength to fight,
But the weakness of the arm
Is more than made up for
By the vigor of the tongue.
Nothing can restrain that tongue of yours
From hurling words that pierce the heart!

Yet he whom you wound
Will not always just go quietly to bed;
The time will come when he will pummel you,
And that will give you no joy.
He will accuse you of infidelity and despise you;
Yours will not be a very good life.

Your husband will suspect
That someone else has made you pregnant,
And his blood will boil.
He will lock you in your room,
Out of earshot of neighbors—
And oh, the agony of your death!

JACOPONE DA TODI

9 THE ADVICE OF ONE FRIEND TO ANOTHER
ON MAKING ONE'S WAY BACK TO GOD

O my brother, before death overtakes you
Come to terms, find your way back to God.
The game you are playing is close to madness;
Before your time is up, start all over again.

> Thank you for your good words, brother,
> For your concern. But I have a family
> To think of, and that makes things difficult.

You have a family to support, but have no right
To support it with the goods of others.
Regulate yourself according to your wealth,
According to what you can afford.
There is not much point in dying for your children.
They'll not thank you much, whatever you do.

> If I change my ways, brother,
> What will become of those sons of mine?
> How can I leave them paupers,
> To be pointed out as "that wretch's sons"?

Come, why not think on death, which awaits
Both father and son? Follow the path
That leads out of the labyrinth.
The irresolute father is in danger
Of ending up with his son in Hell.

> But I've become accustomed to being well dressed,
> To a certain decorum. How can I suddenly change,
> Become an object of people's contempt,
> Have them point to me as that poor idiot?

A baited fish hook looks good to a fish,
But once he has swallowed it
It gives him little pleasure.

84

Very well; but you must remember
That in my weakened condition
I cannot stand fasting,
And poorly prepared food makes me ill.
I cannot do without the things I'm accustomed to.

You might try meditating on dungeons, then,
Where kings and barons and young lords
Used to a higher estate than yours
Have lain, and there been reduced by hunger
To gnawing on their muddy sandals.

Do you expect me to stay awake at night,
To stand for hours in prayer? I would die!
Staying awake till the wee hours
Makes my head spin for all of the following day.

Think of sentinels, how they stay awake.
When encircled by the besieging foe, all night long
They make their rounds, always on the alert,
Intent above all on the defense of the castle.

Your arguments frighten me, brother;
You make me feel the wound of holy love.
The world will no longer deceive me.
I shall go to my confessor,
Denounce my foolish ways.
Better to be a poor beggar
Than to have my riches
Plunge me into blazing fire.

10 HOW GOD LEADS THE SINNER TO REPENT

Who has given you such boldness,
Sinner, that you do not fear Me?
I could hurl you into the abyss,
And with good reason. But I have been patient
So that one day you would be able to repent.

JACOPONE DA TODI

I beg You, gentle Lord, be patient.
I have been misled by a deceitful enemy
And because of my sins
I have lost everything.

And why am I tempted to cast you into the abyss?
Because you abandoned Me for the Enemy, believed him.
You brushed aside My counsel with great impertinence.

    In the world, I was told, I should act
    In a wordly way; later, much later,
    There would be plenty of time to confess,
    They said, and You would pardon me.

And you believed such an obvious ruse?
You know that you have no right to live
For a year, or indeed for an hour.
You made a great mistake
To think you would grow old.

    Lord, the hope in Your pardon led me to sin.
    I trusted that toward the end
    I would be able to return to You.

I grant forgiveness to the man
Who weeps over his sins—
Not to the sinner who hopes
That I will delay in coming.

    After sinning I thought of confessing
    But the Enemy whispered to me,
    "Do you dare? How could you bear the penance
    You would be given for such great offense?"

The punishment in this world is light
Compared to that in the next!

    Out of shame I remained in this wretched state,
    Arguing that I could not possibly confess
    Such abominable sins to the priest.

JACOPONE DA TODI

Better to feel shame before My priest
Than to suffer it in grief
When I shall pass judgment on you,
And all your sins will be trumpeted
In the presence of a vast multitude.

> Say no more. I yield.
> I repent of my transgressions
> And my utter lack of prudence.
> Have mercy on me, O Lord.

Since you have surrendered to Me, I embrace you.
And may this pact endure for all time,
For I cannot abide ingratitude.

11   CONTRITION FOR HAVING OFFENDED GOD

Lord, let me die
Before I offend You any further;
Let my heart stop beating,
Rather than persevere in evil.

Your indulgence, Lord,
Has been of no avail,
So ungrateful have I been,
So unpardonably churlish.
End this life that continues
To place obstacles in Your path.

Better that You kill me, Lord,
Than that You be given
Any further offense;
For I see all too well
That I do not change my ways,
And still burn with the desire to commit evil.

Condemn the impenitent sinner;
He merits punishment.
Carry out the sentence:

Strip me of health,
And all freedom of action;
I have made evil use of those gifts.

May no one take pity on me,
Or feel any affection for me;
I have not been quick
To make friends with the infirm.
Wrest from me that self-confidence
That made me sing in joyous exultation.

Let your creatures gather together
To take vengeance on me,
For I have consistently made ill use of them,
In opposition to Your decrees.
May my suffering, O Lord, serve to avenge You.

My lament comes late,
And late are the tears
I shed for the loss of You.
How can you dwell on this,
O my heart,
Without turning to ashes?

How can you turn your back on Love,
Love that grieves for you?
Deny your heart
To the One who suffered for you?
Put aside all concern with yourself
And weep over the dishonor you have done Him!

12   HOW SIN KILLS THE SOUL

What death is to the body,
Sin is to the soul, but worse.

Bodily death first inflicts the wound
From which life ebbs and then,

JACOPONE DA TODI

When the soul leaves, the body turns to nothingness.
The wound of sin goes deeper than that.
It drives a wedge between God and the soul,
Sows corruption; the soul can no longer do good;
Increasingly absorbed in the vastness of evil,
It is weakened more and more by a vile pleasure.

Death robs the body of color and of beauty,
So undoes it as to provoke horror.
Who can remain unshaken by this sight?
In the same way, sin wounds the soul
And destroys the beauty God imprinted on it.
If one could gaze upon the sinful soul he would die;
Its countenance is terrifying,
Its glance cruel death.

Death makes the body putrefy,
And the vile stench drives away all who approach.
No one, neighbor, friend, or relative,
Can endure the presence of a corpse for a day.
Were all the world's stench concentrated in one place—
Sulphurous fumes of decaying flesh, odor of latrines—
It would be musk and amber compared to that of sin,
The stench with which hell reeks.

Natural death, when it strikes the body,
Deprives it of all good company,
Makes it like a leper,
Bars it from human intercourse.
Sin so wounds the soul that it cuts it off
From the company of God, the angels, and the saints.
The doors of the Church are closed,
And the sinner deprived of all her consolations.

Natural death consigns the body to worms;
It becomes their home,
And they gradually devour it.
Sin does something similar to the soul:
It hands the soul over to devils

JACOPONE DA TODI

Who, as is their wont,
Instead of devouring it slowly
Torment it in endless pain.

Death's last gift to the body is the grave;
No palace or court, but a small, narrow space,
Just barely long and wide enough to hold it.
Sin leads the soul to the tomb of hell,
From which it can never escape.
Renounce the sin, brother, that leads you there.
If these are the wages decreed,
This is what you will be paid!

13   HOW GRACE TRANSFORMS THE HELL OF
SIN INTO BLISS

The vice-ridden soul is similar to Hell:
It has become the abode of the Devil; it is his.

There Pride sits enthroned in demonic fury.
There dark Envy lays her snares;
All vestiges of the good are blotted out,
Such darkness has fallen on the mind.

The flame of Anger dances about,
Drawing the will to evil,
Turning and twisting upon itself,
Biting itself like a thing possessed.

Sloth spreads its bottomless cold
And the soul, bewildered,
Cut off from the comforts it knew,
Is dissolved in terror.

Obsessive Avarice, a worm that knows no rest,
Has eroded the mind with endless preoccupations;
And Gluttony, devouring serpents and dragons,
Is oblivious to the price it will have to pay!

JACOPONE DA TODI

Fetid Lust,
A raging, sulphurous fire,
Smothers the soul
In which it takes lodging.

         *   *   *

Come, people, come,
And marvel at what you see:
Yesterday the soul was hell,
Today it is paradise!

Putting Pride to rout,
God has infused the soul with Humility.
Hatred He has sent away,
And filled the heart with love of neighbor.

He has cast out Anger,
The tyranny that enchains
And maddens the soul,
And lo, once more it is meek.

Sloth is no more,
And Justice is reborn,
Straightening at once
The twisted soul.

Mercy sends Avarice into exile,
And great are the riches she dispenses.
Temperance, reasoned temperance,
Takes the place of Gluttony.

Foul-smelling Lust takes flight and again
The court is resplendent with chastity.
Be grateful, heart, for this God-given good;
Live in love forever, just as the angels live.

JACOPONE DA TODI

14 PRIDE, THE ROOT OF ALL SINS

Many are the offspring begotten by haughty Pride;
The whole world laments the evil she has spawned!

The proud man seeks to subject the world to himself,
Wants to look up to no one at all,
Nor can he find strength
To take joy in his equals.
With unruly heart he oppresses the weak,
For they could never pay him sufficient honor.

When the proud man espies others on higher ground,
Envy is born. Unable to topple them,
And fearful of their strength,
He swells with hate, lays down snares,
Ever ready to condemn and destroy them,
Wanting to be rid of them once and for all.

To gain ascendancy
He imposes his authority,
Creates divisions,
Fans passions into wars,
And pursues relentlessly
What eludes his grasp.

Anger maddens him, he is like a rabid dog;
And once she rules the roost,
Cruelty comes to keep her company.
Not even a massacre would suffice
To satisfy the hatred
Sprung up in the heart.

And then, when Anger can no longer be sated,
She languishes, and Sloth is born
And takes possession of the soul.
All things lose their savor,
And bitterness and desperation
Dry out the marrow of the heart.

JACOPONE DA TODI

Looking for a remedy, Sloth convinces the soul
That a bit more wealth is all that is needed
To restore her flagging courage.
That is when Avarice, lying in wait, pounces;
Using every weapon at her command
She blocks the gates and imprisons the soul.

The avaricious man's whole household
Lives in fear of being robbed—
Wives, sons, daughters-in-law, servants,
Scurry frantically: Listen to their curses!
Each of them invokes the death
Of that demon incarnate!

He does not hesitate to steal, deceive, compel;
Indifferent to the opinion of the world around him,
He insolently expresses his desire to possess
A piece of land, and threatens the owner
If he does not surrender what is rightfully his;
No neighbor this man has not attacked and robbed.

He has fields, vineyards, orchards, woods;
Gold and silver and jewels under lock and key.
He has mills to grind wheat,
And animals large and small,
Plus the houses he's built
To store all his riches.

Grain he piles up from year to year,
Always prepared for the time of famine.
When it goes moldy, and he has to eat it that way,
Oh, the wails, the wails that fill the house!
How he curses his family—
All peace and harmony are destroyed!

Should his wife and children
Put on weight, he is displeased—
The bread and wine in his house
He considers all his.

JACOPONE DA TODI

Listen to his abuse. "Filthy wastrels!
May you all be damned for devouring my wealth!"

You have made a hell of your life,
Avaricious man, and already have a taste
Of the hell that will follow.
Be patient, in time you'll get your fill.
O Pride, this is where you lead—
Man loses his honor, and all revile him.

Five sins there are that reign in the soul:
Pride, Envy, Anger,
Sloth, and Avarice.
Two others, Gluttony and Lust,
Are of the flesh, and these two
Are spread throughout the world.

What Avarice has accumulated Gluttony devours—
In a tavern more than willing to exchange
A piece of property for a glass of wine.
That's how hard-earned money disappears!
And to make sure the money is quickly spent,
Lust keeps Gluttony company.

Lust doesn't think it bad business to trade
A piece of land for a buxom wench;
It's not hard to imagine what joy will ensue!
My soul, be on guard against such guests.
They make Hell your inheritance
And rob you of Heaven.

15   THE SOUL RETURNS TO THE BODY
FOR THE LAST JUDGMENT

Rotting body, I am your suffering soul—
Arise, we stand damned together.
The angel trumpets a fearful blast;
Come quickly, we must take our places.

JACOPONE DA TODI

Remember when you would tell me
That there was nothing to fear?
How foolish I was to believe you!

     Is that you, my soul, so kind and understanding?
     Since you took your leave I have returned
     To nothingness. Hearten me with your company,
     For the faces I see about me terrify me.

These are the demons with whom you are to live.
What you will have to endure I cannot describe,
I could never remember it all;
But if all the oceans turned to ink
There would be enough only for a brief allusion
To what you will have to suffer here.

     How can I answer the awful summons?
     I am close to dying out of fear,
     Feel death's harsh presence close.
     I felt this way when you left me
     And broke my every bone and joint.

We once were bound by love,
Now we are bound in pain by eternal hatred,
Bones rubbing hard against veins,
Nerves against joints, all the humors
At variance with their original state.

     Galieno, Avicenna, Hippocrates
     Never understood how the ills of the body
     Are linked to those of the soul.
     They meet head-on in anger
     And create such a turbulence
     That I wish I had never been born!

Up with you, accursed one, no more delays!
Our sins are inscribed on our foreheads;
What we thought we did alone,
In the privacy of our chamber,
Will now be displayed for all to see.

Who is this mighty king, this awesome lord?
I wish I could burrow my way
Under the earth, he frightens me so.
How can I flee, how escape
The severity of his countenance?
Earth, cover me now
That I may not see his wrath!

He who comes is Jesus Christ, the Son of God.
The sadness in His face shows
He takes no delight in me.
We could have inherited His kingdom.
O evil and vicious body,
What have we won for ourselves now?

16   THE THIRST FOR PRAISE AND
THE ATTENDANT LOSS

What are you doing, O captive soul?

> I stand and suffer;
> Infinite Goodness has fled me.
> Banished from God's presence
> I am in Hell.

You, in Hell? You make me despair.
What of all the perfection you attained?

> A cloistered nun for seventy years,
> My bridal vows were made to Christ;
> Now I am wedded to the Devil.

How can this be? Many there were
Who hoped for your canonization.

> They knew nothing, then, of the cancer
> In the darkness of the heart.
> God, who sees all, was not deceived.
> I kept myself a virgin,

JACOPONE DA TODI

I castigated my body,
Never looked at a man,
So as not to be tempted.

For more than thirty years,
As my sisters can tell you,
I spoke not a word, and practiced penitence,
Even when others could not see me.
Nor did I neglect to fast—
Bread, water and raw herbs—
And kept it up for half a century.

For fifty years I tormented myself
With prickly skins, knotted ropes,
Penitential bands and garments.
I cheerfully endured poverty,
Cold, heat, ragged clothing.
But humility—ah, humility—was lacking
And that is why God has cast me off.

I found mental prayer and devotion
Of very limited interest:
What I thirsted for was praise.
When I heard people call me "the saint"
My heart would preen its feathers;
And now I find myself here in Hell,
With those beyond all hope.

Had I known shame I might have cured
The infection that raged in the heart
And I might not now be here.
But the thirst for praise kept healing at a distance.
O love of honor and praise, I did not understand you—
It was you who killed me. How much you meant to me,
And how much I have paid for that admiration!

If you were to see my face now
You would feel naked terror:
The sinful soul provokes horror
Past all imagining; in torment,

It gives off a vile stench
And blows rain on it
From every side.

There is no end to this suffering,
Nor will there ever be.
Those who inflict the punishment
Never tire, those punished never die—
Imagine how much love is lost between the two!
The pain consumes but the dead soul lives on,
And the suffering never diminishes in intensity.

When I think of the little good I've done
And all the evil, I think I shall be damned.

Do not despair, brother.
You can gain heaven if you take care
Not to rob God of the honor due Him.
Fear and serve Him with loyalty.
If you persevere in this to the end
You will know true humility
And your story will have a happier end.

17 THE LATE BROTHER RINALDO

Brother Rinaldo, where have you gone?
And what philosophical points
Have you made of late?

Tell me, Brother Rinaldo, for I'm not sure
Whether or not you've paid your debts.
Are you in glory or is it warmer there?

I know you died meekly, confessed, were absolved.
But this is the question—were you truly contrite?
Was yours the unction that truly heals?

JACOPONE DA TODI

Now you have come to that school where Truth alone
Judges every word and lays bare every thought.
Now you have come where all facts are clear,

And the cards are on the table, good and evil face-up.
No point now in fashioning clever sophisms to counter
Strong syllogisms, in prose or in rhyme: truth will out.

You earned your doctorate in Paris, Brother;
Great was the honor and great the expense.
Now that you're dead and buried the real test begins.

Tell me now, did you truly feel
That the greatest of all honors lay
In being a poor and despised *fraticello*?

I can't help but wonder if the fruit of your labors
Will suffice to release you from your debt.
Did you pay to your God the tribute that was due?

18 HOW THE WORLD BLINDS US

Man, you have been duped; the world has blinded you
With pleasures, luxury, rich garments and praise.
These delights, where are they now? All gone.
Gone, these hollow seeming-treasures,
And all of them the cause of sin.

And still you refuse to repent
Until you come to the very end;
Only then will you call the priest.
"What have you to tell me?" he asks,
And you answer, "I am very, very sick."

You grieve over your children who will be orphaned,
More concerned for them than for yourself.
When they moan and wail you become so upset

99

JACOPONE DA TODI

That you forget your resolution to make amends,
To return to the source all ill-gotten goods.

When you are close to death they call in the tribe—
They will not let you die in peace,
With a little decorum; they will throw you out!
As they carry your body to church
They'll bemoan their tragic loss;

Once back at the house for the funeral meal
They will gorge themselves and forget about you.
All that money you made—of what use is it now?
O blind man, for whom do you work—for your children?
When you're dead they'll soon devour all that you earned.

19 ON THE MAN WHO FAILS TO MAKE SATISFACTION FOR ILL-GOTTEN GOODS

Sons and brothers and sons of sons,
Give back what I left you of ill-gotten goods.
You promised as much to the confessor,
Now you must keep your word!
Of all the wealth I left behind
You've not given a cent for the repose of my soul.

    True, we promised; did you really believe
    We would do what we said? But leave it to us;
    Tomorrow, as they say, is another day.

When I think of all that I left you—
What have you given me in return?
Oh, the shame I have brought on myself,
Abandoned by those I loved most!

    If you loved us you should have seen
    The port you were heading for.
    We mean to enjoy what you left us;
    Stop wasting our time with your problems.

JACOPONE DA TODI

I left you barrels of wine,
Cloth of wool and of linen—so much—
And now you have forgotten me.

> Yes, you were generous with us,
> But that does not mean
> We have to be generous with you.
> Resign yourself to your suffering:
> You're reaping, after all,
> What you yourself have sown.

I worked hard and did without things
To enlarge the vineyard,
To build up our holdings, and now
You give me not even crumbs?

> True enough, you worked hard,
> But that was your affair. Rest assured
> We'll not waste much time on your problems.

And you are the sons I raised from the cradle,
Flesh of my flesh? How can you do this?
But the day will come, you may be sure,
When you will share my anguish!

20 ON THE WRETCHEDNESS
OF THE PENITENT SINNER

O time ill-used, how often have I, wretch,
Turned you against my Creator!

Once grown to man's estate,
The world was my only delight—
Nothing could vie with it.
Now I must leave what I cherished most,
And suffer eternal torment and pain.

Then my great joy was to eat and to drink,
When not whiling away long hours in bed;

Such pleasures sufficed to fill my days.
Now I see that I was deceived;
And realize the offense I gave to the Lord.

While others were at Mass or listening to sermons
I (with apologies to moderation)
Was sitting down to a proper meal. In those days
I sang a lot; now my song has turned into a wail,
A long lament that's more and more out of tune.

If family or true friends
Would dare to suggest
That I consider changing my ways,
My answer was quick: "Just one more word,
And you'll find yourself dead!"

When out with my friends I'd sometimes see
A beautiful woman who caught my fancy;
With knowing and confident glance I would beckon.
If she turned away and spurned my advances,
I'd slander her name and boast of a conquest.

Pride in my ill-gotten wealth made me lose my soul;
Now I'll get misery in exchange.
There's not enough time left for penance
For death, I feel, presses hard,
Impatient to hand down the sentence.

Chaste Virgin, help me;
Succour me not, and I go to my doom.
Queen of Heaven, mother of that sweetest of Sons,
You are our advocate; we beg of you, intercede,
That exile from the kingdom be not our portion forever.

21   ON BEGGING FORGIVENESS AFTER DEATH

"O merciful Christ, forgive me my sins,
Which have led me here where none escape.
I cannot flee, for death has struck me down

JACOPONE DA TODI

And taken from me the solace of the world I knew.
I stand before You, despairing,
For the Enemy is here, ready to accuse me."

"This is not the time for repentance.
I urged you to confess in the past,
But you were busy with other things.
Now is the time for Justice to rule."

The Enemy appears, ready for the joust:
"Pray, Lord, give ear to the case
I will make against this man,
And let me take him off to prison
If I present enough evidence to condemn him."

The Lord, Justice Incarnate, responds:
"I will listen impartially to the evidence,
For all men trust in My truth and righteousness.
You have examined the defendant,
Tell us what you have found."

"Lord, You created him according to Your good pleasure,
You showered him with grace, endowed him with perception.
Of the commands You gave him he kept not a single one.
In all justice, he belongs to the master he served.

"For he knew exactly what he was doing
When he accumulated riches through usury,
When he short-weighted the poor. In my court
I shall give him proper recompense for those sins.

"When people would say to him,
'Some day you too will die,' he would laugh,
Certain that day would never come!
For this too he will be repaid.

"Whenever he saw a gathering of young people
He would go with his instrument
And sing them new songs,
Winning over the poor wretches.

"There are some in my court who will teach him to sing.
Were I to go into his many sins in detail
It would be proof of my skill but boring for all.
I have mentioned a few just to refresh his memory.

"If I have wronged him in any way,
Let his guardian angel give the rebuttal.
I am sure of his loyalty to me,
And he can not deny it."

"Know, Lord," the guardian angel replies,
"That the Enemy speaks truth.
Indeed there is much he did not mention.
Even as I watched over this man
He had nothing but contempt for me."

"What do you say to this?" God replies,
"What excuses can you make,
For I intend to pass judgment.
How could you justify such arrogance?"

"I have no defense against these charges
Except to beg You, Lord Jesus, to help me,
For the dark visage of the Evil One
Fills me with terror."

"Long have I waited for you to repent;
The sentence is just. Leave Me.
You will no longer look on My countenance.
Call the adversaries to take him away."

"Lord, Lord, how can I leave You?
Help, they gather around, ready to take me away!
Bless me, Lord, as I go. Console me in my grief."

"I damn you and strip you of each and every good.
Begone, you who were so long swelled with contempt!
Had you been My friend they would not be able
To take you away. Now you are damned forever."

JACOPONE DA TODI

The Enemy sends his forces—
A thousand with pitchforks,
Yet a thousand others
That attack like dragons.

Each is impatient to drag the sinner away.
"You are ours," they shout in glee.
Binding him tightly with a chain,
They lead him off to Hell.

Those with pitchforks bellow,
"Out with you, accursed one, out!"
And as all look on,
He is cast into the flames.

22   ON OLD AGE

Two old men, haggard and weak, compare notes.
One is well dressed, the other in rags;
Neither can now take care of himself.

Weeping over his hard-hearted son,
The one in rags bitterly laments,
"Look how I'm dressed by that Jew-son of mine
Now that my money is all in his hands!

"When he comes home his sharp tongue makes me tremble:
'You old idiot, you demon incarnate,
Won't you ever drop dead?
When will I ever be rid of you?'

"But God be praised, my daughter-in-law
Is a jewel of jewels, a gift from Heaven.
Without her I would long ago have been dead;
She washes, de-lices, changes me—God bless her, my joy."

"O my friend," answers the other,
"How it hurts me to listen

JACOPONE DA TODI

When you speak of your daughter-in-law,
So different from mine.

"Let me tell you
What mine is like
And you'll see in a flash
How very lucky you are.

"My daughter-in-law is a clever shrew.
From early morning her forked tongue
And braying speech inform the neighborhood
Of every quarrel under our roof.

"Howling wind and driving rain
Sooner or later spend themselves,
But her malicious tongue
Knows no rest.

"The scalding torrent of her abuse
Rolls over me unrelentingly.
Whenever it comes,
Death will be kind.

"My son, by comparison, a gift of God,
Is gentle and patient, respectful in speech.
Sometimes he beats her for the way she treats me,
But nothing helps; she's got a thick hide."

"My friend, what you tell me
Lightens my burden.
Of all men, I thought,
The least fortunate am I.

"Now I see you are a hundred times worse off.
Is there anything more frightening
Than a vicious woman?
May God in His justice damn her to Hell!"

"My friend, perhaps you remember me young,
Courteous, handsome, gracious, well-bred.

JACOPONE DA TODI

Now I've become the favorite target
For the insults of a money-grubbing tavern slut.

"Her tongue, a jousting lance, unhorses me;
She loves to humiliate me, time after time.
'God has forsaken this house,' she screams,
'Since this old idiot came to nest here.

" 'He's filthy, vile-smelling, capricious and ugly,
With squinting, bloodshot, pussy eyes
And a nose that drips like an old water mill.
His teeth look like those a wild boar might bare,

" 'With gums enflamed and bloody red:
When he smiles it's enough to kill you,
With his horrible face, his foul breath,
His hacking cough and thick yellow catarrh.

" 'His skin is as tough as leather, and scaly,
And he's always scratching himself like a mangy dog.
What a broken-down wretch, almost bent in two!'
All this she says, and more I'll not mention."

"Just to hear this, my friend,
Is to suffer with you.
How can you bear it?
And your heart hasn't burst?"

"Don't worry, I've earned what I'm getting,
I sinned and it's right that I be punished;
I admired inane beauty and now I pay the price.
Small wonder it is that I get on her nerves—

"It's a marvel, considering the state that I'm in,
They don't throw me out in a ditch somewhere,
Like the foul-smelling carcass
Of a dog that's been skinned.

"Dwell on this picture, you who delight in beauty;
Who knows, it might be of help to you.

107

Dwell on this tale of the sad old age of one
Once so handsome they came from afar to seek him out.

"Here I am now, a misshapen and broken thing—
How can one look at me and not feel horror?
Beauty is fleeting, and the morning flower
Is sure to fade away with the sun.

"Filthy world, you have stripped me of all—
False world, false to those who find their peace in you;
Cheating world, my time at your gaming table has cost me dear:
Your smiles and blandishments have made me lose paradise!

"Lord, have mercy, grant me Your friendship;
Forgive me, I beg of You, my many sins.
My obtuseness cut me off from You,
I abandoned You for the enemy world.

"And now that I would want to change
I lack the strength to help myself,
And the tardy recognition
Makes me burn with shame."

23   ON THE WRETCHEDNESS OF MAN

What is there, man, that you can glory in?
Dwell on what we are and what we were,
What we shall be, to what we shall return.
Dwell on that.

Conceived by human seed—how repugnant!
Think but a moment and you will see
There is nothing in which you can glory.
Fashioned of worthless stuff,
Born in pain, brought up in misery,
In the end, you know, you will turn back to dust.

Poor, naked, and wretched pilgrim,
Your first song was a sob and a wail.

JACOPONE DA TODI

You came to this world with nothing at all,
But the Lord, ever gracious, came to your aid.
Think now: if the Lord should decide to take it all back
You would be left with nothing of value.

Proud of rich robes cut to your taste,
You become puffed up when people call you "Sir."
What if the lamb should want back her wool, the flower its dye?
Your taste, your pride, are vain and foolish.
Consider the tree and its fragrant, succulent fruit;
Consider the vine and with what it is laden—

Good grapes, that gladden the heart of man;
Let them ripen a bit and they make good wine.
You, instead, are laden with lice, and their eggs as well,
And they are like servants that give you no peace.
How foolish to glory in your wealth,
When every last shred must be left behind!

24   THE PAIN OF LIVING

Jagged life, unremitting battle,
How you crest in pain!
Still within my mother's womb, I was pledged to death;
How I survived in that close, cramped darkness I cannot say.
When I emerged it was with anguish and pain.

I was wrapped in a sack for a mantle,
And when it was opened
There I lay, bloodied, wretched,
Greeting life with a wail,
My entrance song.

Those around me, taking pity on me, held me in their arms.
My mother was exhausted and in agony:
Mine was a hard birth.
They washed me and put me in swaddling clothes,
Wrapped me up again.

JACOPONE DA TODI

Oh, the helplessness of the infant, his utter dependence!
Not that I gave proper thanks to those who helped me—
I dirtied myself and my wrappings again and again;
That was the soup I served up
To those who cared for me.

If my mother were to come back and tell
What it cost her to feed me!
Getting up in the cold,
In the heart of the night, to give me her breast,
While I would cry and cry, and she would wonder why.

Afraid I was sick and would die,
She would tremble all over,
Undress me and study me intently
As she pulled back the covers,
Searching in vain for the why of my wailing.

O mother of mine, the price you paid for one night!
Nine months so heavily burdened,
Then doubled up in pain,
The birth itself, and the exhausting feedings—
Was that an adequate recompense?

My father, some years later,
Had me learn to read and write;
When I did not do well he gave me a thrashing.
My dread of those lessons
I cannot describe.

I wanted to join the children outside,
But if I dared to play hooky
My father would get his whip and use it.
I could not go on, I felt;
I wished my father would die.

In fights with others boys, how many blows my poor head took!
But I gave back what I took, in good measure,
Pulling out fistfuls of hair, getting in good punches in return;

JACOPONE DA TODI

More than once they knocked me down and trampled me,
Jumping up and down as if they were pressing grapes.

As a young man I took to gambling and acting the part
Of the big-time spender, hobnobbing with people with money.
My father, in rage and anguish, refused to pay the bills;
To pay my debts I was forced to steal,
Since I had squandered more than I had.

Once I got it into my head to lead the life of the rich,
The effect on the family was worse than any illness;
All the gold and silver in Syria would not have sufficed.
Oh, the agony of those shipwrecked ambitions,
The agony of the attendant shame!

The family's income was not nearly enough
To pay for the needs of the day—
The contests, jousting, dress, banquets, good fellowship,
Invitations to friends and relatives, gifts;
Taken all together, they made the well run dry.

If I felt I had suffered a wrong
That cried out for vengeance, with no compromise possible,
And I found it inconvenient to pay the penalty to avenge myself,
The hatred of my enemies would grow and sicken the soul
With rage and pain, since the stain of dishonor remained.

But if, on occasion, I did take armed revenge,
In terror of a vendetta twice the strength of mine
I would close myself in the house, afraid to step out.
Who can describe the pain that stems from hatred,
Hatred that is rooted in evil beginnings?

I wanted a wife, and I dreamed of a beautiful woman, no shrew,
Healthy, of my own people, deferential, eager to please,
With a handsome dowry, gracious, well-mannered and composed:
Visions of this sort rarely leave heaven,
As the dreamer of such visions comes to know!

111

JACOPONE DA TODI

Once married, when no son appeared to be coming, I grieved,
Anxious to leave my goods to those of my blood;
When children did come, they did not yield perpetual joy.
Such is the condition of man in this world,
Where the blind have no notion of the good.

I thought that harvesting and working the vineyard,
I was laying away for the future; but there's no end
To sowing and reaping, buying and selling.
What are we doing but stealing God's time
And breaking His commandments?

Ceaseless labor to put food on the table, noon and night;
And if the table's not set as I like it,
You can be sure I let them know!
O jagged life, look where you have led me,
All the livelong day is passed in tribulation!

My gluttony knows no end:
Tasty dishes, good wine and fresh fruit;
But to furnish a bountiful table is no easy task.
Toil and weariness, will you never come to an end?
And for what? An empty purse and a soul steeped in sin!

Then, of course, there's the pain of fevers,
The ones that doctors cannot heal
With simple incantations.
To prescribe rose syrup or the like
They charge you by the bushel!

The number of woes to which man is subject
Would be hard to set in rhyme.
(Doctors, to be sure, know more than a little about this—
They who write the prescriptions and charge handsome fees.)
Better, then, to make our story brief.

Rain-battered winter comes,
Dissolves into mud,
Oozing and threatening.

Then wind and cold and snow;
But no matter, the work must go on.

Summer approaches,
Hot weariness black with flies,
And at night no relief:
There are swarms of fleas
Ready to take over.

Exhausted, I throw myself on my cot,
Aching for rest;
And then of a sudden,
My cares begin to whirl about me,
Robbing me of sleep.

At daybreak the wheel starts to turn again,
The pressure mounts;
I never seem to do
What I've set out to do,
And by nightfall I get the usual recompense.

To finish one thing is to begin another—
There's no escaping that; there are times
When I just don't know where to turn.
Is this the reward for accumulating riches?
Will this weariness never end?

Following these rhythms,
I stumble into old age;
Gone are all traces of youth—
Ugly, slovenly, repulsive, condemned to die,
And accepting the wages of death.

Life, you cheat, are these my rightful wages?
To be eaten by worms—
Is that proper thanks for services rendered?
And this is the currency
With which you pay all men.

Yet all men are called to another life,
A life without end.
Two cities can be espied on that distant horizon:
One a city of suffering,
The other a city of delights.

Unless you cease to love sin,
Leaping flames will swallow you;
But cast off your old self,
And you will be shepherded among the saints.
Why leave the world in torment?

25 ON THE CONTEMPLATION OF DEATH
AND THE BURNING AWAY OF PRIDE

Proud man, when your confidence and spirits soar,
Pause, bring to mind the tomb; dwell on that image.
Imagine your body in that dark hole.

You who are buried in that blackness,
Suddenly catapulted out of this world,
I see you completely covered with dirt. Tell me,
Whatever happened to the rich robes you wore?

    Gently, brother, gently;
    I can tell you something of use.
    My relatives washed and changed me
    And buried me in rags.

What about your well-groomed hair—
Was it yanked out in a fight?
Or was it boiling water
That made it all fall out?

    My hair fell out when the skin
    All slid off in patches, something
    I never dreamed of when I was alive,
    Strutting about and shaking my golden curls.

JACOPONE DA TODI

Where are your eyes, those deep, clear eyes?
Out of their sockets, and by worms consumed.
Your haughtiness, apparently, did not impress them.

> Gone are those eyes, instruments of sin,
> That knew how to beckon with a furtive glance.
> Oh, the pain of this body decomposing,
> And the soul consumed in flames!

Where is your nose—
Did some illness eat it away?
Or have the worms been here, too,
Now that your pride has crumbled?

> I have no more nose, it has rotted away,
> Something I never dreamed of when I was alive,
> Enamored of a vain and deceitful world.

Where now your razor-sharp tongue?
Open your mouth—I see nothing.
Did someone cut it out,
Or did you bite it off yourself?

> Gone, gone is the tongue
> That once sparked so much discord:
> Something I never dreamed of when I was alive,
> And gorged myself and drank beyond measure.

Draw your lips together to hide your teeth—
Yours is not a pleasant smile, it mocks me.
It frightens me just to look at you;
Your teeth are falling out without being pulled.

> How can I draw together lips that I do not have?
> I never gave much thought to this moment.
> Oh, what will become of me now
> When the soul and I plunge into flames?

Where are the arms that with their brawny strength
Were such a threat to the timid and the weak?

JACOPONE DA TODI

Scratch your head now,
Shake your curls, preen yourself!

> This tomb is littered with my peacock feathers;
> The flesh has fallen from my bones.
> Every glory has been stripped from me,
> And I've been filled to the brim with misery.

Up with you now, you've been in bed long enough!
Take up your arms, take up your shield!
Surely you'll not give up without a fight?

> Stand up, take arms? You must be jesting!
> What a fool I was to make no provision for death!

Call on your family to help you now,
Have them protect you from the devouring worms.
In truth, they were quicker than the worms
To strip you and divide your property and clothing.

> I cannot call them, for I am gagged;
> Have them come and see my plight.
> Let those who are intent on buying lands
> And expanding their holdings look at me now.

> O you who are worldly, meditate on me;
> Renounce vanity before it is too late.
> Remember, fools: be your empire ever so vast
> It will sooner or later be narrowed to the grave.

26 CHRIST'S LAMENT OVER THE SINNER

O man, you whom I want to save,
Why do you flee Me, and grieve Me sorely?

For you I took flesh from the Virgin Mary;
I struggled—to no avail—

JACOPONE DA TODI

To lead you to a safe haven;
And still you persist in your ingratitude.

I am not cruel or arrogant—why do you turn your back on Me?
I brought into being all other creatures
That they might serve you, do your bidding;
Why do you show no concern for Me?

As a father who loves an ungrateful son alternates threats
And gentle counsel to turn him from his evil ways,
Just so I act toward you, threatening Hell
And promising Heaven, if only you will turn back to Me.

Flee no longer, child of My heart:
Shielded from evil,
All sins forgiven,
I give you a kingdom as your inheritance.

Long have I sought you, dearest of brothers;
My Father has sent Me to bring you back.
Return in love to His joyous court,
Come and let us rejoice together.

How can you continue
To reject such love?
Put an end to your ingratitude,
Which cost Me such pain.

Long and bitter was the pilgrimage I made for you.
Look here at My hands: see the price I paid for you.
Let the ice in you begin to thaw,
And your heart rejoice in your newfound riches.

Look here at My side: see the price I paid for you.
Here the spear tore through My flesh,
Here the iron pierced the heart.
Your name is writ therein, writ by Love.

In flight from Me you have let flesh deceive you,
You have abased yourself for pleasure,

Mindless of what is to come.
Flee no more, My son, or you will stumble.

The world puts on a gladsome face
To persuade the unwary of its goodness;
Its emptiness and falsity it carefully conceals, knowing
That as you approach Me, I raise you up and crown you.

Demons, too, are watching your every move,
Intent on blocking your return to that lofty state
(The loss was yours, and the fault as well)
From which with bloody violence they made you fall.

Are you not aware, O wretched one,
That world, flesh and devil encircle you?
How will you overcome these enemies?
Do you think you can do so without My help?

Had you abandoned Me for a valiant lord,
Your rejection would not have made Me suffer so,
But to leave Me for a traitor
Who leads you to the torments of hell!

To flee from My mercy and run toward vengeance!
My judgment on you for your evildoing,
For your hardness of heart,
Will be delivered in sadness.

But I find no comfort, you worsen each day.
Be punished, then,
Now that all else has failed,
Now that you've given your final "no."

27   THE SOUL CRIES OUT FOR HELP
AGAINST THE SENSES

O Blessed Christ, Love source of all delight,
Have pity on my wretchedness!

JACOPONE DA TODI

Have pity on me, a sinner, long in error.
I have merited the fires of hell,
For I abandoned You for the blind and venomous world,
The world which has lavished me with suffering.

The pain of sin swells within me,
My soul sags; unillumined
By the light of Your justice,
I live in shadow.

Once free from sin,
I'll be bathed in Your light,
But now I am a blind man
Fallen into a pit.

Three enemies have led me to this dungeon;
The strongest of them, with deceitful mien,
Clasps my soul and binds it in chains.
False friends, in secret they wound me.

Beaten, mocked, stripped naked, I feel my strength ebb,
Oozing out of sores that have festered too long.
The abscesses must be lanced, the proper salve applied;
Not treated, they will never heal.

Help me escape from the deceitful Enemy, O Lord:
His arrows, shot from afar, are aimed at the cleansed heart.
I cannot see the hand that wounds me;
To suffer thus is more than I can bear.

Making a bow of this world's delights,
The Devil sends arrows winging toward me.
The eye and the ear and all the senses,
Reel from his insidious assaults.

The nose seeks pleasure in scent, the palate something good to taste;
And all the senses seek to make me subject to them.
Nor are they satisfied when I grant them what they want;
They complain bitterly at the skimpiness of the portion!

The sense of touch complains it has a right to certain satisfactions:
"All your life I'll nag you!" But what choice have I?
If I release the brake that keeps my miserable body in check,
The anguish of remorse overwhelms and crushes me.

28   THE IMPATIENCE WHICH MAKES US LOSE
ALL WE HAVE WON

I work hard to lay away treasure—
If only I could hold on to what I've gained!

I am a friar. I've studied Scripture, I've prayed,
Endured illness with patience, and helped the poor.

I've patiently kept my vows of obedience and poverty,
Gladly practiced chastity as well as I could;

Meekly accepted hunger, heat, and cold,
And made long, hard pilgrimages.

I've risen early for divine office—from beginning to end—
Terce, none, and vespers, and vigils after compline.

But let someone say something harsh to me,
And I am quick to take offense, and spit out fire.

Now see the good the habit has done me,
The riches and ease it has won for me!

Let someone make just one comment that upsets me,
And I can barely find it in me to forgive and forget!

29   HYPOCRISY

I have strayed from the path trodden by the saints,
Strayed far, twisting my way into hypocrisy.
People consider me one of the illuminated,

And so I seem on the surface, as if humility dwelt in my heart;
But refuse me honor, and watch me sulk!
The man who has faith in me, in him I delight.

I also take pleasure, of course,
In displaying my virtues;
But let me hear one word of criticism,
And see how fast I take my leave.
Even my leave-taking is a stratagem
To persuade people of my sanctity.

I work hardest at giving the impression
That I've left the world behind;
My dress—sheep's clothing—proclaims the fact,
But within myself I know the cruel and ravenous wolf.
I enjoy affecting a lean and hungry look,
A sure-fire way to ensure admiration.

Should I hear some other ascetic
Praised as much as I,
I scowl within—that praise bothers me;
I put on a good face at the time,
But as soon as I'm alone
I relieve myself with an obscene gesture.

Shabbily dressed and austere, I beg from house to house;
I always ask in the name of God, and insert some edifying phrase,
But shake the dust from my sandals in anger when I get not a cent.
If brusquely dismissed I plead poverty and tremble with cold;
I smile on him who opens his purse,
Vent my spleen on the one who sends me away.

30 ON JUSTICE AND THE SEMBLANCES THEREOF

It is God above I wish to please;
What others think of me matters not.

Were John the Baptist to return and denounce
The sin of the world, once more they'd cut off his head.

JACOPONE DA TODI

The world today is in the grip of Pharisees;
Confronted with Christ's goodness, they would murder Him again.

The Pharisees were the religious of their time,
Envious and resentful,
Careful to seem unconcerned with honor,
The real object of their desire.

O false religious with swollen hearts, answer me!
Your pride oppresses and confounds the humble;
You crucify Christ in their souls,
You put Him to death with your Ciceronian rotundities.

Draw yourselves up to your full stature
And thunder me a sermon for the mote in my eye.
You scorn me, oblivious of the beam in your own.
Tend your own wounds, so wide and deep they cannot heal.

Students of Scripture, you want to preach,
And point out the darkness in my life, ignoring yours;
You make a show of your exterior, and have little love
For anyone who would search your heart instead!

The Order has given you a banner like the one they give a Lord
    Mayor:
Does that imply virtue or goodness in you?
If a Lord Mayor is derelict in his duties the court condemns him,
Puts a chain around his neck, calls the people to witness his
    disgrace.

That I am a son of Saint Francis fills me with pride;
How far I have strayed from his teaching
And from his example is clear for all to see!
He who defiles the whiteness of snow deserves to be condemned.

The man blinded by sin who leads others
Often guides them to the edge of the pit.
Why, then, does the preacher
Not first live what he preaches?

JACOPONE DA TODI

Why does the friar, spurred by the Devil,
Renounce poverty and become a bishop?
First poverty—then chastity?
It's but a short step.

The captains have betrayed the troops;
Our regimental flags have been trampled in the dust.
Help us in defeat, O Lord our God,
For we know not where to find refuge.

We were a mighty host, encamped on the heights,
But the waters of the flood have risen and covered us,
And taken from us the power to pray,
Which alone could keep us afloat and heal our wounds.

31 HOW AMBITION AND IDLE KNOWLEDGE
DESTROY THE PURITY OF THE RULE

That's the way it is—not a shred left of the spirit of the Rule!
In sorrow and grief I see Paris demolish Assisi, stone by stone.
With all their theology they've led the Order down a crooked path.

Our honored professors get special treatment
In the wing of the monastery reserved for guests,
While the others eat herbs and oil in the refectory.

Should the master of theology pick at his food,
They stand on their heads to try to please him;
Let the cook fall sick and who will pay him a visit?

In chapter meetings they keep passing new rules
And the first to introduce one
Is always the first to break it.

See how these theologians love one another!
One, like a young mule, watches and waits
For the right moment to kick the other in the chest.

Dare disagree with one and he will crucify you,
Laying snares until he succeeds
In sending you far, far away.

All day long he gossips and jokes with women;
A friar who just glances their way
Is apt to end up behind bars.

No matter if his father was a shoemaker
Or a butcher, to judge from his bearing
You'd think he was of royal blood!

32   THE NEED TO GUARD ONESELF AGAINST
     WOLVES IN SHEEP'S CLOTHING

O faithful soul, intent on salvation,
Beware the fangs of the wolf.

Beware the wolf who comes by stealth;
In the guise of a friend
He gains entry to your house,
Sure of deceiving you with his pious talk.

> The Lord bless you for the counsel you give me!
> You help to disentangle me from this web;
> Their assaults have cut me off from help,
> And I know not where to find refuge.

Be on guard; remember the Lord's warning
About the wolf disguised as a lamb.
By stealth he comes among the flock,
Then suddenly attacks and scatters them.

> I will tell you a story that's hard to believe:
> One came among us pretending to be a learned healer,
> And once unmasked, set himself to poisoning those
> Who had discovered and exposed his fraud.

Speak up; do not be afraid;
Now that you know, defend yourself.
Remember, once the wolf has you in his grip
He sinks his fangs into your throat.

But how can I defend myself when I am besieged
By those from whom I should expect counsel?
They act like lambs until I drop my guard,
And then quick as lightning they pounce.

Wisdom lies in trusting no one;
He who is bitten by a snake comes to fear the lizard.
Keep a wary eye on all sheep you do not know,
And your conscience will not reproach you.

33   THE COUNTERFEIT LOVE THAT OFFENDS THE VIRTUES

Counterfeit love, empty husk of virtue,
You cannot attain to the heights where true love dwells.

A storm-battered ship without a captain,
A stallion running wild—
No virtues to guide it, this false,
Unbridled and intemperate love.

A weak love, it is subject to mortal illness;
Adversity crushes it, and success all the more—
Applause for a lying exterior, for the false lovers of God,
And their hosannas in song and dance!

God loathes this counterfeit love,
A love whose words soar heavenward,
Hollow and false; men guilty of this pretense
Do violence to true love.

Love that knows not wisdom or prudence
Is unaware of excesses, is love gone mad.

JACOPONE DA TODI

It breaks laws and statutes, ignores established custom,
Claiming its exalted position frees it from the yoke of law.

For this love without faith,
Love gone astray, there is no sin.
This is abominable teaching, heresy!
All men do well to avoid its company.

Love not sustained by hope cannot find the truth,
Since in fleeing light it cannot see.
How can one turn to heaven if friendships bind him to earth?
Outside the law there is no freedom!

O Charity, true life—for every other love is dead—
You break no laws, but obey them all; and in the heart
In which there is no law, you bring it into being.
He who flees from you cannot know the sweetness of your fruit.

All acts are licit,
But not for one and all:
For the priest, sacrifice;
For husband and wife, the begetting of children;

For civil authority, the execution of criminals;
For judges, handing down sentences;
For lawyers, the presentation of evidence;
For doctors, healing the sick.

Not everyone has the right to kill a thief—
Only those invested with the proper authority.
The eye does not pretend to digest,
The nose to speak, nor the ear to walk.

He who lives without the law will perish without it;
And the path he follows will plunge him into Hell,
Where grievous sufferings are heaped up high
And companions in sin will be comrades in misery.

JACOPONE DA TODI

34 ON THE DIFFERENCES BETWEEN TRUE
AND COUNTERFEIT LOVE,
ACQUIRED AND INFUSED KNOWLEDGE

O Freedom, subject to all creatures,
You reveal the depths of the goodness of God.

He who sins has lost his freedom,
For he has betrayed his nobility.
Caught in the painful web of vice,
He becomes base; the Godlike strength and beauty
Mirrored in man becomes twisted and deformed.
The kingdom he then inherits is Hell.

Carnal love, malodorous cesspool,
Blazing sulphurous fire, reason turned brutish,
Stinking lust, sick and abominable,
Worshiper of the full belly;
O ash-covered land of Sodom and Gomorrah,
New friends rush to you, feverish with desire.

Counterfeit love, sterile harbinger of evil,
Both heaven and earth elude you.
The whole of your life
Is dread and pain; death is preferable
To this house of grief,
The gate of Hell.

Spurious, bastard self-love,
Deprived of reason by God omnipotent,
Your sloth and cowardly ways bar you forever
From the celestial kingdom, the royal people.
O the folly of loving created things alone,
Folly that makes you base and vile-smelling!

Natural love strengthened by philosophy
Bears some resemblance to spiritual love,
But in moments of crisis and pain
Its strength ebbs; when it is caught

JACOPONE DA TODI

In the tangle of suffering and illness,
It lacks the wings to soar above them.

Spiritual love, once infused in the heart,
Immediately becomes love of neighbor, so strong
That it gives all of itself to its beloved.
Its violent strength makes whole
Any love that is malformed,
As it lowers itself to heal.

If lofty love does not swoop down
It cannot touch creation's meanest plane.
The feebleness of our insight weakens the good
And defaces the temple of love.
I see this by the light of reason, and God revealed it
By humbling Himself to take human form.

Virtue is made strong
In trials and testing;
There is no easy leap, as there is none
Between intuition and realization,
Between theory and practice.
It is perseverance that leads to mastery.

Acquired knowledge, however long its meditation,
Cannot engender properly ordered love.
Infused knowledge, as soon as it touches you, fills you
With burning love, makes peace between you and God.
It makes you humble, edifies your neighbor,
And gives you knowledge of the truth.

A symmetrical balance of strength, judgment, and the will to do
    good,
Infused knowledge conveys an image of the Trinity.
Strength shorn of wisdom destroys the harmony—
If we grope our way in the dark we are bound to fall;
A crooked beginning leads to no good end,
And past a certain point it's too late to repent.

JACOPONE DA TODI

When the will overbalances judgment and strength,
There are no defenses against madness,
The trinity crumbles and falls apart.
Our vision blurs, and we find,
Contrary to our expectations,
That evils have no end.

What folly to pride ourselves on our lofty estate,
Perched on top of a rickety ladder!
Should the ladder break we plunge to earth,
And future generations will mock our madness
In song and legend. O the unpardonable stupidity
Of not trying to foresee the ends of our actions!

35   OF NOBLE ORIGIN, THE SOUL SHOULD TURN
SWIFTLY TO DIVINE LOVE

My high-born heart, take care!
Do not fall and plummet into the commonplace.

Yours is true nobility, hold it dear.
The gift of some small bauble binds us to the giver;
Will you show less gratitude to the great Lord
For the long and bitter pilgrimage made because of you?

Were the only daughter of the King of France, beloved of all,
Fairest of the fair, draped in the white stole of royalty,
To fall from her station and give herself to someone unworthy,
What would you think of that?

You, worse, have given yourself without a struggle to a shabby
    world.
The body God gave you as a servant is now your master—
Remember, he who allows his servants to assume authority
And give him orders is a negligent lord.

JACOPONE DA TODI

And still the body and the senses are not satisfied:
The sense of hearing is jealous
Of the satisfaction the eye takes in sight,
And the delight of one sense makes the others grumble.

Sight wants to enjoy more than one world;
Show the eyes a thousand worlds and still they hunger for more.
Stripped of all pleasures, the desire for them persists,
And the feeling of having been defrauded.

The senses, your vassals,
Want more than the world—
How foolish of you to give them your heart!
To satisfy them you will die in travail.

Come back, then, come back to the heart that will give you life!
Three kingdoms you have—memory, intellect, and will;
Because of your blindness
They are slowly dying of hunger and neglect.

Created on the heights, yours is a noble nature:
Dwell on your origins and you will find new strength and purity.
In all creation there is nothing truly worthy of your love;
Your heart should belong to the Lord alone.

See reflected nobility in the mirror,
The semblance in you
Of the Lord your God:
Rejoice in this likeness.

The infinite reduced to human measure,
The whole of earth and heaven
Compressed into one tiny vase.
O fair vase, held with such nonchalance!

Not meant to be circumscribed by creation,
Your heart must reach out for other worlds,
Soar to its Creator,
Who alone can satisfy its needs.

JACOPONE DA TODI

Let it wing swiftly to Love:
Give Him your heart
And He will give you His, on one condition—
That you possess it unconditionally.

O priceless Love, You give Yourself utterly,
And draw all things to You!
Your nobility pays God proper honor;

For men have often wondered at God's madness—
To redeem a creature of such little worth,
And share with it
His limitless domain!

36 FROM VIRTUE TO GLORY

Only the fair soul crosses the threshold of paradise;
Come unadorned and no heavenly host will greet you,
The great doors will not swing open as you approach;
And once you are dead it will be too late to change.

If you yearn for such beauty
Let your faith be living and strong.
Living faith gives the soul its delicate lineaments,
Not faith without works, which is dead.

Hope, the friend of the Heavenly Court,
Will give you a royal bearing
And lead you to the throne of God.
Stay close, and put your trust in her.

Soar with the wings of charity,
For charity is life-giving;
The love of God and of neighbor
Will sweep you up to the highest peak.

Deck yourself with prudence, Soul,
For prudence will teach you the ways of love

JACOPONE DA TODI

And prepare you, bride of quiet wisdom,
To enter the King's chamber and court.

Come to the gate naked and forlorn
And only death and confusion will greet you;
Put on the joyous mantle of justice, glistening with gems,
The robe of a bride approaching her bridegroom.

Soul, you lack the strength to scale such heights—
Arm yourself with fortitude for your darkest hour.
When death comes you will not fear,
For you will know you go toward life without end.

As you wing upward, adorn yourself with temperance,
Humble in her great riches.
She will point out the way,
And steady your heart.

Adorned with these virtues,
You will see a mighty host moving toward you
And greeting you with great rejoicing;
For you the doors will swing open in the sun.

"Come to us, sister and friend,"
The chorus of Fathers sings;
"For your faithfulness, come and abide,
Come and be one with us."

"For the hope that adorns you,"
Echo the Prophets,
"Come to us, beloved,
Come and share our measureless joy."

"For the robe of charity
We see draped about you,
Come to us," cry the Apostles,
"Come and share our bliss."

The Doctors praise the prudence with which you glow,
And ask that you join their company.

JACOPONE DA TODI

"One law we have and one reward;
Do not refuse our invitation."

The martyrs honor you
For your fortitude,
Invite you to gaze upon Divine Beauty,
And drink of measureless mirth.

For your temperance
Confessors and Virgins call out,
"Come join us now,
And taste our abundance of joy."

Because you wear the ornaments of justice
Prelates ask you to join them:
"Come gaze on the Majesty
That deigned to save us."

O blessed inheritance of the saints,
Glory and joy for law observed and sin refused!
How can we question the value of penance,
Which fosters virtue and smothers the fires of hell?

37 ON CHASTITY AND ITS NEED TO BE ACCOMPANIED
BY OTHER VIRTUES

Chastity, fair flower of long-stemmed Love,
Scented lily of soft vermilion,
Your fragrance rises to the Trinity.

Mirror of beauty without stain,
Custodian of the soul's purity,
I falter when I try to speak of you.

Radiance of white light,
Praised by many but cherished by few,
Your noble countenance is pleasing to God.

133

JACOPONE DA TODI

Treasure beyond price of gold or silver,
The man who does not hold you dear
Will smell of corruption.

Fortress that guards a great treasure,
Granite from without, honey-sweet within,
Your sentinels must never sleep.

Chastity, you are manna; you safeguard
The soul's garlanded virginity;
When it leaves the body it beholds its Creator.

O soul bedecked in chastity, slowly you move
Toward your Spouse—He, like you, a virgin.
Heaven will open its gates and pay you homage.

Betrothed, delight of your Beloved,
Guard the candor of your image
That you be not dishonored and cast aside.

One gown, remember, will not suffice;
Enhance your comeliness with others
And you will be resplendent.

You must robe yourself with virtues—
With all the virtues, lacking none.
Hasten, then, to make them yours.

To adorn you Christ was stripped of all,
He was wounded to heal your wounds;
To give you strength His heart was pierced.

Think what you have given Him in return.
Prompted by the body, your lover,
You have abandoned Him for vile pleasures.

That body is sworn to destroy you.
Be on guard against it: it is evil
And treacherous and knows how to entice.

JACOPONE DA TODI

38 THE DIFFICULTIES OF ATTAINING
TO THE VIRTUOUS MEAN

Virtuous mean, unremitting self-discipline,
To find you and cling to you is no easy task.

Love compels me to love the lovable;
The hatred of evil is a part of love.
Love and hatred, that is to say,
Are locked in unending struggle
In the selfsame heart.

Love seeks to possess what it loves,
And impediments sorely distress it;
The tongue has no words
For the pain to be borne by the heart
In which joy and apprehension vie for dominion.

The hope of salvation leaps up like a flame
And quickly burns down to ashes of despair.
Who can describe the tumult of the household
Where hope and despair
Live together under one roof?

In joyous daring I look with contempt on suffering and death;
A moment later, terror opens an abyss at my feet.
If such confidence dwell in the same court as fear,
Who can count the times one gains ascendancy,
To be replaced in a trice by its rival?

My sins drive me to fury;
Peace, when it comes,
Convicts me of the sin of rage.
Torn between rage and peace,
How can I stand erect, strong against the wind?

I delight in tasting what I long for,
And am dejected when it is taken away.
The heart is in constant turmoil—

JACOPONE DA TODI

Delight and distress at odds,
Constantly grappling with one another.

If I speak to my neighbor of my state of soul
I scandalize and distress him;
If I do not speak I am less than honest,
And it is my soul that feels the turmoil.
How can I escape the anguish of this contradiction?

The disorder in my neighbor's life angers me,
And I see the wisdom of avoiding his company.
Yet my heart bursts with love of his soul,
Which once issued pure from the hand of God,
And I know not how to express that love.

Self-hatred has me punish myself,
Yet discretion cautions against going too far.
Who ever heard of a man who detested himself
For his own good? And experiencing this hatred
Goes well beyond hearing it described!

Fasting does me good,
And so do long periods of abstinence:
They keep this donkey of a body from getting out of line.
And yet I want my body to be strong,
So that I can persevere in penance.

The contempt others have for me gives me joy,
And so does going about in rags;
But enhancing my reputation, it nourishes my vanity as well.
There are dangers wherever I turn—
Lord, help me! Who can escape unharmed?

To contemplate, I must do my best
To cut myself off from the outside world;
I also have an obligation to be active
And put time to good use.
Will these conflicts never cease?

JACOPONE DA TODI

I bask in silence, the guardian of tranquility,
But doing God's work robs me of that silence.
How can I defend myself
Against the onslaught of contradictions?
It is triumph enough not to feel the wounds!

If I love my neighbor, I want to give him what he needs;
Yet love of poverty finds such trafficking repugnant.
Can these extremes be reconciled?
It may be a vice to go to either,
But to embody the mean is no small grace.

Offenses against God make me want to avenge His honor;
The love of neighbor inclines me to forgiveness.
I am caught between the two blades of the scissors,
Each of the blades cutting into me.
Enough!

39 HOW THE LIFE OF JESUS IS THE MIRROR
OF THE SOUL

To see my deformities in the mirror of truth,
The life of Jesus Christ,

To see them, Lord,
In that blinding light!

Once I looked on myself as a person of some importance
And my self-esteem helped to brighten my days.

But as I peered into that mirror the reflected light
Lit up my life, in mired depths.

Looking into that mirror and then
At the vile-smelling pit into which I had sunk,

I wept bitterly
At the chasm between the two.

137

JACOPONE DA TODI

I saw my faith—it was diffidence;
My hope was presumption, full of vanity;

I saw my charity—
Love half-spoiled;

One look and my world dissolved
In dizzying, turbulent confusion.

In that mirror I saw my notion of justice—
A denial of true virtue, robbing God of His honor,

Condemning the innocent
And sparing the evildoer.

Oh, the iniquity of it all! To love myself, the malefactor,
And deny love to Him to whom it is due!

My prudence, too, I saw mirrored there:
The obtuseness of the brutish soul;

Heedless of the law of the Lord,
I had given my heart to the world.

And to what effect? I, endowed with reason,
Had become animal, and something worse!

The reflection of my temperance
Was no more reassuring—

A total lack of control,
Unable to bridle the passions of the soul.

Though outwardly orderly and composed,
The heart, ever bolder, coveted all;

Its flood waters had submerged reason,
That reason it was meant to serve.

JACOPONE DA TODI

In that mirror I saw my fortitude—folly to name it that,
But there is no right term for such weakness,

It is beyond description. Once again I wept
For seeming virtue, and vice in hiding.

And I had the gall to sell
Such shoddy wares to the Lord?

Insinuating deformity into the heart of light is defilement,
And merits the wrath of God. Let me flee this error.

Nothing that is mine can give Him delight, and indeed
I soil what is His when I try to bring them together.

Justice bars the sinful man from entering the kingdom;
To rejoice with those on high one must strive for virtue.

Nothing can harm the virtuous man,
And the evil man, no matter where he is, cannot see God.

In your light, O Lord, I have seen my nothingness,
My less than nothingness. The vision compels humility,

A sense of my worthlessness,
A consciousness that my will has become Yours.

The humble man does not abase himself to be the lowest of the low,
But so as to be ennobled by virtuous love.

I cannot be reborn unless I first die to myself,
I cannot be annihilated without surrendering myself.

No man can taste the fruit of this glorious *nihil*
If not led by the hand of God; of himself he can do nothing.

O glorious state, in the quiet center of the void,
The intellect and the emotions at rest!

JACOPONE DA TODI

Compared to this high state,
All I have seen and thought is vile and repugnant.

I cannot swim in that ocean of fathomless depths,
I will sink beneath the waves, a man drowned;

Overwhelmed by the infinite glory of my sweet Lord,
I settle into the sands at the bottom of the sea.

40 THE ANGELS ASK THE REASON
FOR CHRIST'S PILGRIMAGE TO THIS WORLD

Christ Omnipotent, for what distant land are You setting out?
Why this pilgrimage? A journey such as this is for the despairing,
Not for someone of Your rank and station, not acquainted with
    grief.

> I come to the world sent by My Father;
> Consumed by love of twisted, degenerate man,
> I wish to possess him, make him Mine.

What need have You of man, that You should suffer so?
It is he who fled You—no great loss—
His is the heavy unpayable debt.

> I will make good for the whole of his debt
> And establish peace between God and man;
> I will seal the pact so it cannot be undone.

But how can you bring peace between God and worldly man?
Man seeks to be God, and God demands his submission—
The conflict cannot be resolved.

> If I become man, man will attain to his proper end;
> The act of submission to God will be Mine.
> I will bring them together in a common joy.

JACOPONE DA TODI

How will You come into the world?
It is good that man know of Your coming.
Spread the word, let him know You come to heal him.

> I've let it be known that all men must come
> To learn from Me the things of God;
> I thirst to teach man, and for this I come.

Before the lessons begin, pray,
Where can man find You, where should he go?
It is good that You tell him, good that he know.

> Tell him My dwelling place will be humility;
> The man who comes there will truly find Me
> And pay nothing, for I will pay the price.

Tell me again, what is it You will teach?
Let everyone know, let the word be proclaimed,
So they will come from all over to learn at Your feet.

> I come to teach men how to love;
> He who masters this art abides with God—
> If he holds fast, he will know eternal joy.

What of those without a book, how will they learn?
Where can the book be purchased?
If you do not tell the student, he has a good excuse.

> I am the book of life, sealed with the seven seals;
> When I am opened you will find five signs,
> The color of red, red blood. Ponder them.

Perhaps the words in that book
Are beyond understanding for all but a few;
Others might turn away in anguish, unable to comprehend.

> No, this is a book that all men may read,
> And all will profit from its reading—
> Here the elephant can swim, the lamb can wade.

JACOPONE DA TODI

41 THE ANGELS MARVEL AT
THE PILGRIMAGE OF CHRIST

Christ Omnipotent, where will Your journey take You?
And why do You set out in the guise of a poor pilgrim?

> I took a bride and gave her My heart;
> With jewels I adorned her that she might do Me honor.
> She has dishonored Me,
> Abandoned Me, and left Me to suffer.

> I fashioned her to My image,
> Gave her memory of celestial joy,
> Inscribed My will in scarlet in the center of her heart,
> And she has deceived Me, abandoned Me, and left Me to
>   suffer.

> I crowned her with faith
> To perfect her understanding;
> With hope and with charity,
> The love of the ordered will.

> That she might lack nothing I gave her a body,
> To adorn her with beauty and serve her as well—
> A beautiful instrument it was,
> But now how out of tune!

> So she might rule graciously over a kingdom
> I brought into being
> All other creatures; in return,
> She offers not love but enmity.

> In a mantle of four virtues I tenderly draped her,
> And she has soiled it with every sin.
> She has dishonored Me,
> Abandoned Me, and left Me to suffer.

If we should find her, Lord,
And she should want to return,

JACOPONE DA TODI

Shall we say You forgive her,
That her wretchedness can come to an end?

> Tell My bride to come back, all wrongs forgotten,
> To save Me from the cruel death she will have Me die;
> Joyfully adorned with My tender love,
> Have her come back to Me.

O sinful soul, once fair bride of the Lord,
How can you continue to lie in this filth?
How could you abandon Him,
The Lord who loved you so?

> When I think of His love,
> Death and confusion invade my soul—
> All the honors He bestowed on me, and I flung them away!
> Painful death encircles me.

Return to your spouse, ungrateful bride.
Do not despair: remember,
In the anguish of His wounded heart,
He is dying for love of you.

> Wretch that I am, how could He ever take me back?
> I killed Him when I abandoned Him;
> And still He binds me so with His love
> That I no longer know where I am.

Do not doubt His welcome.
Come without delay,
Make your avowal of love
In bitter tears.

> O merciful Christ, my Love, where shall I find you?
> Show me Your face or the pain will destroy me.
> Who has seen my Lord?
> Tell me, who has seen Him?

We have seen Him hanging on the cross;
He was dead when we left Him, beaten and bruised;

143

It was you He died for,
You He redeemed at great price.

> I wail and lament, I wail and lament!
> Who killed You, my Love? For love of me You died.
> Where did it lead You, O Christ,
> This drunken love? They hung You from the tree!

42   THE SOUL BEGS THE ANGELS
TO HELP HER FIND CHRIST

Show me where my Lord is, I have heard He loves me;
Tell me where to find Him, I can wait no more.
Long it is He waits for me in sorrow.

> To seek the loving Christ in earnest,
> You must pass through the valley of humiliations.
> We can show you the way, for many have dwelt there.

Help me, I beg of you, in my affliction;
Point out the path,
That I may not lose my way.

> The valley is approached through a narrow pass,
> But once within, the road opens wide
> And leads to great rejoicing.

Open to me! Open, I beseech you, the gates,
For if the loving Christ is within,
Then you speak truth, many have found Him there.

> You may not enter. We have sworn to open
> Only to those with spotless robes;
> Yours are lurid and smell to the heavens.

If they do, then off with them!
O heart of mine, sustain me,
That I might see Him again.

JACOPONE DA TODI

Strip yourself of the world,
And of every worldly love;
A dead weight they are, an illness, a vanity.

Here in your sight I strip myself,
And put aside the love of all created things—
May they no longer have a place in my heart.

> You must do more. You have yet to despair of the world.
> You still hope in it with a false and evil hope:
> Strip that away too; let your heart be beyond reproach.

I will strip myself of all hope,
And flee all who would succor me.
Better to die of starvation than be bound to the world.

> There is still more to be done:
> You are richly robed in spiritual friendships—
> A mighty wind that has shipwrecked many.

O harsh demand, to renounce those friendships!
Yet I see that therein lies honor for no one.
In the name of self-abasement, I now renounce them.

> You need not flee their company completely,
> But you must not open your heart to them.
> Thieves come in through that door,
> And strip you of all you have earned.

Open, open, I beseech you,
That I might see Christ, in Whom I place my hope.
Answer, my Love, my Life, hide Yourself no longer.

> Soul, since you have come to Me,
> Gladly will I answer you. Come,
> See, this is My bed—the cross.
> Here we will be one. Come to Me
> And I will quench your thirst.

JACOPONE DA TODI

O my Love, naked will I scale that cross,
To suffer and die with You.
Lord, clasped close in Your embrace,
In joy will I suffer and die.

43 ON MERCY AND JUSTICE AND
HOW MAN WAS MADE WHOLE—
AN ORATORIO FOR SEVERAL VOICES

Virtuous as he left the hand of the Creator,
Man in his folly showed contempt for those origins.
The fall was perilous, light turned into darkness;
To rescale those heights is a cruel endeavor.
To the blind the attempt seems madness, but others
Come to the summit and see glory, new life, heaven now.

When man sinned he brought down in ruins the order of Love,
For in clinging so tightly to self-love
He placed himself above the Creator.
Justice, outraged, stripped him of honor,
The Virtues abandoned him,
And the Devil was allowed to use him at will.

Mercy grieved to see man fallen to such low estate,
For with him were lost all his descendants as well.
Gathering her children about her she deliberated
How she could come to his aid.
They decided to send a messenger
To tell despairing man he would not perish;
Lady Penitence was chosen to bring the news.

She sent a courier ahead to prepare her lodgings—
Contrition by name; he brought with him the basic needs.
But on contemplating man carefully it was plain to see
There was no place in him where Penitence might dwell,
So Contrition sent instead for her three sons
To scour man's heart and prepare a place.

JACOPONE DA TODI

The first to appear was Fear, who troubled the heart of man
And cast out arrogant and false Security.
Fear was followed by Shame,
That man might recognize his wretchedness and deformity;
And in his train came Grief overwhelming,
For the offenses man's sin had given to God.

Seeing his own sinfulness, man sighed disconsolately;
As he wept without cease, Compunction came to his side:
This was the moment for Penitence and her children
To enter his heart and take up their abode.
Confession spoke to them, but there was no way
In which man could make satisfaction.

Since man was responsible for his fall,
It was man who must learn again to stand erect.
He despaired of his own efforts;
No angel could help him, no choir of angels:
God alone could rebuild the house that had crumbled—
God, who was under no obligation to do so.

Penitence sent Prayer to inform the Heavenly Court
Of man's plight, and his despair,
And how he was barred from making satisfaction.
"I cry out not to Reason but to Mercy;
She it is I choose as my advocate.
My offering is the tears of a bitter and contrite heart."

"Sire," Mercy began, entering the Court,
"I have been wronged by Justice.
When man first sinned and fell from Your grace,
My good offices should have been asked for.
Justice has mortally wounded me as well as man,
And stripped me of my honor."

Justice, before the throne, answered the charge:
"Sire, man was given a law and he willfully transgressed it;
The responsibility is his.
The punishment meted out to him everyone knows;

JACOPONE DA TODI

It was in keeping with the gravity of the offense.
Study the sentence; if excessively harsh, revise it."

"Sire," countered Mercy, "the harshness of the sentence
Is not the reason for my complaint.
My lament is that no role was assigned to me,
I count for nothing in the proceedings of the court!
I was with you *ab initio*, and have never been confounded—
I have just cause for my grief and my bitter lament."

Moved by Charity, the Father all-powerful
Handed down His judgment,
Opened the treasure of Largesse
And gave it to Mercy, that as His advocate
She might give man consolation,
While Justice still reigned in truth, no harmony destroyed.

The Father Omnipotent, in whom all power rests,
Softly deliberated with His Son:
"O my Son, Wisdom past telling,
Yours is all discernment; reconcile man to Us,
And to Our company. Play this music,
And make all the Heavenly Court rejoice."

"My gentle Father," answered the Son,
"In whom I abide from the beginning,
In reverence and love I obey Your injunction.
Choose a suitable place for My stay on earth
And I will make a new pact between God and man,
One that is fair to both Justice and Mercy."

Then out of His infinite goodness
God called into being a maiden;
Beauteous body and sanctified soul
In an instant He created, preserving her
From the sin the first man had sown,
A sin that had made all of his progeny suffer.

O soil without tangle of thorns and travail,
Bearer of every good fruit, laden with grace and virtue,

148

JACOPONE DA TODI

You put an end to our suffering,
Punishment for Eve's transgression.
O Mary, restorer of our ruined estate,
Yours is the fullness of blessings.

Of yore the jealous and wily Enemy
Came to Adam and his wife,
To tempt and deceive them.
Then You, Father, in Your gentleness and mercy,
Sent Gabriel to the Virgin Mary, hidden in her humility,
To announce to her she would conceive a child.

"*Ave, gratia plena,* blessed are you among women."
Pondering the salutation, the Virgin was afraid.
"Fear not, Mary, for you will see
All prophecies have come to fulfillment in you.
You will conceive and bring forth a son,
And He will rescue a fallen race."

"How is this to be, when I am a virgin?"
"The Holy Spirit will come upon you,
And the power of God will overshadow you.
You will remain a virgin, and as a virgin
Give birth. Behold, Elizabeth too,
Old and barren, has conceived.

"With God nothing is impossible—what He wills He does.
Consent to His counsel, give me your answer."
"Behold the handmaid of the Lord,
Be it done unto me according to your word."
And in that instant she conceived the Christ,
Remaining a virgin beyond all shadow of doubt.

Adam, Scripture tells us, was fashioned out of earth;
Christ, the Redeemer of mankind, was born of a virgin.
After nine long months in Mary's womb
He was born in the winter, in deepest cold,
And the land of His fathers offered no hearth,
Offered no swaddling clothes.

JACOPONE DA TODI

He soon came to know insult, cruelty, and villainy;
From Heaven to earth He came, to suffer for our offenses!
Long had we pleaded for a Messiah,
That He might heal our every illness,
And look—He lies naked under the sky,
With no one at all to take pity on Him.

The Virtues in chorus then made loud lament,
"Lord, we are widowed by the sins of others;
Give us in marriage to one who will be kind,
Take away our disgrace,
Have pity on our wretchedness,
And restore to us our honor and esteem."

"Go to my Beloved, daughters,
Take Him as your spouse.
Go rest with Him, I leave you in His hands.
All peoples will pay you honor,
And you will render Him so perfect
That I will exalt Him above the heavens."

Hearing news of the wedding, the Gifts of the Spirit came running.
"Lord, what will we do in the Celestial Court?
Will ours be a perpetual widowhood? What will be said
Of our lamentation while the rest of the Heavenly Court rejoices?
If we, too, play our Christ-instruments and break into song,
All of the palace will be filled with joy."

"Come, come all together, O My children,
To render honor to My Court.
Embrace My beloved Redeemer Son,
Join the Virtues and perfect them
So that with them you may be blessed
In the Court of Love."

Hearing this, the Beatitudes joyfully rushed to the Court:
"Lord, shelter us, we who belong to Your family.
Through winter and summer, bitter days and trying nights,
We have journeyed as pilgrims, no home in sight.

Wherever we come they send us away, sure of acting wisely;
They hate us worse than death."

"Until this time no man was worthy to harbor so noble a treasure;
I now give you Christ, come dwell in Him. You will hold Him
    dear,
And He will be a token of the fruits you will gather
In My Kingdom, where you will be draped in the robes of My
    Court.
You will show forth Christ as a sign:
'This is the author of the world's salvation.' "

Then, in the name of man,
Our most gentle Redeemer addressed Justice:
"What do you ask of sinful man?
What is he to do to pay for his sin?
I will pay his debt, all that he owes; out of love
I will help him, and am ready to pay the price."

"Lord, if it pleases You
To pay man's debt, You can do so,
You who are God and man;
Indeed, You have already begun.
Gladly will I make a pact with You,
For You alone can satisfy my demands."

Then turning to Mercy, who had pleaded for man,
Christ asked, "What is it you want for the son of Adam?"
"That he be pardoned, Lord, and released
From the sentence of exile from his native land.
Since his fall I have suffered, years without comfort;
Console me, Lord, I who took pity on man.

"Unless You take his trespasses upon Yourself,
Sins of past and present and future,
A creature so weak can never be healed;
You must reform his strength, intelligence, and will.
That will console me,
Dry my long and bitter tears."

JACOPONE DA TODI

"There is wisdom in what you would have Me do.
I am so drunk with love
They will call Me mad,
To pay such a price for such shabby goods.
That man may know the strength of My love
I will die to satisfy for his sins."

"Lord, man is so covered with filth,
Unless he first be cleansed,
Who can endure the stench?
He must be healed, and soon;
Who but You will heal him? Abandoned,
Barely alive, he lives in anguish."

"I have asked of My Father the most precious of waters,
From which man will emerge as white as snow:
This is holy and glorious Baptism,
Which heals man of all his ills.
Those bathed in its waters are sweet-scented,
If they do not lapse again into sin."

Justice, on hearing this, then spoke her turn:
"Lord, in this new pact with man
He must acknowledge that he is a servant.
Breaking the previous pact, he thought he was God:
Now I demand that he humble himself,
Be faithful, and instantly obey all my commands."

"Answer, man: do you give Justice your word?"
"Lord, I promise to be a servant,
And renounce the Devil and all of his house.
I promise to keep faith,
In all times and all places. Faith,
Without which we perish, will save me."

Mercy stepped forward; "Here, Lord, is man baptized.
But he will need strength and skill
If he is to join Your forces and combat the Enemy.
For the Foe is an able warrior,

And long a master of deceit.
If You do not strengthen man, he cannot but go astray."

"Remember, Lord, that when man erred the wound cut deep.
Foolishly, he expected that I, Justice,
Would not demand satisfaction. I want him
To acknowledge his fault, always have it present.
Let him, then, bear a mark on his forehead
To remind him that sin is hateful to me."

"Lord, gladly will I bear the mark of the new creation,
Newly remade in Your image, and protected from the Evil One."
"I will mark you with the sign of the cross on your forehead,
A sign of chrism, to buttress your strength.
Take heart, My kingdom belongs to him
Who, faithful and valiant, fights the good fight."

"Lord," Mercy pleaded, "Man has fasted so long,
He will faint if he is not fed."
"To give him strength, I give him My body,
And the blood that flowed from My side;
Bread and wine of the Sacrament,
Which the priest on the altar will consecrate."

"Before You give this food to man,"
Justice cautioned, "first have him promise
To love the Lord his God above all,
And always seek his neighbor's good."
"Lord, I promise to do this.
I must, and I will."

Still, Mercy was cautious in her victory:
"Were man to lapse again," she asked,
"What could he do to save himself?"
"Penance, your friend, is the medicine I prescribe;
Should he once again be overcome by evil,
Penance will make him well again."

"But man must cling to me with his dying breath,"
Justice insisted, "for me endure pain and evil fortune."

"I will keep my word," answered man,
"Endure suffering, and remain loyal to the end.
If I obey, You will open those gates of Heaven
Closed to me because of my sins."

"Lord," said Mercy, "Man, clothed with flesh,
Knows the flame of passion;
Give him a remedy against the torments of lust."
"Man and wife, companions together,
Will together be wary of all the dangers
That might sully the purity of their love."

"Marriage lived in temperance, Lord,
Will give man peace and shield him from sin."
"Lord, though my flesh is inclined to sin,
I will use all my strength to bend it to my will;
For flesh is a friend to be kept at a distance,
A friend that causes the fall of many."

"But Lord," begged ever-solicitous Mercy,
"To whom should man turn?
Who will dispense the signs of Your goodness?"
"Broad authority I give to My priests,
To bless and to consecrate,
To bind and to loose."

"This help," Justice countered, "will come to naught
Unless the priest is robed in prudence,
From which all other Virtues flower.
Let the priest ascend seven flights of stairs
And be cleansed of every ugly stain;
Let him never again turn back to earth."

Seeing how hard it would be for man at the end,
His three great enemies converging in their attacks,
Mercy cried out, "Lord, come to his aid,
Give man the means to ward off the Foe.
Anoint him with holy oil before he dies,
That the Enemy will not be able to hold him."

JACOPONE DA TODI

Then Justice summoned Fortitude,
Who fights valiantly in moments of adversity,
Endures the most painful assaults,
And knows how to checkmate the Enemy.
The Sacraments, in convocation with the Virtues,
Agreed to stand fast, not to be divided.

Justice then drew up the pact,
Insisting on the strict practice of the Virtues.
But Mercy demurred: she demanded the inclusion
Of the Gifts of the Spirit.
And so Justice and Mercy together
Besought Christ to come to their aid.

The Gift of Wisdom was then given
To strengthen Charity;
The Gift of Understanding was given
To strengthen Hope, Heaven's ally;
The Faith that storms Heaven
Was infused with the Gift of Counsel;

And the Virtues were given in marriage
To the Gifts of the Spirit.
Fortitude came to aid the practice of Justice,
Knowledge imparted beauty to Prudence;
Piety sustained Temperance,
And Fear of the Lord girdled Fortitude.

Poverty of Spirit was born of Faith and Counsel;
The child born of Fortitude and Fear of the Lord
Was Meekness, totally scorned.
Justice and Fortitude gave birth to holy Grief,
And the offspring of Prudence and Wisdom
Was called Hunger for Justice.

Temperance and Piety brought forth Mercy;
Understanding, Hope, and Celestial Love
Generated Purity of Heart;
While Wisdom and Charity endowed the heart with Peace.

JACOPONE DA TODI

Let us now pray the Glorious Trinity
To forgive us all our sins.

44 THE PETITIONS IN THE OUR FATHER

There are, I believe, seven modes of prayer,
As Christ taught us when He gave us the Our Father.

Our first request of God should be
That He sanctify within us His holy name.
Baptized into Christ and Christians called,
Our life is to be unblemished.

Then we should ask Him to come into our hearts,
Hearts made ready for Him,
And preserve them in purity, reign in them forever,
For to turn out such a guest would be shame beyond telling.

The third plea the Lord would have us make
Is that He be obeyed here as He is in Heaven;
That we give His will primacy,
And place ourselves, body and soul, under His law.

We then ask for bread in threefold form:
Bread as devotion—the soul in God enkindled;
Bread as sacrament, the consecrated bread of the altar;
And lastly, the daily bread that sustains our body.

Bread in the first form brings us joyously close to God;
In the next, to our neighbor, in the congregation of the faithful;
In the last, we have from day to day
Our body's need, the necessary food.

The fifth prayer is for the forgiveness of sins.
Do not come before God when angry with your brother:
Threaten one of His adopted children with a knife
And He'll not receive you kindly!

156

God graciously receives the man who loves his neighbor;
Let him beg forgiveness of his sins,
His prayer will be heard in full,
And grace will shine upon him.

The sixth request is not to be led into temptation:
Should He abandon us we will be led into captivity,
Chained by the world, the flesh, and the Devil,
Which sully us more than I once could see.

If the Lord is with us, let the storms of adversity pelt us,
We will be led to triumph in travail;
Enemy legions will be put to rout
And our joy will be in God's good company.

The seventh prayer is that He save us from evil—
From our sins, that lead to the raging fires of Hell,
Where all that is unacceptable to God
Is gathered together and heaped up high.

45. THE FIVE WAYS IN WHICH GOD REVEALS HIMSELF

The Lord appears to me in this life in five ways:
He who ascends to the fifth has scaled a great height.

The first is the state of fear, the second healing love;
The third manifestation is of tender sustenance,
Followed in turn by fatherly love
And lastly by conjugal love, the love of the bridegroom.

In the first stage the Lord God in His power
Raises my soul from the dead;
Putting to flight the demons who bound me in error,
He touches the heart with contrition.

The reawakened and still fragile soul
Is then visited by the Healer,

JACOPONE DA TODI

Who nurses and comforts
And strengthens with Sacraments.

My Love then appears as the noble companion
Who succors me and saves me from my wretchedness;
He endows me with virtues that lead to salvation.
Can I leave hidden, unsung, the good He has wrought?

In the fourth mode He appears as a tender father
With gifts of great largesse;
Once the soul tastes of that goodness, that love,
It exults in its inheritance.

In the fifth mode Love leads me to the conjugal bed
And I lie in the embrace of the Son of God. O my soul,
Led by grace, you are the queen of the angels,
In wondrous fusion transformed into Christ.

46   HOW FAITH LEADS THE SOUL
TO THE REALM OF THE INVISIBLE

With the eyes in my head by the light of noon
I see corporeal things.

With the eyes in my head I see the Blessed Sacrament
As the priest on the altar raises it high.
In appearance it is bread; to the inner eye,
The eye of faith, that bread is something more.

Four of the senses concur: this is bread as we know it.
The sense of hearing alone dissents—
Christ is hidden under this visible form;
Thus, in this mystery, does He give Himself to the soul.

"How can this be? I want reason to account for the change."
Should Divine Power be subject to reason?
It pleased God to create the heavens, and no one questions how;
Why then should this transformation provoke such endless debate?

JACOPONE DA TODI

The blind man leans on the cane of faith;
He comes to the Blessed Sacrament sustained by firm faith.
Hidden within, the Lord bestows His blessings
And the grace He gives us weds us to Him forever.

Holy Mother Church is the hall for the wedding.
Enter by the door of obedience and be mantled with faith,
And she will then set you before the Lord as His bride.
Sing a new song for the bride now wedded in faith!

Here is born the love of the invisible God; the soul feels,
Though it cannot see God, that all evil is hateful to Him.
A wondrous change—Hell is transformed into Heaven!
Weeping over its sinful past, the soul is overcome with love.

Oh, the lustful, worldly, hateful life I led,
The life of a sow, wallowing in its excrement,
A life contemptuous of the fragrance of the rose of heaven!
How can I remember without bitter tears?

O churlish, ungrateful, arrogant life,
Holding Heaven in high contempt, insolent toward God,
Indifferent to His holy law and word—
And yet He saved me, did not damn me.

My soul, how will you make amends?
So much cause for lamentation!
Let tears, then, and sighs and suffering
Be my daily fare as I ponder my sin of ingratitude.

The Lord I cannot see has transformed me into another,
Rooted out the love of earth and given me the love of Heaven.
You, the Giver, I do not see, but I see and touch Your gift:
You have reined in my body, which once covered me with filth.

How is it, O Chastity, that I now hold you dear?
From whence comes the light that gives such understanding?
It comes from the Father of Light, who breathes forth His
    blessings.
I know with certainty that He has showered me with His grace.

JACOPONE DA TODI

Poverty, why do I now take such delight in you,
You who in the past filled me with horror?
The very thought of you was a torment worse than fever,
And now I love and desire you intensely.

Come, come see this wonder—now I love my neighbor,
Bear the injuries he does me,
And find it easy to forgive him.
Nor does this satisfy me—I burn with love of him.

Come, come see this wonder—I now endure shame,
That shame I loathed and kept at a distance;
In sweet embrace shame binds me to God,
And in that embrace I find my joy.

O fierce-shining Faith, you led me to this fruit!
Blessed be the day and the hour I believed in your word.
This is the foretaste of the joy of Heaven:
You have taught me to love my inheritance.

47   HOW THE ENEMY WAGES WAR

Listen and I will tell you—it may be of help—
How the wily Foe wages war against me.

Most insidiously—how well he knows my weak points—
He slowly tightens the noose around my neck.
"Brother," he begins, "Brother, you are a saint,
Your fame has spread far and wide.
God has been good to you, now and in the past;
You must be very dear to Him. Rejoice,
For you have good reason: can you have any doubts
As to the reward you will receive in Heaven?"

> "How well you know how to insinuate yourself, my clever
>   Foe!
> You once-glorious angel, once of that luminous company,
> Whose disordered desires sent you plummeting from Heaven.

JACOPONE DA TODI

Would that you had kept God's favor! We make a fine pair—
You an evil spirit, I a demon incarnate,
Since times past counting I have offended my Lord."

The answer does not faze the Enemy.
He strikes back, attacks violently:
"Scum of the world, have you no shame?
How do you dare to open your mouth,
You who in so many ways have sinned against God and man?
For a single offense I was instantly condemned;
And you, you sin-ridden thing, expect to be saved?"

"Ah, my evil Foe, it is not my strength that will save me;
My hope is in the goodness of the Lord.
God is good, and goodness must be loved:
His goodness has drawn me to Him and made me love Him.
Were I not to be saved He would be no less deserving of
    love,
For all my Lord does is just and acceptable."

Now the attack comes from a different direction:
"When will you start to do penance,
To take advantage of the propitious time?
You fatten your flesh for the worms in your grave;
The time has come to torment it for the evil it's done!
Pay no more heed to the body, entrust it to the Lord;
The evildoer doesn't deserve the comfort of food or clothing."

"Hypocrite, I'll nourish my body, not kill it!
I know your ruses, and they make me smile.
I will nourish my body, which helps me serve God
And win that glory which your fall made you lose.
The fault is yours, Father of Lies,
If I must struggle so to sustain corruptible flesh
So as to flee from you and win Heaven."

"It seems to me, though, that you go too far;
Why torment your body without reason?
Have pity on it, consider its age and condition.
Love your body as you love your soul;

JACOPONE DA TODI

Its health, you know, is a matter of some importance.
Add no more burdens, demand no more sacrifices."

    "Fear not, I give my body its needs,
    And we've agreed to live in poverty.
    Orderly abstinence has strengthened it
    And cured it of the ills of its excesses.
    There's medical art to penitence,
    It regulates the senses."

"One shortcoming you seem to have, however, a sin against charity:
You have no compassion for the humble poor.
Accept, Brother, the money people want to give you,
To help the needy who are ashamed to beg.
To accept alms would help those who give and those who receive."

    "I am not held to love my neighbor more than myself
    (And I have renounced him to give myself completely to
        God.)
    If I took it upon myself to provide for him,
    In buying and selling I would lose my peace.
    Were I to accept money and distribute it among the poor,
    It would never be enough to satisfy their needs,
    And the donor would take little pleasure
    In seeing me pass it on."

"One more flaw in you: you do not practice silence.
In its holy name many saints went into the desert.
How edifying, Brother, if you were to practice that art—
How many would admire you and turn to God!
Scripture, you know, commends silence,
Since the tongue often leads man to sin."

    "If you were speaking out of holy zeal,
    What you say would be true.
    But you want to persuade me to be silent
    For your own unworthy ends.
    When we ought to speak out, silence is a sin,
    As when we fail to proclaim the goodness of God.

JACOPONE DA TODI

There is a time for silence and a time for speech,
And this holds true until the very last."

"One more failing—you don't hide the good you do;
The Lord, you remember, tells us to do good in secret.
To exhibit the good one does is vainglory,
A scandal to all those present.
The Lord, who sees you, will give you your reward—
Do not make a display of virtue to have your brother praise you."

"I offer to my Lord the secret prayer of my soul,
And lock the door to my heart
So my brother cannot see within.
But my brother ought hear vocal prayer;
So as not to give him scandal
I also pray out loud to my God.
And I do the same, for similar reasons,
With works of piety."

"Enough, enough! You have bested me, Brother!
What can I say? In truth you are a saint,
So well do you defend yourself.
I have never been so roundly defeated,
Checkmated at every point.
You have nothing further to fear from me,
There's no point in my ever trying again."

"This is the moment I fear most,
The moment of your most dangerous lie!
If I trusted you now I'd be worse than mad.
I'll still keep watch, my lying Foe,
Against you and against sin."

On the alert, my soul!
Hoping to make you trip and fall,
The Enemy never sleeps or nods.

JACOPONE DA TODI

48. THE ILLS AND EVILS FRATE JACOPONE
CALLED DOWN ON HIMSELF
IN AN EXCESS OF CHARITY

Send me illness, O Lord,
I beg of You, out of courtesy!

Hurl down quartian ague, tertian fever,
Chills every day and swollen dropsy!
Give me toothache, headache, and stomach cramps,
Pains in my guts and spasms of choking.
Give me pleuritis and burning eyes,
Let my left side swell with a tumor;
Visit me with a violent case of tuberculosis,
Let me suffer perpetual delirium.

May my liver grow inflamed,
My spleen swollen, and my stomach bloated,
My lungs hollowed out, with vicious coughing and paralysis.
Let me suffer fistulas and thousands of boils;
Let my body be filled with cancers,
Suffer gout, hernia, dysentery, and hemorrhoids;
And be afflicted, on top of that,
With asthma, fainting spells, and rabies.

Let my mouth be full of ulcerous sores,
Have me suffer from epilepsy, falling into fire and water,
My whole body utterly broken by illness.
Come blindness, loss of speech and hearing,
Wretchedness, poverty and palsy.
May my stench keep everyone at a distance,
With no one to help me in my misery:
Let them abandon me in the horrible gulch of Rigoverci.

Ice, hail, storms, lightning, thunder, darkness—
Let me not escape a single adversity.
Because of the folly of my sins, let devils minister to me,
Tormenting me with every evil at their command.
May this be my life until the Last Judgment,
And then when death strikes let it strike me hard.

JACOPONE DA TODI

Let me be buried in the stomach of a ravenous wolf,
Who will shit the relics in a bramble patch.

Let those who come there, expecting miracles after my death,
Be accompanied by evil spirits,
Feel howling terror, have doomsday visions.
Let anyone who hears the mention of my name shudder
And cross himself to ward off the danger of an ugly encounter.
All this I call down on myself, O Lord, is not adequate vengeance,
For You created me as Your beloved,
And I, ungrateful wretch, put You to death.

49 ON CONSCIENCE AT REST

Now you give me lasting rest, O Conscience;
Such was not your custom in times past!
Then, I remember, you gave me no respite,
Voiced unsuppressible dissent.

You never passed by without noticing,
But constantly murmured against me,
Spelling out all my sins in detail,
No matter how carefully I sought to hide them.

This is my God-given nature, from the moment of birth,
And at all times I have been faithful to it.
Righteous judgment is the law of my being,
And I keep a careful record of all your deeds.

Why are you now mute, and no longer molest me?
You now give me peace and happy companionship,
Ever since I ceased to rebel against you.
Your displeasure, I remember, cut to the bone.

I am silent with good reason—
You have accepted right judgment.
Now you love justice,
And have put yourself into her hands.

JACOPONE DA TODI

You no longer impose conditions,
For you love what justice decrees:
There lies the secret of peace
And the end of my fury.

50   THE BATTLE AGAINST THE ANTICHRIST

Now if he appears we shall see
Who has faith and constancy:
I see the tribulations prophesied,
See them converging from every direction.

The moon is black, the sun darkened, stars fall out of the heavens;
The ancient serpent has broken out of captivity,
And the world follows in his train.
Having drunk all of the surrounding waters he turns
To the River Jordan, impatient to devour the people of Christ.

The sun is Christ, Who makes no move
To impart His strength to His servants;
We see no miracles to sustain them in their faith.
Evildoers mock God's absence, laugh in scorn;
Even if we explain the reason, they will not change their ways.

The moon is the Church in Christ, dressed in mourning;
Guided by other popes and cardinals it once illumined the night,
Now that radiance is blotted black. The whole clergy
Has spurred it to a mad gallop along the path to destruction.
Lord God, who shall be saved?

The stars that have fallen out of heaven
Are the religious orders, fallen on evil days.
The flood waters have risen,
Submerged the mountains and plains;
Help us, O Lord, or we drown!

The cracks in the world grow wider and wider,
And ruin hovers over the chasms.
The world is like a man gone mad,

166

And doctors despair of medicine and incantations;
We can sense the approach of the death agony.

I see a vast multitude in three groups divided,
Marked with the several signs of the ancient serpent;
He who escapes one temptation is assaulted by the next.
Avarice first takes to the field, routing and slaughtering many;
Few have the strength to continue to battle.

Those who survive this onslaught
Are tempted by the vanity of knowledge;
Knowledge puffs them up and makes them proud.
In their presumption they enumerate the sins of their neighbors,
Carefully concealing their own: too much talk and no action.

Those few who have escaped from these two perils
Are caught in yet another snare:
They ache to perform miracles, signs, to heal,
They hunger to speak in tongues and to prophesy.
Should any overcome this temptation, praise be to God!

Gird yourself, then, and pray that you escape this death,
For no other trial has ever been harsher,
Nor will any to come be more bitter.
Saints dreaded such testing:
For us to confide in our strength would be folly!

51 TRUTH WEEPS OVER THE DEATH OF GOODNESS

Weeping over the death of Goodness,
Truth calls all to see where she lies slain.
All creation joins in the dirge and the wailing;
Heaven and earth, sea and fire, make loud lamentation.

"Wounded in Adam," Innocence begins in tears,
"I was reborn in Christ; now once again I die and am lost.
Infinite majesty of God, avenge our wrongs!
May man recognize sin by the suffering it brings."

JACOPONE DA TODI

Natural Law joins in the dirge
With its pitiful wail:
"Who, O noble Goodness,
Will avenge the evil done you?"

The Law of Moses with its ten commandments
Raises its voice in lament:
"O noble Goodness, how great your suffering!
Who will avenge the contempt they have shown you?"

The cry of the Law of Grace
Pierces the heavens with its anguish:
"Father all-powerful, are You asleep?
Why do You tolerate the assaults of the Enemy?"

Heard high above all other voices,
The Life of Christ, His Incarnation, rings out,
Demanding justice and judgment for His Passion and Doctrine:
"Lord, honor Me, avenge Me."

Holy Scripture and Philosophy lament,
"O most noble Goodness, our treasure and our life,
What wretches are those
Who despised and rejected you!"

The Articles of Faith in chorus accuse:
"With grief and desolation
We watch them destroy all we labored to build;
Life is no longer bearable in this all-embracing sin."

"Our anguish is past telling,"
The Virtues cry out with bitter tears;
"O most noble Goodness, our treasure and song,
There is no remedy for such a loss, or our unimaginable grief."

Then the Sacraments come weeping and wailing:
"Since the death of Goodness we find no joy in life,
We wander about, emptied of hope.
Avenge, O Lord, that wrong!"

They are echoed by the Gifts of the Spirit:
"Avenge us, O Lord, O high and holy light!
Save us, or our foundering ship
Will be dashed against the rocks!"

"O Lord," cry out the Beatitudes,
"Look down upon our misery.
They look upon us with contempt,
As if we were heinous sin."

The religious orders join the lament:
"Lord, look down upon us and on our torment;
Since the death of Goodness we are destroyed—
Our life is as dust in the path of the wind."

"Avenge the betrayal of the Roman Curia,"
Reecho the Fruits of the Spirit;
"Let us attack it with all our fury,
Let us dismantle it!

"The members of the Antichrist call themselves Your Church:
No longer, Lord, let this be so. Cleanse her,
And may he who in this Church leads an evil life
Be sent to the place where his sins will be purged."

52 THE LAMENT OF CHRIST FOR
THE CHURCH OF ROME

This is the lament of Jesus Christ for the Church of Rome,
Contemptuous, indifferent and ungrateful for His love.

*   *   *

After the Incarnation, after I took on human nature,
I endured suffering and the cruelest of deaths.
I took as My bride the Church, faithful and pure,
And loved her ever with a burning love.

JACOPONE DA TODI

In poverty I sent My disciples wandering through the world
And enflamed their hearts with the Holy Spirit.
Through them I sowed the seed of My most holy faith,
And many were the miracles I performed to lead man to Me.

The blind world, on seeing these signs,
And hearing wisdom from the unlettered tongue,
Was overcome with wonder. They believed and were baptized,
Convinced that they too would make men marvel with miracles.

To consider My signs as magic
Led to idolatry, the gravest of errors;
It blinded nations, kings, and emperors,
And they put to death every envoy I sent.

Yet such was the fervor of the first believers
That for every one killed a thousand heirs sprang up;
The slaughter wearied the executioners,
The perseverance of a martyred faith bore abundant fruit.

Heresy then asserted itself,
Sowed weeds and cockle with the semblance of truth.
It waged war against the faith,
And the cruel struggle was not quickly won.

I sent the Doctors of the Church, sustained by My Wisdom;
They revealed truth without a shadow of error;
Refuting and rejecting all false beliefs,
They demonstrated the prudence of a well-ordered life.

Consider My anguish, then, at what I have been reduced to!
A faithless clergy has slain and destroyed Me,
Laid waste My work and spoiled its fruit.
The suffering they have inflicted on Me is worse than death!

170

JACOPONE DA TODI

53 THE TEARS OF THE CHURCH ON
SEEING ITSELF REDUCED TO A SHAMBLES

The Church weeps, weeps and laments,
In torment to have sunk so low.

"O gentlest, kindest Mother,
Why do you weep? I can see
Your anguish is past all measure;
Tell me, why do your tears know no end?"

"I weep, my son, in my bereavement—
Gone father and spouse,
Brothers, sons and their children all lost,
And my every friend captured and bound.

"Bastard sons, cowardly in battle,
Surround me on every side—
How utterly unlike my true sons,
Undaunted by sword or arrow!

"My sons were of one accord;
These are always at odds.
It is because of their scandalous lives
That infidels call me 'the whore.'

"Their one concern is for ecclesiastical office;
They have sent Poverty into exile.
How utterly unlike my true sons,
Who armed with austerity scorned the world!

"My bastard sons have made many enemies
By letting gold and silver back into their lives
And setting their opulent tables;
They have lost all virtues and all respect.

"Where are the Fathers, strong with faith,
And those ready to lay down their lives in its name?
I am slain by the lukewarm,
With no one to intone the dirge for me.

JACOPONE DA TODI

"Where are the Prophets, rich in hope?
I stand abandoned in my widowhood;
All around me arrogance has become brazen
And its followers grow and grow.

"Where are the Apostles, filled with fervor?
I have none to comfort me in my suffering.
Self-love attacks me from every side,
And I see no defenders in sight.

"Where now is the fortitude of the martyrs?
I stand a widow alone.
Easeful life has taken up arms against me,
And fervor has been undone.

"Where are the just and zealous priests
Whose lives were balm for ill mankind?
Pomp and haughty pride have come forth
And stained the noble sacerdotal office.

"Where are the Doctors and their prudence?
Many I see raised high by knowledge,
But their lives do not pay me homage.
They have cast me aside and wounded my heart.

"O austere religious,
The great joy I once took in you!
Now I go from monastery to monastery,
But find few to console me.

"The wounds you have inflicted on me, O bitter peace!
While battles raged I stood erect,
But now ease and repose have taken their toll.
The demon of drunkenness has poisoned me.

"Christ has died in each of these stations,
And no one comes to grieve with me.
O my life, my hope and my joy,
I see you smothered in every heart!"

JACOPONE DA TODI

54 EPISTLE TO CELESTINE V
(IN THE WORLD, PIETRO DA MORRONE)

What now, Pier da Morrone?
This is the test.

Now we'll see what comes
Of all those meditations in your hermit's cell.
Disappoint those who have placed their hopes in you,
And they'll rain curses on your head.
The fame of your sanctity rises high and spreads far afield;
Tarnish it at this point, in the closing years,
And think of the scandal you will give to the good!
Their eyes turn to you as truly
As an arrow speeds toward its target.
Do not short-weight them.

This is the test: we'll see if you're gold, iron, or copper,
Whether your yarn be coarse wool or fine.
The papal court is a crucible
In which the gold is separated from the dross;
Should too much copper be mixed with the gold,
The whole will be reduced to coal and ashes.
Should you take delight in your power,
That would be the worst, the most infectious of ills.
In exchange for this morsel,
You would lose God, be damned.

I wept for you when you announced, "I accept."
Oh, the yoke you placed around your neck,
A yoke that condemns you
To an unremitting struggle!
In the midst of a storm the brave standard-bearer
Finds the strength to hold his regiment's banner high.
You have accepted the most awesome of offices:
Its difficulties and responsibilities
Are no less awesome. Remember,
All of your comrades are not of one heart.

JACOPONE DA TODI

55 CANTICLE OF BROTHER JACOPONE IN PRISON

What now, Fra Jacopone?
Now you're put to the test.

You did penance for a year and a half
In that siege of Palestrina;
You caught the illness that was raging there,
And for that you now find yourself in prison.

This is the benefice they gave me in Rome: gone is my good name,
When people mention me it is to curse me.
They've awarded me a new type of prebend—
My hood taken away, a life term before me, chained like a lion.

My prison, underground, opens on a latrine
Whose odor is not quite the fragrance of musk.
No one is allowed to speak to me, except for one attendant,
And he has to report every word that I utter.

I am fettered like a falcon,
And my chains clank as I move about—
The attendant outside my lodgings
Can hear me practicing my new dance steps.

When I'm lying down, if I turn over
My legs get all tangled up in the chains.
There's a basket dangling from the wall,
High enough to be beyond the reach of rats;

It holds, I suppose, five pieces of bread,
Bread left over from the day before,
With an onion to add a little flavor.
Now there's a fine pack for a hobo!

After they finish singing None
My meal is set out;
Each and every crust is gathered up
And readied for that big stomach of mine.

JACOPONE DA TODI

They bring some soup and dump it into a pail,
And when they lower it down to me
I drink and wet my lungs,
After slicing enough bread to satisfy a baby pig.

How's that for an ascetic, a new Saint Hilarion?
After I've finished (elegant fish in a peppery sauce!)
The meal is rounded out with an apple—
Crowning touch for a gourmet spread.

As I eat I'm getting colder and colder,
So I get up every now and then
And take mincing steps like a hobbled horse,
Stamping my feet on the wooden boards.

As for my bill, I say eight Our Fathers
For each penny I owe the Divine Inkeeper;
That's the only kind of currency I have
To settle my account.

If the friars who go to the papal court
And come back home mitre-cuckolded
Had laid away more of this kind of treasure,
They'd be better off.

If they had this advantage,
They wouldn't bother rushing down
To Rome, raiding enemy territory
To bring home ecclesiastical offices.

How few are they, O Poverty,
Who take you and love you as a spouse!
They abandon you for a bishopric
Without a second thought.

Some friars there are who lose this world;
Others leave it as if in a trance;
While others yet abhor it.
The three types are quite diverse.

JACOPONE DA TODI

Those who lose it rather than reject it are lost;
Those who leave it regret having done so;
Those who abhor the world reject it with loathing
If it is offered to them again.

Those who resist the world
Are opposed by it in return,
While the other two groups do everything possible
To get as much of it back as they can.

Once all shame is gone,
Who will stay in his appointed place?
There is a break in the fence of the sheepfold;
If that were repaired the sheep would remain at the manger.

With all my talk, all my asslicking around the Roman Court,
I've gotten myself thrown into prison.
Wallow, wallow in this pigsty, while they fatten you up—
Come Christmas, there'll not be enough lard on me to cut off a
      slice!

The monastery that agreed to hold me in custody
Will end up complaining of the cost.
So far they have gotten nothing
For all of their trouble.

Do what you will, Brothers,
Unlucky enough to have me on your hands,
You'll only lose money—
No income from my room and board!

But I have other riches: I am accustomed to evil days;
And this champion of mine will prevail against pain.
He is armed, and self-hatred is his shield;
As long as that protects him he cannot be wounded.

O admirable self-hatred that masters all suffering,
Nothing can injure you, for to shame you is to exalt you.
You have no enemies; all are your friends.
I am the only enemy that stands between me and salvation.

176

JACOPONE DA TODI

The suffering they've inflicted on me—
For thirty years I have loved it,
For thirty years longed for it,
And now the day of my consolation is here.

Wearing the long hood of the friar on probation
Is nothing new to me—
For ten years I wore it as a wandering penitent:
It was then I learned to bear shame and derision.

All these humiliations are like the air in a child's balloon.
The enemy is scattered, shame scorned,
And Jacopone, surrounded by his companions-in-arms,
Raises the glorious standard high.

One phalanx put to rout,
Another takes its place;
Jacopone's troops stand fast,
On the alert for another attack.

My good name,
I entrust you to a braying ass.
Let your place be behind the ass's tail;
That will be your reward.

Here, letter of mine, the prisoner Jacopone
Sends you to the Court of Rome;
May every nation, tribe, and people
Give you ear:

"Here I lie in Todi, underground,
Imprisoned for life.
This is the handsome benefice
I have won at the Court of Rome!"

56   LETTER TO BONIFACE VIII

O Pope Boniface, I bear the marks of your preface—
Anathema, and excommunication.

JACOPONE DA TODI

You have wounded me with your forked tongue;
That selfsame tongue can soothe and heal me,
For in no other way but through absolution
Will the deep wound close. I beseech you,
Say the words: "I absolve you";
And then the other punishments,
If you wish, I will suffer to the last.
If you would test yourself and duel with me,
Use other weapons, not excommunication.
Wound me fairly, when I lower my guard,
And I'll hold you a good swordsman indeed.
For I have two shields, and unless I lay them aside
No steel can pierce my flesh, *per secula infinita.*
The first shield is on the left, the other on the right.
The one on the left has been proven as hard as diamond,
No weapon can penetrate it:
This shield is my self-hatred, bonded to God's honor.
The shield on the right is of ruby;
It blazes like fire, flames leaping high:
It is made of ardent love of neighbor.
Step closer and you'll feel its heat with a rush.
Do what you will, this love will overcome you.
I should like to talk to you; I think it would help you.
Farewell, farewell, farewell.
May God free you from all evil
And give it to me instead as a grace,
That I might endure it with serenity.
So much for this treatise, we'll draw it to a close.

57 SECOND LETTER TO POPE BONIFACE VIII

Because of my sin the shepherd has cast me out of the sheepfold;
For all of my bleating he will not let me come back in.

O shepherd, let this bleating cry awaken you to pity;
Rescind, I beg of you, the excommunication.
Should the sentence of life imprisonment not suffice,
Wound me with some other lance—you have many to choose from.

178

JACOPONE DA TODI

I have written and called out to you untiringly, to no avail.
My pleas are ignored, you never open when I knock.
If I am not back in the sheepfold of my Order,
It is not for want of trying.

The blind man rebuked by those around him cried out all the
    louder,
"Have mercy on me, O God, for I am blind!"
"What would you have Me do?" "Lord, that I might see again,
That I might sing again the hosannas of my childhood!"

Like the centurion's servant, a paralytic wracked with pain,
I am not worthy to have you come under my roof.
It is enough that I see the written words, "I absolve you";
Those are the words that will free me from the pigsty.

Almost paralyzed, I lie at the pool near Solomon's Portico;
The waters have been moved with a host of pardons,
And now the season has drawn to a close. When shall I be told
That I should rise, take up my bed and go home?

Because of my sickness and stench I have been sent away;
Neither in church nor at table can I share my brothers' bread.
Sing out the gladsome news, I beseech you:
Let me hear you say, "Be thou made clean."

A demon has made me deaf and dumb;
Heal me, I pray you, instantly and completely:
Cast out the devil that I might hear,
And loose my tongue, silenced by your command.

My soul's death is harsher than that of the daughter of Jairus;
Take my hand, I beg of you, give me back to Saint Francis,
Who will set me down at a table again,
Where I may take my humble meal.

The members of my Order weep for me
As I stand on the brink of Hell;
Let me hear a mighty voice proclaim,
"Old man arise, let your lament be turned into song."

JACOPONE DA TODI

I am four days in the fetid tomb,
But with no Martha or Mary to plead for me to the Lord.
Would it not be to your honor to call out, "Lazarus, come forth"
So that I might once more be son and brother?

I have been told of a cure for my illness;
But I cannot turn for that remedy to one who is far away,
So I am writing to him to ask him to allow
That the words of healing come from the tongue of Fra Gentile.

58   THIRD LETTER FROM JAIL TO POPE BONIFACE VIII

Pope Boniface, you've had a good deal of fun in this world;
You'll not be very lighthearted, I suspect, as you leave it.

The world does not usually let its servants
Take their leave joyfully;
No special privilege will exempt you from this rule,
Allow you to turn down the gift you have coming.

You had your fill, I thought at one point,
Of the world and its dealings;
But once you found yourself on the papal throne
Those past ambitions seemed modest indeed!

Ingrained habit becomes second nature:
You were always intent on accumulating riches,
But now you find licit gains are not enough;
You've taken to stealing like a vicious highwayman.

Body and soul, sweeping aside all sense of shame,
You've given yourself to advancing your family's fortunes.
You have built your house upon sand,
And there's never any future in that.

Just as fire renews the salamander,
So scandals give you new life, confidence, and boldness.
The care of souls doesn't seem to interest you much:
When you die you'll see the abode you've prepared for yourself.

JACOPONE DA TODI

Should a bishop of no account
Have a bit of money laid aside,
You know how to deal with him:
You send him to the papal chamberlain.

There are hints at the possibility
Of removal from office;
If he comes across with a contribution
He'll find he can live in peace again.

Should a castle in the country strike your fancy,
You drive a wedge between the brothers who own it—
To one an embrace, to the other the flash of a dagger,
And you threaten to use it when you meet with resistance.

You think with craftiness you will rule the world;
What you build one year crumbles the next.
The world is not a horse you can bridle,
To be mounted and ridden at your pleasure.

The day you said your first mass
Darkness fell over all the land;
Such a storm came up not one candle was left burning,
There in the church where you stood at the altar.

On the day of your enthronement
(There was no want of witnesses)
Forty men were killed as they were leaving the palace,
A clear sign of God's displeasure.

Of all men living you considered yourself
The most worthy to sit on the papal throne.
You called on Saint Peter to speak in your favor,
To confirm that you know more than he ever did.

You placed yourself on a level with God
And challenged His sovereignty;
As with Lucifer, ruin followed immediately:
A prisoner in your own house, no one can help you.

JACOPONE DA TODI

Behold, a new Lucifer on the papal throne,
Poisoning the world with his blasphemies!
Nothing good is left in you—only sin;
I'd be ashamed to mention some vices you're accused of.

Blaspheming, for no good reason,
You condemn religious orders.
God will let you perish in this turbulence,
And all men's tongues will curse your name.

Your tongue is murderous in its arrogance,
Heaping injury and humiliation on all;
Not even an emperor or a king
Can leave your presence without suffering an affront.

O vile greed, thirst that grows and grows,
With all you drink you are never sated!
Have you ever thought, you wretch, that those for whom you steal
Have stolen from you something you were not aware of?

In Holy Week, when people stay at home in mourning,
Your servants were going around Rome,
Jousting, breaking lances, singing and dancing;
God will punish you severely for this.

In the heart of Saint Peter's, near the Holy of Holies,
You sent your servants to dance and sing.
The pilgrims, scandalized, cursed you,
And cursed your gold and your shining knights.

You thought that magic could lengthen your life,
But you cannot know the day or the hour.
In sin, life often comes to a sudden end,
And death looms abruptly in moments of joy.

I can find no one who can remember
Any pope of the past who was so vainglorious.
To have cast aside, as you have, the fear of God
Is a sign of either heresy or despair.

JACOPONE DA TODI

59   ON HOLY POVERTY, QUEEN OF CREATION

Lady Poverty, burning with charity,
Vast is your dominion!

France and England are mine, from sea to sea;
So firm is my grip,
No one takes up arms against me.
Mine is Saxony, mine is Guascogne,
Mine are Burgundy and all of Normandy.

Mine the kingdom of Prussia and that of Bohemia,
Hibernia and Roumania, Scotland and Frisia.
Mine is Tuscany and the valley of Spoleto,
The Marches of Ancona and the land of the Slavs,
Sicily, Calabria, and the plains of Puglia.

Mine is Campagna, the Roman hills, and the plains of Lombardy;
Mine are Sardinia, Cyprus, Corsica, and Crete,
And unknown kingdoms and numberless subjects beyond the seas—
Medes, Persians, Elamites, Syrians, and Mongols,
Georgians, Ethiopians, Indians, and Moslems.

My lands I give to my vassals to cultivate,
And in my generosity I grant them
The fruits of their labor, year after year.
Land, fields full of flowers, trees,
Succulent fruits, livestock—all at my command, all mine.

Lakes, rivers, and oceans teeming with fish,
Air, winds, birds—all pay me joyful homage.
Moon and sun, sky and stars, are but minor treasures:
The treasures that make me burst into song
Lie beyond the sky that you can see.

Since my will is centered in God, who possesses all,
I wing with ease from earth to heaven.
Since I gave my will to God
All things are mine and I am one with them
In love, in ardent charity.

JACOPONE DA TODI

60 HOLY POVERTY AND ITS THREEFOLD HEAVEN

O love of poverty, tranquil kingdom
That knows not strife or hatred!
Out of reach of thief and tempest,
Yours is the sure way.

Having made no testament,
You die in peace;
You leave the world as it lies,
And your passing sparks no discord.

You need not pay
Either judge or notary,
And smile at the avaricious man,
Fretting over his money.

Poverty, deepest wisdom, you are slave to nothing,
And in your detachment you possess all things.
To have contempt for things is to possess them without risk;
They cannot block the path to perfection.

The man who desires possessions is himself possessed,
Having sold himself to the thing he loves;
Let him think on what he has received in exchange,
And ponder the bargain he's made.

How unworthy of us to allow ourselves
To become vassals of vain possessions,
To smudge our likeness
To the Living God.

God does not dwell in a heart that's confined,
And a heart is only as big as the love it holds:
In the great heart of Poverty
God has room to dwell.

*   *   *

To the man on earth whose vision is clouded,
Poverty is an overcast sky;
But he who has ascended to the third heaven
Senses the mysterious presence of God.

The first heaven is the starry firmament
Where we must strip ourselves of honor—
For honor in any form
Is an impediment to serenity.

To kill the love of honor
We must shed all riches,
Silence knowledge,
And flee a reputation for sanctity.

The accumulation of riches is a poor use of time,
Knowledge leads to vainglory,
And hypocrisy likes to lodge in the man reputed as holy.
The man who strips himself of all three is a starry heaven.

Another hidden sky there is,
Of frozen waters crystal-clear;
The winds of fear, hope, pain, and joy blow over this sea,
And they trouble the mind of man.

To strip oneself of these four is more demanding:
Those who do not understand would consider this error,
But we must cast aside the fear of Hell, the hope of Heaven,
Joy in the good and sorrow in adversity.

We do not understand the source of virtue—
The cause lies outside of us
And all unknown to us, day by day,
It heals us of our infirmities.

Defenseless, virtue and vice fall to earth,
Mortally wounded. With the death of the vices,
The virtues come to life again,
Sustained by the soul's impassivity.

JACOPONE DA TODI

Higher than all, the third Heaven in its infinity
Lies beyond the reach of the imagination.
It has stripped you of every good and every virtue,
And what you have lost has been replaced with true treasure.

This heaven is founded on *nichil*,
Where purified love lives in Truth.
You see that things are not as they seemed to you,
So high a state has been reached.

The proud win Heaven and the humble are damned;
Between aspiration and realization yawns a great gap,
And the man who thinks he has succeeded
Is often the loser.

The name of this heaven is Nonbeing—
All affirmations are forbidden
There where Love is a prisoner
In that dark light.

All light is shrouded in darkness,
All darkness bright as the noonday sun;
This new philosophy
Has burst the old wineskins.

Where Christ enters in, the old world is swept away,
Lover and beloved are fused in wondrous union.
Love no longer needs the heart,
Nor knowledge the intelligence—our will is His.

To live as myself and yet not I,
My being no longer my being,
This is a paradox
We cannot pretend to understand!

Poverty is having nothing, wanting nothing,
And possessing all things in the spirit of freedom.

JACOPONE DA TODI

61 ST. FRANCIS AND THE SEVEN VISIONS
OF THE CROSS

O truly poor Francis, patriarch of our times,
Yours is a new banner, emblazoned with seven crosses.
Much has been written on the meaning of each,
But I'll spare the reader and try to be brief.

The first vision, soon after your conversion,
Was one of a noble palace. Within, it was filled
With shields marked with the cross—
The shields of those entrusted to you.

Another time, as you prayerfully meditated
(The mere remembrance of the vision
Always reduced you to tears), you caught fire
In the love of the crucified Christ.

That Christ you saw said to you,
"Come and lovingly embrace this noble cross;
If you would follow Me, become as nothing,
Hate yourself and love your neighbor."

Still later, when again you were meditating on the cross,
In clear, strong tones He called you thrice by name
And then, "My Church has lost its way—
Set it once more on the right path."

On the fourth occasion, Brother Silvester
Saw a golden cross shining over you,
And your blazing words put to rout
The cursed serpent that had encircled Assisi.

In similar fashion, as Brother Pacifico gazed at you, Francis,
Worthy of all praise, he saw a cross of two swords—
One reached from your head to your feet,
The other followed the line of your outstretched arms.

As Saint Anthony was preaching, Blessed Brother Monaldo
Saw a vision of you in the air, on a cross,

187

JACOPONE DA TODI

In the act of blessing your friars; and then,
According to the account, you vanished from sight.

The seventh apparition came as you prayed with great devotion
On the craggy heights of La Verna—
An awesome vision of a six-winged seraphim, crucified.
It sealed you with the stigmata—side, hands, and feet.

The man who hears a brief account finds this hard to believe,
Yet many there were who saw these marks
While you were still alive and well,
And on your death many came to touch them.

Among others, Saint Clare came,
Bringing with her her sisters;
Greedy for such treasure she tried in vain
To pull out those nails with her teeth:

The nails were made of flesh, hardened like iron,
The flesh was as fair as a child's.
It had lost the traces of the many winters;
Love had made it radiant, beautiful to gaze on.

The wound in your side was like a scarlet rose.
All that saw wept at the marvel:
Its likeness to that of Christ
Made the heart sink into an abyss of love.

O happy weeping, full of wonder—
Joyful weeping, full of consolation!
How many tears of love were shed there,
To see and touch the new Christ's wounds!

They flowed freely as the friars gazed upon this vision
Of fiery love. The precious balsam of holiness
That lies hidden in the heart
Had burst forth from the wounds of Francis.

That towering palm tree you climbed, Francis—
It was with the sacrifice of Christ Crucified that it bore fruit.

JACOPONE DA TODI

You were so closely bound to Him in love you never faltered,
And the marks on your body attested to that union.

This is the mission of love, to make two one;
It united Francis with the suffering Christ.
It was Christ in his heart that taught him the way,
And that love shone forth in his robe streaked with color.

The burning love of Christ, whose depths are lost to sight,
Enfolded Francis, softened his heart like wax,
And there pressed its seal, leaving the marks
Of the One to whom he was united.

I have no words for this dark mystery;
How can I understand or explain
The superabundance of riches,
The disproportionate love of a heart on fire?

Who can measure the intensity of that fire?
We only know that the body could not contain it
And it burst out through the five wounds,
That all might see that it dwelt therein.

No saint ever bore such signs upon his body—
Sacred mystery, revealed by God!
It is best to pass over this in silence;
Let only those who have experienced it speak.

Wondrous stigmata, manifestation of the holy,
You give witness to the awesome presence behind the awesome
    sign.
All will be clear at the end, when the last joust is over,
In the presence of those who follow the cross!

O my arid soul, dry of tears, run—take the bait;
Drink of these waters and never turn away
Until you are drunk with love.
Oh, that we might die at this sacred spring!

189

JACOPONE DA TODI

62   ON SAINT FRANCIS AND
THE ENEMY'S BATTLES AGAINST HIM

O Francis, beloved of God,
Christ made Himself manifest in you!
The deceitful Enemy, adversary of the Lord,
Dreading that his lost power would devolve to man,
Approached him and through fraud led him
To disobedience and to the loss of paradise.
The Enemy gloried in his triumph,
For with man's fall he was raised,
And became the Prince of this World.
Then God became man, wounded him mortally,
And wrested from him that dominion.
The humility of God changed the Enemy's fortunes,
And holy poverty checkmated him.
Long after his defeat the Devil tried again,
And man did not escape his snares.
Seeing the Enemy was carrying the day,
The Lord God sent in the cavalry with an able commander;
Saint Francis was chosen to lead the troops,
And he accepted into his ranks only those
Who despised and rejected the world.
The three great steeds that would carry them into battle
Were poverty, obedience, and chastity.
Francis wore the arms of his Lord,
Who loved him with such a great love
That He marked him with His own signs.
And so intense was the love in Francis's heart
That his body was adorned with five magnificent jewels.
He was like a fig, whose great value is not visible to the eye,
But is hidden in the center, honey-sweet.
The Lord God then showed Francis how to skirmish,
How to deliver blows and how to take them,
And taught his tongue the language of peace.
The sight of Francis struck fear into the Enemy,
For he much resembled the Christ, who with His cross
Had once before stripped him of his prize.
"If he is the Christ, the victory will be His;
Against Him there are no defenses.

190

O misery, to be defeated by such an enemy!
But I will not lose heart, I will tempt him.
Nothing ventured, nothing gained!

"Francis, take care—
That strict fast you've begun will kill you."

  "I fast with discretion,
  For the body, properly disciplined,
  Is a good and useful servant."

"The whole world knows you are a saint;
We have seen in what esteem the Lord holds you,
May His holy name be praised."

  "I want to conceal the good in me,
  And show the world I am a sinner.
  My heart is with the Lord
  When I bow my head low."

"What do you plan to do? Don't you want to work,
And with your earnings help those in need?"

  "I shall go about in rags and beg for my bread;
  In my love of God I go about like a drunken man."

"What good will that do? You will die a miserable death,
And your followers will grieve that you left them penniless."

  "I will stay on the true path, with neither purse nor bag;
  I have told my followers they must never touch money."

"Go then into that lonely wood
With your ragged band of heroes;
In that solitude you will edify man,
And God from His throne will smile on you."

  "I did not come into this world to shirk my duty;
  Pressing on, I will lay siege,
  Pitching my tents around your citadels."

JACOPONE DA TODI

"I fear your tactics: with this Order of yours
You will take many souls away from me.
At least leave me the women—
Your friars shouldn't be mixing with them."

> "I have upsetting news for you:
> I have founded an order of sisters,
> And they too will wage war on you."

"What woman would ever have the impudence
To move against me, the conqueror of the world?"

> "In the Valley of Spoleto lives a virgin,
> Of sovereign virtue, a temple consecrated to the Lord,
> Clare, the daughter of Donna Ortolana."

"Married people should not mix with friars and nuns—
You can let them go, leave them under my patronage."

> "I will trouble you even more:
> I have founded an order for married penitents."

"At least leave heresy, your enemy, alone;
If you touch that it will be too great an offense."

> "I mean to fight the heresy that dwells in your mansions,
> And those infected with it I'll have thrown into prison."

"Oh, I am poor and wretched indeed!
What has happened to that sharp hook of mine?
You've put a bit in my mouth and are reining me in!
Francis, you have annihilated me and retaken the world,
So bereaved me that I am utterly destroyed.
Enough! I shall call on the Antichrist,
Whose coming has been prophesied."

> "And I will deal you both the final blow.
> I will win back the world and free those you have
>   imprisoned,

Sharing with them the striped robe of the fool,
Mad with the love of the Lord."

"The prophetic texts do not reassure me;
The last part foretells the victory will be yours:
Then truly will I be undone."

In this harsh and bitter struggle
Many will be wounded and slain,
And the rewards of the victor
Will be more than ample.

63   LETTER OF CONSOLATION TO
BROTHER JOHN OF FERMO
KNOWN AS JOHN OF LA VERNA
FROM THE PLACE HE IS RESTING—
THE PROSE PART TRANSLATED FROM THE LATIN

To Brother John of La Verna, who is passing the winter
Shivering and trembling with fever,
I send this message, which he is to read:

> I have always held, and still do, that it is a great thing to be filled
> with God. Why? Because humility is then wedded to reverence. But I
> have also always thought, and still do, that to know how to suffer His
> absence, how to endure that fast when He imposes it, is even greater.
> Why? Because faith is then attested to without witnesses, hope with-
> out expectation of reward, charity without signs of benevolence. Such
> are the foundations of the holy hills. They lead to that summit where
> rocks have the sweetness of honey and stones the savor of the finest oil.

Farewell, Brother John, farewell!
Accept your suffering with equanimity!
It is hammer and anvil that give a vase its beautiful form,
And the vase must be heated to be beaten into shape;
Otherwise, if beaten when cold it will crack,
And be thrown out with the rejects.
Do all you can, then, to call on the Lord

To send you every evil and ill that the world dreads.
Malum pene, the evil of suffering, is glorious
When due to no faults or sins of our own.
Should the suffering be due to sin,
That is another affair, hardly the same sort of thing.

64   A CANTICLE OF THE NATIVITY

A new canticle I hear,
To dry the tears of the afflicted!

I hear it begin with a piercing tone,
Whence it slowly descends several octaves,
For it celebrates the coming of the Word. Never was heard
A descending scale of such exquisite melody!

The joyous chorus is that of angels
Singing sweet songs around the manger
Before the Christ Child,
The Word Incarnate.

"Glory to God in the highest," they sing,
"And peace on earth—
An end to war and to all evils;
Praise and bless the Infant adored!"

The sacred notes, I see,
Are inscribed on parchment, skin of the lamb;
In the Lamb—our penetrating eye discerns—
Is all song, whether solo or choral.

The hand that moves across the page
Is the hand of God,
And it is God in His mercy
Who teaches us to sing.

Here, robed in firm faith,
The singers around the manger

JACOPONE DA TODI

See the Godhead Incarnate,
And their hearts leap up in hope.

Here they hear unceasing songs of love;
That love conforms itself to God,
And finding in Him the law of its being,
Seraphim-like, darts flames.

Led by the soaring voice of Stephen,
Hosts of martyrs chant the first office of the night—
The chorus of those who gave their lives
To Christ, that flower burgeoning with seed.

The second sequence is taken up by the Confessors—
The voice of John the Evangelist heightens the splendor.
No voice ever soared to such piercing heights
In such exquisite melody.

The Holy Innocents sing the third sequence,
They who for all time abide in the presence of the Child.
"We praise you, God," they intone,
"For Christ our Lord is born this day."

O sinners who have served an evil master,
Come sing with us—now man can find God,
Who has appeared on earth as a child,
And all who seek Him can take and hold Him.

Come sing, O ye who have strayed,
Now you are called to penitence,
Which cancels error and grants truth
To those who humbly seek it.

Just men who have labored hard and long,
Come, you too, and sing!
God invites you to glory in a kingdom
And fulfills the longing of every heart.

JACOPONE DA TODI

65 SECOND CANTICLE OF THE NATIVITY

Honor and praise to the Love made flesh,
Who came to give Himself to us!

Honor Him, O my soul, for He comes to save you.
Come, hasten to greet Him!
He does not hold back—all of Himself He gives
In His desire to be one with you.
Will you not give all of yourself to Him?
Will you not hasten to embrace Him?

Think of what He gives you, and what He demands—
That you be as generous as He.
Leaving Heaven behind, all alone,
Without the trappings of wealth or glory,
No servants to minister to Him, no palace to house Him,
He manifested Himself on earth in a stable.

"Why did You leave the golden throne resplendent with gems,
Why did You put aside the dazzling crown?
Why did You leave the order of cherubim,
The seraphim, that joyous court of ardent love,
The honored servants and courtiers you loved as brothers—
Why did You leave them all, O Lord?

"In place of Your glorious throne,
A manger and a little straw;
In place of a starry crown,
Poor swaddling clothes
And the warm breath of an ox and an ass;
In place of a glorious court, Mary and Joseph.

"Were these the actions of someone drunk, or out of his senses?
How could You abdicate kingdom and riches,
A renunciation that verges on madness?
Did someone promise You other and greater treasure?
O measureless love that would cede
Such glory as Yours for such humble estate!

JACOPONE DA TODI

"High-born Love, who is it You love
So deeply and tenaciously and wildly?
Love holds You bound so tightly
You give all of Yourself—this You can hardly deny.
And this love will lead You to Your death,
For it gives no signs of diminishing or cooling.

"Such disproportionate love has never been known,
So powerful from the moment of birth!
You sold Yourself for us even before You were born;
It was Love that purchased You, and You held back nothing.
The decision was made—You would die of love,
Suffer death in agony on the cross.

"Love imposed these terms when first it wounded You;
It struck with such force it stripped You of all—
Stripped You of wisdom, life, and strength,
Drawing them to itself as a magnet draws iron.
From such heights You were drawn to such wretched depths,
To a stable, not repelled by stench or poverty.

"It was almost as if You did not grasp or sense
The depth of the descent, when You came among us.
It was almost as if Your understanding was darkened,
Your power and insight lost. Wounded by Love,
You did nothing to defend Yourself;
Surrendering to Love, You gave it Your strength.

"I know that all knowledge and power were Yours
Even when still a child; how could so much be contained
In such a tiny frame, made of common clay?
There is no limit to Your charity,
For Your wisdom, strength, and worth
You kept concealed within You.

"Wrapped in poor swaddling clothes,
You were utterly dependent.
Dear humble cloth in which the most high God
Was wound and bound, as if He had nothing—

JACOPONE DA TODI

Humble cloth which enfolded treasure
That puts to shame all gems and gold!

"The disproportionate love of the Omnipotent God,
How could one ever describe it?
No love of son or father rises to such heights.
Love never so bound a human heart
That it stripped itself of strength and let itself
Be sweetly drawn beyond all awareness of self.

"Nature compels a father to love his son,
And a mother to give him her heart.
Yet I cannot imagine a father who strips himself of wisdom,
Counsel, strength, and honor in favor of the son he loves.
I see that a father forgives himself for not wanting
To die or to suffer torment for his son.

"Who would ever renounce life in order to find love,
Renounce all cherished possessions,
Buy poverty with a pearl of great price,
And suffer for that love a mortal wound in his heart?
In the natural order of things he who gives wants to receive,
He who loves wants to be loved in return.

"What can a creature offer You, O Highest Goodness,
In exchange for Your gift of Yourself? Whatever a man's worth,
It is less than nothing, compared to Yours.
Why, then, did You give Yourself to him?
What can he give You in return for Your love?
Can we in our illness bring You any joy?

"Your love, I think, brought You no gain.
Does gold need tin for its splendor to be seen?
For love of man You seem to have gone mad!
And think what You will receive in return—
For joy, reproaches; for riches, niggardly recompense.
Is it not folly, in the name of love, to surrender mind and will?

"Yet so great is Your strength,
Disproportionate love,

JACOPONE DA TODI

That You make Divine Majesty
Stoop down, abase itself!
You have wounded the heart
Of Beauty itself,

"Which now loves us in our ugliness
And wants us for His bride.
Jesus cannot cure Himself of love;
He seems to be out of His senses.
Love has so wounded Him
That pain seems to Him sweetness.

"O enamored God, speak to me of this love,
Which renews and gives joy to the lovers.
If I might see Your face and rest with You
I will desire nothing more.
Tell me, how did Love find You?
I too would want to feel its ardor."

"My bride, the wonder of this exchange of love!
When you beseech Me, you command Me;
Love makes Me suffer, drives Me mad,
Drawing Me outside of Myself and closer to you.
Delay no longer, My bride, yield to Me; take Me,
As I give Myself to you, and give Me your heart.

"Yield to Me, My desire, My love;
Be one with Me, bride of My heart.
Satisfy My longing, come and be My spouse.
Caught on the hook of Love, I yearn for you.
That is why I call to you, My bride, embrace you chastely,
Come down to you in the ardor of My love.

"For you I put aside riches and embrace poverty,
Leave every delight to endure suffering,
Yield sweetness and accept adversity,
And true peace exchange for a life of pain and need.
Let this perfection of love now be recognized—
Know it, and render love for love.

JACOPONE DA TODI

"If you cannot enrich Me with wealth,
Or with joy or with knowledge,
What can you offer Me other than yourself?
You can offer Me nothing of value;
It is the love you have in your power that drives Me mad,
It is your heart I have always sought.

"This is the prize I want to give you—
Myself and all My riches,
The treasure I brought with Me when I exchanged
The glorious life of Heaven for a cruel death.
Take the sweetness I offer, give Me pain in return;
The Love that never wanes has made Me prodigal.

"All this I give you, and ask for little in return;
I will hold back nothing—I want to die for you.
Think on what I ask, on the yoke I am taking upon Me—
Will you still hold back the love I seek?
Love, you are driving Me to madness; I can do no more.
You have made Me more reckless than the worst of gamblers.

"A bride gives a dowry to her husband,
She does not receive one from him;
And that arrangement precedes the wedding.
To give his wife a dowry
A husband would have to be mad,
Unless her lineage would exalt him.

"My bride, I do not expect from you rank or riches,
And for love of you, for your sake,
I accept need, shame, and servitude.
Love Me forever, then,
For it is I who will give you a dowry—
My blood shed for you in pain on the cross.

"I give you infinite riches never dreamed of,
Your every desire will be satisfied:
These gifts are kept for you in Heaven,
Beyond the reach of thieves and time.

JACOPONE DA TODI

You shall be robed in radiance brighter than the sun,
But first I must cleanse you of guilt and stench.

"Yours will be a crown of stars;
Your robe will be resplendent with pearls and gems,
Your throne with gold and precious stones,
The bridal chamber and wedding bed richly draped.
(I speak to you in images—
The chaste splendor is beyond your imagining.)

"To raise you to this height,
I descended to an ugly stable.
Let My high love and festive joy
Be swiftly reciprocated;
Let your heart not delay in answering
The fervor of My love with ardent embrace.

"Give Me love, I beseech you, My bride,
It is love I desire; I ask for no more.
Love has no mercy—it strips Me,
Binds Me, enflames Me ceaselessly.
Love Me then, My much-loved bride:
I bought you dearly, and have given you all."

"Jesus, my sweet spouse, tell me
How I can love You as You deserve;
After the fall, You endured all suffering
To save me. You, Divine Majesty,
Came to draw me out of the mire,
To make of a servant a queen.

"I am Yours, my Creator and Redeemer,
You who saved me from death!
He who finds what he has lost
Guards and loves it all the more.
You alone have rights over me, O Lord;
You paid the price, shield me from evil!

JACOPONE DA TODI

"More than myself I would give You if I could—
The world and all its fruits, were they mine—
But that is beyond my power.
What I have I will give You with all my heart:
My will and my hope,
My love and my desire.

"You receive little in return for Your love, I know,
But You do not ask for more than I can give.
I give You what You demand: a will that does not go astray,
Or spread itself out in all directions,
But remains fixed firmly on You forever.
A thousand lives my wounded heart would give You, Love!

"Do you ask more of Your bride,
Who longs to embrace You?
O sweet Life of mine, put an end to my suffering;
Let me gaze forever on Your fair countenance:
If You could not defend Yourself
Against Love, how can I?

"Have mercy on me, then;
O compassionate Jesus, never leave me;
Without You I weep and suffer and die.
Without You, my Spouse,
The world and all its beauty
Tastes bitter indeed!"

I sing for the birth of my Love;
He has redeemed me and slipped on my finger His ring;
I burn with love for Him who now appears in the flesh,
And embrace Him, He who is now my brother.
O sweet child, I have conceived You in my heart
And held You in my arms, crying out "O Love!"

Lovers, come to our festive wedding;
Where Love is, there is joy.
He is one with us in loving riches and delights.
Soul, you are created anew—

Hurry to embrace your spouse
Who gathers you into His joy—O love, love!

Love, keep us drunk with love;
Keep us in Your embrace, in Love that unites.
Watch over us constantly that we may not be deceived.
Let our hearts be ever filled with love and lifted up to You.
You, Love, were born for us; nourish us with that food
Whose sweetness is all unknown to scribes and pharisees.

66   THE LAMENT OF THE SOUL FOR GRACE IN HIDING

Who will weep and lament with me?
Let me find someone who will take pity on me,
Someone to whom I can voice my anguish.
O God of righteousness, why have You hardened Your heart?

You have justly punished me,
Laid bare my fault,
And fled from me;
Your absence is my just privation!

No longer can I find that compassion
That always led me back to the heavenly court.
I hear the gate as it shuts,
And ingratitude bars me entrance.

Neither tears nor sighs nor prayer nor meditation
Will prepare the way for my return.
O my wretched and forlorn heart,
No words can express your pain!

Tongue cannot say,
Nor can mind conceive;
They only approach the threshold of pain—
Pain deeper and wider than the sea.

Have You no pity, Lord,
No compassion for my distress?

JACOPONE DA TODI

I would want to move others to pity,
But my tongue is tied.

I would want to find someone able to understand—
He could not but weep with me.
Will You abandon me here, O God,
Unarmed and surrounded by enemies?

I shall go into battle like Uriah, unarmed,
And I know I will die in the fray.
Nor is there anyone who will mourn my passing—
I will die in shame and disgrace.

What has become of the arms with which
I used to defend myself,
Those weapons that always routed the foe?
Like Samson I am captured and chained.

I seek out Your nativity, Lord,
Seek out Your suffering;
There is no joy in the quest,
For love has gone cold.

Your providence is reason enough for loving You;
I count Your gifts, go over them one by one,
Trying to find my way back to You, but to no avail:
You have hidden Yourself from me.

Contemplating my own grief I weep,
The dry tears of a heart in ruins.
That precious, inaccessible sweetness—
Where has it gone?

67   THE SOUL LAMENTS THE DISAPPEARANCE OF GOD

Love, beloved Love, why have You left me?
Tell me, Love, why have You left me in grief and uncertainty?
Is it my vileness that repels You? Let me make amends.
If I reshape myself, will You not come back?

JACOPONE DA TODI

Love, why did You give my heart such sweetness,
Only to strip it then of joy?
To give and take back is not chivalrous.
I speak as if out of my mind, but with good reason.

Suddenly bereft of You, I know not where I am;
Confused, I look for You all about,
Look for the sweetness that all unawares,
Little by little was taken from me.

Love, a thief when caught must make restitution;
In tears I beg the Heavenly Court
To bring You to justice—
You are the thief who has robbed me, Love.

Once the ill-gotten gains of a merchant are exposed
He loses his good name and the trust of his friends;
And the partner who defrauds his associate
Is clearly guilty of theft.

Should a merchant eager to sell his goods
Turn his back on the man who would buy?
He should not say he wants to sell
If in his heart he knows he will not.

Had I never caught a glimpse of what You offer,
Love, I would not now suffer so,
But I saw and desired it, and the memory throbs.
What You did You did with cunning, Love, to make me die.

Love, is it to the honor of a rich man
If his betrothed should go about begging?
Your riches, Love, cannot be counted;
You could satisfy me, but it seems You will not.

Love, You have taken me for Your bride;
Is it to Your honor if I have not one penny to spend?
I have given myself to You, put myself in Your hands,
And all despise me, fallen to low estate.

JACOPONE DA TODI

He who shows a starving man
A piece of bread, Love,
But does not want to give it to him—
Is he not held to blame?

You have showed Yourself to me, Love,
And now You see me dying;
You could come to my aid,
But it seems You will not.

Love, my heart is crushed,
Starved, close to death.
Will You wait until it is lifeless
To give it back to me?

The man who leaves his lodgings, Love,
Without first settling accounts,
Is he not compelled to return and pay what he owes?
What I seek is just, and to Justice will I appeal.

Hear Me, you who make such loud lament:
I will answer in brief.
I made My abode in you
And I wanted to stay,

But you cast Me out
And welcomed the world.
You are less than honest, then,
In your complaints against Love.

You know the price I paid when I dwelt with you,
And how pleased you were with the changes I made.
I scoured a house that was filled with filth
And made it pure so that Love could dwell there.

When I left, the Love I took with Me was Mine;
You know that yours had become displeasing to Me;
How can you say, then,
That I took anything that was yours?

JACOPONE DA TODI

When something loaned is not appreciated
The lender is right in taking it back
From the ungrateful borrower unable to see
Who it is Who loaned him Love.

You know how many times I came to lodge,
And you to your shame cast Me out.
Perhaps you wanted Me to remain there
While you heaped insults on such a noble Love?

O Love, you have put an end to my murmuring:
You put me to shame, I bow my head.
But do not punish me, I beg of You,
Conceal Yourself no longer, Love.

Though you cast Me out with malice,
Because of your repentance I shall return,
So that someone like you can never complain
That I betrayed a loyal love.

68   THE SOUL WEEPS OVER
THE DEPARTURE OF ITS LOVE

Weep, my suffering soul,
Fallen into the hands of the Enemy,
For you are widowed of Christ's love!

Weep, suffer and sigh,
For you have lost your gentle Lord;
May these tears yet bring Him back
To my disconsolate heart.

I weep for good reason,
For I have lost both son and father.
Comely Christ, lily in flower,
Has left me, and the fault is mine.

O Jesus Christ, have you abandoned me,
Ringed about by enemies, in desolation?

JACOPONE DA TODI

From every side my sins assail me,
And I am drained of every strength.

O Jesus Christ, how can You allow me
To die such a bitter death?
Give me leave to deal myself a mortal blow,
For I would gladly do so.

O Jesus Christ, if You could let me die
A death still harder than that!
You have left me bereft, closed the gate,
And it seems my cry does not come unto You.

O wretched heart, what is the root of this pain
That holds you so tightly in its grasp?
It is brimming over, the vessel is full;
Yours no grief that could be endured in silence.

O my eyes, continue to weep,
For you have good reason!
You have lost a great inheritance,
The contemplation of pure splendor.

O my ears, why do you find solace
In the weeping of a grieving fellowship?
Do you no longer hear the voice of the Beloved
Who made you rejoice and break into song?

Oh, the sad, sad memories!
Harsh death gradually consumes me;
I am neither alive nor dead,
In torment, cut off from my Savior.

I no longer seek the company of my fellowman;
What life is left for me to live
Will be a life of solitude,
For I have lost my Redeemer.

JACOPONE DA TODI

69   THE TREE OF A HIERARCHY SIMILAR
TO THAT OF THE ANGELS
BASED ON FAITH, HOPE, AND CHARITY

Let me teach you to make your way
To the three heavens of faith, hope, and charity,
And to the top of the three trees
That soar to the height of each heaven.

I ask forgiveness for any errors
To be found in these my glosses;
It is not for myself I write, a person of no account,
But for those with a higher understanding.

Earth-dweller, created for eternal life,
Look upon this tree and learn from it.
Come, do not delay,
Begin to climb.

Dwell on the nine hierarchies of angels,
Each on a level higher than the last;
Consider the nobility of your nature—
You can rise to their highest level.

The first tree, planted deep,
Is rooted in faith;
It rises past the starry heaven
And reaches hope.

The first small branch represents
Sorrow for my sins;
It exhorted me to confess
And resolve to sin no more.

The second branch imposed
Satisfaction for sins—
Sins that in my case
Sent me as far as Rome.

JACOPONE DA TODI

The third branch bent down to me and said,
"If you would want to love Christ
And understand His example, be poor."
I then stripped myself of all possessions.

The man who reaches this state
Considers himself among the saved,
Since he has risen to the first choir of angels.
Let him persevere!

Drawn up to the fourth branch,
I was led to join the Order,
And there taught penance
And the fear of Hell.

Not long after,
The fifth branch drew me up,
Urged me to pray
If I wished to remain chaste.

Then the sixth branch
Taught me the virtue of silence,
And that obedience to superiors
Is worth more than sacrifice.

He who has climbed up to this branch
Is one with the Archangels;
Blessed be the day
And the hour of his creation!

Drawn up to the seventh branch,
One that is much despised,
I was badly beaten and cast aside,
And I found it hard to bear.

On the eighth branch,
I was tempted by pride,
For I found I had power
To make the lame man walk.

JACOPONE DA TODI

From where I stood with the others
I looked up above me
And the ninth branch commanded:
"Do nothing," and then began to heal me.

He who has risen to this state
Is among the Thrones,
For faith shows him the way
And he can live above the starry heaven.

Meditating on the tree
I could not but marvel,
And felt impatient
To leave my body behind.

I realized then, and to my sorrow,
That I had deluded myself the power was mine,
Because it used my body as an instrument.
I had been unaware of my nothingness!

*   *   *

I then looked at the vermilion tree
Which is the symbol of hope.
No man still in the world
Has even desired it.

As I looked up the tree smiled and said,
"What do you wish to do? It is not easy to climb me."
Trembling, I answered, "I have no choice;
Driven by love, I seek my Lord."

"Come," the tree answered,
"But first leave behind all possessions;
Be cruel to yourself,
Do not let pity deceive you."

Yet this was the limb that bore the flower
That lifted me up to the second branch,

JACOPONE DA TODI

Where I found the fruit of Love,
And began to weep.

On the third branch, love increasing,
I asked God for Hell;
In loving Him and losing myself,
All suffering was sweet to me.

He who rises to this state
Finds himself with the Dominions,
Where to love the Devil
Is to incur no risk.

Raised to the fourth branch,
My intellect became clouded;
I was in the hands of the Devil,
And knew not what to do.

The pain was so strong on the fifth branch
That I could not endure it;
I went to sleep and then
The Devil appeared to me in a dream.

On the sixth I awoke;
The world was covered with darkness
And I was encircled by terrifying enemies
Who were bent on making me lose all hope.

Memory came to my aid and made me feel God's presence;
My heart, taking comfort, sought to embrace the cross.
He who clings to the cross will find Christ comes to his aid,
And he will receive lordship in eternal glory.

Greeted with joy on the seventh branch,
I was given two lights—
The Enemy was routed
And could no longer deceive me.

But in the guise of an angel
He returned to the assault

And showed me a crumbling church
I was called to repair.

In great fear,
Having learned from the Fall,
I turned my back on him
And looked up to the eighth branch.

Then showing himself to me as Christ he said,
"I am your Teacher; take delight in me and I will console you."
I answered, "But Christ said that I was not to cling to Him
Unless I saw Him in the Father, in perfect clarity."

The Devil then appeared to me as an angel of light
And said, "You are worthy of being adored."
"All honor," I replied, "belongs to the Creator;
My heart tells me you are not what you seem to be."

Seeing I was shielded by prudence,
The Enemy left in defeat,
And I continued upward to the last branch,
The branch of contemplation.

As I praised the Omnipotent
My mind opened to the light,
And I saw God present
In the things I was contemplating.

This is the crystalline heaven
Where hope fades away;
He who shares this glory
Reigns with the Powers.

*   *   *

Gazing fixedly on the third heaven,
More radiant than the sun,
I became enflamed with the desire
To soar to that height.

To do so one must climb the tree of charity,
Whose highest branches are lost to sight.
As I was getting ready the tree said to me,
"Hold on tight, and may all go well with you.

"But listen closely: You have won two battles—
Against the Enemy and against the world.
Now if you would climb my heights,
Make sure that your mind is pure."

I answered in the spirit of charity,
"All sensual love has left me;
The splendor of charity has revealed this to me,
So that I might obey your every command."

I made a shield out of the light
And a spear out of the darkness,
And with the greatest of prudence
I began to climb.

On the first level I came upon Sloth;
Looking at her I cried out,
"A curse on you, woman,
You are the source of all evil!"

She was not alone; with her I saw
Gluttony and another companion, Lust.
"This is an evil company," warned my soul;
With my lance I dashed them to the ground.

When I climbed to the second branch Vainglory approached,
Intent on lingering with me, as in the past;
When I denounced her for what she truly was,
Anger took her part and answered me:

"We are of noble lineage,
And our Queen is Avarice;
She maintains her power
By storing away all we earn."

JACOPONE DA TODI

Confronted by that company,
I clasped my shield tightly,
Charged into their midst,
And put them all to flight.

The increase in my strength, I saw,
Brought me in joy to the third branch,
Where I found Ignorance,
And I cursed her.

She looked about and found Pride,
Who was ready and eager to block my way;
They were followed by an efficient handmaiden
Who served them well—Voluptuousness was her name.

Seeing their maneuvers I cried out,
"The torch, the torch!" and set the three ablaze.
He who defeats the vices reigns in Heaven with the Virtues,
Their concordance assuring his salvation.

Then I climbed one more step
And I found myself divided—
Having much and having little,
And loving God in either case.

With joy I then climbed
Up to the fifth branch,
A still more virtuous state,
For my Spouse had me obey His commands.

There all heaviness left me
And I felt surrounded by riches,
And the Highest Power said to me,
"Make good use of these."

I rose to the sixth branch without a struggle,
In harmony with the Power of the Father,
In the deep Wisdom of the Son
And the pure Will of the Spirit.

He who soars so high
Rests with the Cherubim;
Full glory is his,
And he truly sees God.

When I saw myself on these heights,
Holding within me the images of all these things,
I heard a voice say to me,
"Spend, now is the proper time."

I looked at the Creator—
He agreed to my ascent,
And in His honor I glorified
Every order of creation.

Then I came to the eighth branch
And in the name of the Lord I love
I praised the choirs of angels
In the ascending order of their nearness to God.

Still higher I rose, to the ninth branch,
There where I praised the Omnipotent Himself.
He who comes to this point is filled with the Holy Spirit;
Seraphim-like, he contemplates the Trinity.

He has left all stages behind
And the three trees as well.
Shattered are the three heavens;
He now lives in God.

You who have come to this height,
For your honor and our good,
Pray to our Hope
That we may follow you.

70 ON THE FOUR CARDINAL VIRTUES

The four lofty virtues we call cardinal
Bring our nature to its highest perfection.

JACOPONE DA TODI

Just as a door is supported by its hinges,
So are our lives by this fourfold custom.
Adorned with this glorious robe,
The soul is noble, bedecked with gems.

The first virtue is Prudence, light of the intellect;
The second is Justice, which properly channels the affections;
The third, Fortitude, brings constancy amidst trials;
The fourth, Temperance, is a shield against empty pleasures.

Most noble Prudence, mistress of reason,
You indicate at the proper time
Good, better, and best, as well as their obverse,
Whose choice leads man to his damnation.

Prudence, you find the useful
In the humblest of things;
The man who practices you is blessed,
Noble and worthy of high estate.

Without the other virtues
Prudence cannot operate;
She calls on Justice to accompany her
And translate her judgments into action.

Justice from the very start
Inscribes one law in our hearts:
To love God above all, with all our strength,
For in loving Him so we do Him honor.

Justice also demands
That we love our neighbor;
For to be true, love—like gold—
Must be tested and proven by fire.

Fortitude sustains you in brotherly love
When your neighbor does you harm,
When he robs, deceives and threatens you:
To love him then is proven love;

For it is another thing to love one's neighbor
When he is twisted and rooted in sin,
To love him for himself and abhor his evil ways—
This is a sign of proven love.

I have mastered the body and its desires;
Bridled it with Temperance, for it feeds on evil
And fights like a madman against every good.
So deep-rooted is its illness, it is not easy to cure.

Sight now renounces form and color,
The ear grows deaf to the vanity of sound;
Taste, when we limit our food, loses interest;
And scent despises the perfumed robe.

As the body ceases to take delight in things
The soul is induced to find other joys.
Faith points out where true happiness lies,
And Hope leads you there, where blessed Love abides.

71 AS THE BRIDEGROOM WITH HIS BRIDE CHRIST RESTS WITH THE VIRTUOUS SOUL

You who enjoy talking, consider—
Does all that talk serve any purpose?

To go on and on is to tire the listener:
Our preference is for a concise style.
So I'll give you a brisk account, to the point
(Though not without some useful implications)
Of the soul and God at rest, like a bridal couple.

God rests in the good man's soul, for that soul is His bride.
The mind, with its well-ordered passions, is the bed,
The first leg of which represents Prudence,
The light of the intelligence, which makes clear distinctions
Between good and evil, and tells us how to follow the good.

JACOPONE DA TODI

The second leg of the bed is Justice,
Which translates love of the good into practice.
(Prudence comprehends, Justice implements.)
Fortitude, the third, faithful companion of truth,
Assures its triumph in adversity.

The last is Temperance,
The sense of limit in times of abundance,
Humility in prosperity.
The articles of faith are ropes
Binding the headboard to the legs of the bed.

There is a big sack of straw—
The recognition of our sins and unworthiness,
And on that, the mattress—
Christ mad with love of me,
Come to possess me.

At the head of the bed,
Christ climbing onto the cross,
Dying in pain, with a thief at His side.
The sheets are spread out—winged contemplation,
Through which man enfleshed can mirror divinity.

The blanket is Hope, which gives me confidence
I will one day dwell in that holy place.
Charity then approaches,
And makes me one with God,
Joins my unworthiness and His goodness.

And of that union is born
A love that impregnates the heart,
Full of desire and flaming mystery:
The fecund soul melts and in mortal weakness
Gives birth to ecstasy.

It is swept up past human heaven,
Past that of the angels,
Into the third heaven,

JACOPONE DA TODI

The realm of darkness,
Where it finds the Son of the Virgin.

All motion ceases in God, One and Three,
The mind and the emotions are in repose.
The soul falls into a dreamless sleep
For it possess all truth,
And rests in the heart of God.

Farewell, farewell, farewell.
Climb up these steps,
For to stumble here would lead to a mighty fall.

72   THE RARITY OF TRUE LOVE OF NEIGHBOR

I would like to find a man who truly loves:
Many I've found who do not.
I used to think that I was loved;
Now I know the extent of that illusion.

I examine closely the why, and see
It is not I who is loved,
But what belongs to me;
I recognize false love.

Rich and powerful, I find many to love me,
But the same men would shun me if they saw me in rags.
That love distinguishes carefully—
It loves my possessions and despises me.

Only a fool would rely on such love.
Nobility, stripped of riches and power,
Appears contemptible to many,
Who then accuse it of baseless pretension.

The man who helps others is loved by many
And by many abandoned once he falls sick.
The man in good health has friends in abundance,
When bad times come all his friends disappear.

As long as they find some profit in it
Our fellowmen will love us;
When we no longer serve some useful function
They will not hesitate to slander our name.

I flee from counterfeit love
That would steal my heart,
And return to the Lord,
The only true love.

73   ON THE HIGH PRICE PAID FOR SHODDY GOODS—
     THE SACRIFICE MADE BY CHRIST FOR MAN

Dwell on the price paid for you, you shoddy goods—
It will make you feel drunk; and indeed,
Such a price would only be paid
By someone drunk with love of you.

That price, come down from Heaven, is madness—
Why would the King of Paradise pay it?
Look at the treasure God the Father lavished on us:
Angels, Thrones, and Principalities
Marvel that the Word of God, to save me,
Should hand Himself over to death!

Heaven and earth and all creation look on in wonder—
To fight my battles God has taken my nature;
To conquer my pride He has embraced shame!
O drunken excess of love, why?
Why should You have wanted to come?
To save me, a sinner, You gave Yourself up to death!

What can I do but go mad,
Since You have shown me the way?
Since the Wisdom of God is drunk with love,
What will you do, O my wisdom?
Will you not follow the example of your Lord?
Is there a greater honor than to share in His folly?

JACOPONE DA TODI

O celestial paradise,
You are crowned with thorns,
Bloody, beaten, and bruised,
So as to heal me. Surely,
My illness must have been mortal
If it needed such medication as this!

Beneath the thorn-crowned head,
I see the scourged body,
Every member sharing in the agony;
To give me consolation
My Lord hangs from the cross,
And I all the while pursue pleasure!

O my Lord, this is not right:
I am richly clothed and You are naked;
I am satisfied, You endure hunger;
You suffer shame, and I aspire to honors;
You a beggar in rags, exhausted because of me,
And I, a sinner, rich, fat and at ease in the world!

This is not as it should be—
I at rest and You in torment.
O my Lord, You are utterly destitute,
Without land, without house or home,
And I have strayed so far from You:
How vile not to want to follow You!

Renounce, then, O my soul, all consolation:
May shame, affliction, and pain be my joy,
And may I die in torment. O great treasure,
Beyond speech, sight, or hearing,
Beyond understanding! The infinite reigns in You,
And all our powers are submerged in the flood.

The intellect is barred
From the feast of love;
Once it is caught
And drowned in the measureless,

JACOPONE DA TODI

Love soars ever higher in its yearning,
In its quest to embrace the infinite.

The sense of wonder restrains love's impetuosity,
That it may not fall into presumption or lack of reverence.
The soul is infused with God's will, its own annihilated.
Then man acquires eyes with which to see
And begins to understand the price that was paid;
And what he feels then no tongue can describe.

74 DIVINE GOODNESS COMPLAINS
OF CREATED AFFECTION

Goodness laments that Affection does not love her,
And Justice is called to render a verdict.

Before all creatures and before the just God,
Goodness clamorously demands punishment of the evildoer
For the offense he gives to the Good
With his love for the semblances thereof.

Justice immediately takes Affection into custody,
Imprisons him with his bodyguards,
Serves notice that he will be convicted of evildoing
And documents the charge with irrefutable evidence.

Affection, now subjected to Reason,
Almost goes mad, for he was accustomed to freedom.
Goodness, taking pity on him, offers him a sliver of grace,
And Affection comes back to his senses.

Having tasted grace *gratis data*, he senses a new mode of existence
(Intellect, with the aid of memory, has transformed him completely)
And with changed will he weeps over his past offenses.
Overcome with desire for God, he will not be consoled.

Affection has learned a new language, one word above all—"Love."
Tranquil in fear, he weeps, laughs, laments, and shouts with joy.

JACOPONE DA TODI

Outwardly he seems to be mad,
But he is no longer aware of appearances.

Goodness tolerates the fury of this love
For it destroys the world of darkness
As it burns away lust and eliminates
The vile smell of the cesspool.

Goodness having deprived Affection
Of the joy it found in feeling,
The imprisoned Intellect
Can then come out to contemplate.

Affection lives in torment,
Complaining bitterly
That Intellect steals from him
The time he needs to grieve and lament.

Once Intellect samples Wisdom
He finds it much to his taste
And so marvels at what he now can see
That he no longer seeks other joys.

Affection, which takes little delight in seeing,
Cries out against Intellect's rapture,
For his stomach demands what he can digest,
And he weeps disconsolately over the loss of his feelings.

"Be still," urges Intellect,
"Do not disturb me; the glory I contemplate
Is a great feast; do not cloud my vision,
But satisfy your hunger by sharing my joy."

"I am in torment, and you continue to banter?
All that seeing of yours is nonsense—
I grind my teeth in an empty mouth;
I continue to fast and you mock me."

"Take no offense if I contemplate the goodness of creation,"
Returns Intellect. "Through it I come to know divine goodness—

To refuse to contemplate it would be sheer ingratitude.
You should take pleasure in what I am doing."

"But in all this contemplation you offend faith
And restrict its immensity; so fine and subtle are your points
That things no longer hold together. And what is more,
You take from me the time I need to make amends."

To this Intellect answers: "It seems to me that Love,
Governed by wisdom, is more glorious than your ideal.
If I strain to understand who gives it and to whom and how much,
Love is ennobled and becomes more all-embracing."

"On the contrary," answers Affection, "it seems to me
That here you offend wisdom, diminish its scope.
Nothing is grasped when you contemplate created being;
I am kept in perpetual suspense, and will die in expectation."

Goodness, taking pity on troubled Affection,
Suffering from his long fast, has a table spread before him.
Intellect marvels at this, and Affection sits down to eat.
The argument is over.

Intellect savors the taste,
Affection chews and swallows the food with gusto.
The nourishment, prepared with love,
Permeates the body and gives it new strength.

75 TWO DIFFERENT MODES OF CONTEMPLATING THE CROSS

I flee the consuming cross and its fires;
Their heat drives me back and I flee from Love.
Nowhere can I find refuge—
The flames continue to blaze in my heart and my mind.

> Why, Brother, do you take flight
> From that joy which I insistently seek?

JACOPONE DA TODI

How unworthy of you to run away,
To flee its delights!

I am in flight, Brother, because I have been wounded,
And wounded close to the heart;
You know nothing of such pain.
I pray you, say no more.

The cross is in flower, Brother,
And all my thoughts
Are bent on its beauty;
It inflicts no wounds on me but joy.

I, instead, find it full of arrows
That speed from the side,
Piercing my armor and my heart.
The archer aims them straight at me.

Once I was blind, now I see,
And this change I owe to contemplating the cross.
The cross is my guide, which I follow in joy;
Without it I live in torment.

That light has blinded me
With its searing intensity;
I go about sightless
Though my eyes are open.

Now I can speak, though once I was mute,
And the change is due to the cross;
I have tasted of its sweetness
And now I can preach it to many.

And I who once could talk am now made mute;
My heart has plunged into such an abyss
I can find almost no one to whom I can speak
Of the horror of this void.

I once was dead and now I live;
The change came about as I contemplated the cross.

JACOPONE DA TODI

When it leaves me I die,
When I feel its presence I have life.

I am not dead, but close to death—
God will that it come quickly!
Oh, the agony of enduring its assaults
And never, never wrenching free!

The cross is my joy, Brother,
Do not call it torment;
Perhaps you have not become one with it,
Not embraced it as your spouse.

The cross warms you but sets me on fire;
For you it is joy, for me searing pain. How can I stay
In this blazing furnace? Not to have experienced it
Is not to know the heat of the flame.

I do not comprehend you, Brother.
Why do you flee Love?
If you try to explain,
You may help me to understand.

Brother, you have barely sipped,
But I have drunk of this new wine,
And no iron bands could contain this pressure,
Which threatens to split me stave from stave.

76 ON THE HEART'S JUBILATION

O heart's jubilation, love and song,
Joy and joy unceasing,
The stuttering of the unutterable—
How can the heart but sing?

Joy shooting upward uncontrollably,
Where is the heart to contain it?
O shouting and singing oblivious of all,
Joy brimmed to overflowing!

JACOPONE DA TODI

O jubilant joy and somersaults of happiness,
Pray, learn to be prudent:
Sensible people with sensible smiles
Cannot understand the wildness of your ecstasy!

Learn to conceal the bliss
Throbbing thickly beneath the surface;
There is meaning all unknown to sensible people
In the joyous gyrations of the wounded heart.

77 SILENT LOVE

Wordless love hidden in silence, unheard by those without,
Hide your riches beyond the reach of the wiliest thief.

To seek to conceal your fire is to make it leap higher yet;
The man who feels the wild desire to speak of you incurs wounds.
If he is beside himself enough
To speak to others of this hidden love
(Even if his intentions are pure when he begins)
The wind will come with a mighty rush
And disperse the gifts he has received.
The lover who has lit his candle should hide it,
If he would have it burn without danger to himself or others.
Let him close all doors so that the wind
Will not come and blow out the flame.

This love has imposed silence on sighs,
Blocked the gates so they cannot escape.
It makes them give birth within the house
So the soul will be centered only on love.
Sighs that escape precede the flight of the soul,
Which then wanders and becomes enmeshed in vanities.
When it comes to its senses once more
What has been lost cannot be found again.
Such love has hunted down false and evil glory
And its perilous tribute of honor,
And banished hypocrisy from its domain forever.

228

JACOPONE DA TODI

78 TRUE LOVE AND COUNTERFEIT DISCRETION

Intent on seeking dominion over the Heart,
Love is challenged by Discretion.

Storming the ramparts of the Will,
Love wounds the Heart with sweetness
And leaves it in a frenzy,
Mad with love of God.

As Love continues to press against it,
Noble Discretion makes use of the weapons of persuasion:
She turns to Reason, in whose house she abides,
For help in her defense of the Heart.

But Love lunges against Reason
And hurls his spear,
Intent on taking the Heart prisoner
And making the body suffer.

Drawing close to the Heart,
Discretion lays its snares,
Flesh, aware of the danger,
Strengthens his defenses.

Then Love sends life-giving provisions
To the besieged Heart,
Which feeds with difficulty
Upon that flaming food.

"Deny me as your lord," Discretion threatens the Heart,
"And see how your ardor will cool."
In answer, Love secretly hurls a dart at Flesh,
Who finds the pain of the wound hard to endure.

Discretion whispers softly to the Heart:
"Climb slowly, now, or you will grow faint."
But for Love this counsel is madness; he confides
In his own strength and in divine largesse:

JACOPONE DA TODI

He pleads that God shield him from evil.
"Be careful," Discretion continues to urge,
"Many who set out to pursue their desires
Come quickly to the 'I-can-do-no-more.' "

This admonition does not trouble Love;
Paying no heed, it draws back the string of its bow
And the flashing arrow enflames the Heart
With love for the Lord without peer.

Flesh then calls out to Reason, "I surrender;
Come, for I am in need of your help.
Love would want to consume me, though I know
A thousand such would not satisfy his hunger.

"He wrestles with God and thinks he can devour Him,
Clings to Him with all his strength, unable to say what he wants.
He allows no one a moment of peace,
Not even to spit or to clear his throat!

"He takes the side of Heaven and fights against me;
He knows the art of deception, and with honeyed tongue
Speaks to me so gently that he draws me away from others
And holds me so tightly that I cannot breathe.

"Help me, I beg of you, restrain him for awhile;
His thoughts wound me and shake me to the roots.
I will not let him cut me off from others,
For then I am too weak to oppose him.

"I will take every precaution:
The world will protect me,
Provide the distractions I need
To shield me from his assaults."

"It will all be to no avail," answers Reason,
"Love is certain to overcome you.
If he does not find you under the noonday sun,
He will take you when darkness falls."

JACOPONE DA TODI

79 ON DIVINE GOODNESS AND THE HUMAN WILL

Infinite Goodness yearns for infinite love,
For mind, heart, soul, time, and being.

Long and faithful Love, eternally enduring,
Suffused with hope, higher than the heavens,
And all-embracing charity, dwelling
In the depths of the humble heart!

Led by grace, the created will becomes one with infinity,
Drawn upward in a steep ascent,
Like iron to a magnet. The will rejoices,
In the sky of unknowing, in the beloved Unseen.

The ignorant Intellect makes its way gropingly,
Barred from rising into that dark sky.
It would be an offense to try to measure infinity,
To grope for what lies beyond our powers of comprehension.

The ignorant Intellect thus swears fealty,
Makes an act of faith in the Omnipotent, and promises
Not to call on reason to resolve faith's difficulties;
It lives in humility, drowned in the depths.

O wise ignorance, led to such heights,
You have risen miraculously to the point
Where there is neither word nor tongue,
And there you stand in a stupor, marveling.

"Tell me, O most noble soul, what you see."
"I see something unseen, and sense a smile;
(I cannot say more, nor do I understand.)
I see in all its splendor a place of wonder."

"Tell me, now, the fruits of that vision!"
"A life well-ordered in every respect,
And a heart, once impure and lower than Hell,
Now the abode of the Trinity, a bed made holy."

JACOPONE DA TODI

My heart, you have sold yourself to the great Emperor;
Let no created thing henceforth claim my love;
To so honor any creature
Would be to my shame.

Should a creature seek my love, let him turn to Goodness
Who has love to share; I have given mine all away.
Goodness may do with it what she will,
For she has bought the abundance of my love.

Time has taught me that in not serving my King
I have shown little love for His law.
O time, time, time, how you bury in evil all those
Who, living in idleness, do not use you wisely!

80   THE THREE STAGES OF DIVINE LOVE

Do you know of the Love that has swept me up
And continues to hold my heart,
That keeps me imprisoned in its sweetness—
The Love that would have me die in pain?

> The love about which you inquire
> We know in many forms;
> Yet if you do not speak of your beloved
> We know not how to answer you.

The Love about which I am asking
Is the first and highest, unique and eternal;
You have no knowledge of it, it seems to me,
If you can speak of the many forms of love.

> What you have said is true—
> We do not know the love to which you refer.
> Pray, speak to us about it,
> Tell of its worth.

The Love I ask about has one form alone,
And that fills heaven and earth;

232

JACOPONE DA TODI

So pure it is it cannot dwell
Where there is stain of impurity.

The Love I ask about is most humble;
It enriches the heart
In which it comes to rest,
And in its goodness it humbles the proud.

Infusing fidelity in my heart,
It keeps it from forbidden things
And inclines it to use with temperance
What is proper and acceptable.

This love helps me to detach my hope from this world
And fix it on Heaven instead;
It makes us pilgrims on the road to Heaven,
Citizens of a great city.

In that commonwealth order prevails,
There we are schooled in charity;
The inhabitants of the city
Love one another as brothers.

There Love is threefold, in ascending steps,
The good, the better, and the loftiest of all.
The highest good wants to be loved
For itself alone.

It is folly for me, ignorant of theology,
To speak of this highest Love,
But Love in its wildness
Forces me to shout out its praises.

With so much to say, I know not how;
And though I know it would be better
For me to remain mute,
I cannot hold my peace.

How can this overflowing love be suppressed?
The jubilation will out,

JACOPONE DA TODI

As Elias once learned,
In prophetic song.

But let us leave this discussion
And turn our attention
To the first two states,
And dwell on them awhile.

The better is always higher than the good.
If you love your neighbor as yourself,
But do not love yourself in a proper way,
You are a blind man leading others like you into a ditch.

First put order into your love,
Learn from God how to love.
A wise and strong love lasts,
Like chain mail that will not unravel.

Neither hunger nor thirst nor death
Can crush this love; always ready for battle,
It will endure pain and every suffering,
And do so with serenity.

It has subjugated the body,
Ordered the senses,
Made them servants obedient to reason,
And justly punished their excesses.

The house is still and quiet,
The work equitably divided;
Should differences arise
They will be fairly resolved.

The judge who resolves them
Is called Conscience;
No prayers for intimidation
Can influence his decisions.

Neither the rich nor the poor
Win special favors from him,

Nor can wrongdoing be concealed;
All fear and obey him.

When the soul is in harmony with conscience
It takes joy in the love of its neighbor.
Then without doubt it is true love,
Then we can call it charity.

Love then joins the lover
To his suffering brethren;
And in his compassion he suffers more
Than the man whose suffering he shares.

While the brother who was suffering
Finds respite from his pain,
The compassionate man suffers anguish,
Day and night without repose.

No man can comprehend how this can be
If the understanding is not infused in him by charity—
That charity which lies hidden in suffering,
Waiting to give birth.

Now let us put these thoughts aside
And turn to Christ our Lord;
May He pardon us all
And grant us His peace.

> Your words, Brother, fall on willing ears,
> Because what you say is true;
> We too will follow this road,
> Which will lead us to our salvation.

81   IN PRAISE OF DIVINE LOVE

O Love, divine Love, not loved in return,
Your friendship is fullness of joy,
To taste You is to forget all sadness.

JACOPONE DA TODI

O loving Love, consuming Love,
You fill with throbbing life
The heart that shelters You.

O happy wound, full of delight,
He whom You wound
Is joyous indeed.

Love, where did You enter the heart unseen?
Lovable Love, joyful Love, unthinkable Love,
In Your plenitude You lie far beyond the reach of thought.

Love, jocund and joyous,
Divine fire, You do not stint
Of Your endlessly bountiful riches.

Who are Your friends, Love?
Not great barons, whom You leave aside,
But the poor and the destitute.

Those who, to all appearances,
Are of no worth or consequence—to them
You give Yourself as if You were straw.

The man who goes in search of You
So as to see himself grow in knowledge
Will never savor Your presence in his heart.

If it is not lodged in a humble heart
The knowledge that we can acquire ourselves
Is nothing but a mortal wound.

Love, you impose form on desire;
Your terse lesson
Illumines the Gospel.

Love, perpetually burning, enflaming the hearts of Your own,
You transform their tongues into arrows
That pierce the hearts of others.

JACOPONE DA TODI

Generous Love,
Gracious Love,
Your riches are beyond imagining.

Freely given Love,
Full of delights, gentle Love
That satisfies the heart!

Love, You teach us the art of winning Heaven;
You give us the pass we need to enter,
And a foretaste of what we will find.

Love, faithful companion,
Love so poorly repaid, You make me weep,
That I may be cleansed of my sins.

Sweet and gentle Love, key to Heaven,
You lead the ship to a haven,
Safe from the storm.

Love, infusing with light all who share in Your splendor,
You teach us that the true light
Is not to be found in the light of this world.

Light that enlightens, light that teaches,
He who is not illumined by You
Does not reach the fullness of love.

Love, You give light
To the intellect in darkness
And illumine the Object of love.

Love, Your ardor,
Which enflames the heart,
Unites it with the Incarnate One.

Love, life made secure,
Riches without care,
You are measureless and eternal.

JACOPONE DA TODI

Love, You who give form to all
Take poor deformed man
And reform him.

Love, to the man who yields himself to You
You are pure and clean,
Wise and playful, lofty and deep.

Generous and noble, You spread a table
For those who place themselves
Under Your protection.

You rout foul-smelling lust
And adorn the cleansed soul
With the fragrance of chastity.

You, Love, are the hook
With which I have been caught,
The desire of my hungry heart.

A cure for illness, however grave,
You, divine Love
Are the medicine that heals all.

"O proud tongue, how have you dared
To speak of holy Love?
Human speech cannot rise to such heights.

"In speaking of this Love
The tongues of angels falter—
And you feel no misgivings and shame?

"You reduce Love
To the measure of your words;
This is not praise, but blasphemy."

I cannot obey your command to be silent;
As long as I have breath in me
I will sing of Love's glory.

It is not right
That time should pass
Without my singing the praises of Love.

My heart and tongue call out, "Love, Love, Love!"
Should a man taste of Your sweetness
And say nothing, may his heart burst!

If his heart does not shout
The praises of Love
He will surely suffocate and die!

82   HOW THE SOUL THROUGH THE SENSES FINDS
GOD IN ALL CREATURES

O Love, divine Love, why do You lay siege to me?
In a frenzy of love for me, You find no rest.

From five sides You move against me,
Hearing, sight, taste, touch, and scent.
To come out is to be caught; I cannot hide from You.

If I come out through sight I see Love
Painted in every form and color,
Inviting me to come to You, to dwell in You.

If I leave through the door of hearing,
What I hear points only to You, Lord;
I cannot escape Love through this gate.

If I come out through taste, every flavor proclaims:
"Love, divine Love, hungering Love!
You have caught me on Your hook, for You want to reign in me."

If I leave through the door of scent
I sense You in all creation; You have caught me
And wounded me through that fragrance.

JACOPONE DA TODI

If I come out through the sense of touch
I find Your lineaments in every creature;
To try to flee from You is madness.

Love, I flee from You, afraid to give You my heart:
I see that You make me one with You,
I cease to be me and can no longer find myself.

If I see evil in a man or defect or temptation,
You fuse me with him, and make me suffer;
O Love without limits, who is it You love?

It is You, O Crucified Christ,
Who take possession of me,
Drawing me out of the sea to the shore;

There I suffer to see Your wounded heart.
Why did You endure the pain?
So that I might be healed.

83   ON THE LOVE OF THE CRUCIFIED CHRIST
AND THE SOUL'S DESIRE TO DIE WITH HIM

O sweet Love, You who have killed Your Beloved,
I beg of You, let me die of Love!
Love, You who led Your Lover
To such a hard death, why have You done this?
Was it that You did not want me to perish?
Do not spare me, let me die in Love's embrace.

You did not spare Him whom You loved so dearly;
Why then be indulgent with me?
Catch me on Your hook,
Like a fish that cannot get away—
That will be a sign that You love me.
Do not spare me: I long to die drowned in Love.

Love is fixed to the cross—
The cross has taken Him and will not let Him go.

JACOPONE DA TODI

I run and cling to that cross
That my anguish may not drive me mad.
To flee would lead me to despair,
For my name would be canceled from the book of Love.

O cross, I fix myself to you and cling to you,
That as I die, I may taste Life!
For you are adorned with honeyed Death
And I am wretched not to have tasted you!
O daring soul, impatient for wounds,
May I die heartbroken with Love!

I run to the cross and read
Its blood-stained pages—
This is the book that makes me
A doctor of natural philosophy and theology.
O book inscribed with golden letters
And all abloom with Love!

O Love of the Lamb, vaster than any sea,
Who can dare to speak of You?
He who has drowned in You,
And no longer knows where he is;
He to whom folly seems the right path,
Who goes about crazed by Love.

84   TO BE CONSIDERED MAD BECAUSE OF
THE LOVE OF CHRIST IS THE HIGHEST WISDOM

It is right and fitting, I believe,
To go mad over the fair Messiah.

A great wisdom it is, indeed, to go mad,
Out of one's mind with the love of God.
The University of Paris has yet to formulate
A more profound philosophy.

He who is mad with love of Christ
In appearance is troubled and distressed—

241

But in truth he is a doctor
In natural philosophy and theology.

The man who enrolls in this school
Will discover a new discipline;
Only those who have experienced this madness
Have an inkling of what it is.

He who joins in this dance finds love beyond measure—
An indulgence of a hundred days to anyone who insults him!
The man in search of honors is unworthy of Christ's love,
For on the cross Jesus hung between two thieves.

Those who seek shame and humiliation
Will soon come to their heart's desire,
And have no further need of the University of Bologna
With its doctrines and philosophies.

85   HOW WE ARE TO LOVE CHRIST
FREELY AS HE LOVED US

"O Love, You who love me, catch me on Your hook,
That I may love even as I am loved!

"O loving Love
Not loved in return,
The man who climbs Your branches
Always proclaims himself undeserving.

"O soul crowned with a nobility you did nothing to merit,
Completely submerged in the Wondrous One,
You could never climb with your own meager strength—
It is Love Who answers you in your need.

"O active Love, in futile search of the soul
That can reach the fullness of love,
Love whose name is 'I Love,' You are One and One only;
We drink from Your spring, the love You lavish on us.

JACOPONE DA TODI

"Love, show me the 'how,'
For no man can grasp the 'how much';
The measureless weight of that knowledge
Would crush him in an instant."

"I showed you the 'how' with My Incarnation;
For you I became a pilgrim and died on the cross.
To know 'how much' can only be desired,
For this secret has never been revealed to a creature.

"This is not through any lack
Of graciousness in God,
But because of man's nature—
No created being can sound God's depths.

"That infinite Love
Should reveal Itself
To finite creatures,
Limit and define the limitless!

"The saints are submerged in that abyss of Love,
Overcome by its vastness.
Infinite is its height
And length and depth and width.

"Is there any greater sign
That Love could have given
Than to become the last,
The most derelict of men?

"Who would ever be mad enough
To turn himself into an ant
So as to save an army of ants,
An undeserving, ungrateful army of ants?

"My madness was greater yet:
To abase Myself,
To take this road
And become a suffering man.

"I did not love you for My pleasure
I loved you for yourself;
What I did for you
Added nothing to My joy.

"I was not made greater because of you,
Nor could your lack have diminished Me.
Love drew Me to you,
That you might be remade.

"To love Me out of a desire for glory is venal;
To look toward My throne
And think of reward—
That is the love of a mercenary.

"You do not love Me for love;
You have the price written in your heart—
Cancel that price
And your love vanishes!

"If it is your own interest that draws you to Love,
Adversity will change that love to something else.
If love is disinterested then desire is noble,
Imposing no prerequisites.

"This love lays down no conditions, demands no interest;
It is total union, and knows not change.
From within lovable Love comes a marvel of love,
Immutable for all eternity."

86, CONSIDERED APOCRYPHAL IS OMITTED

87 ON DIVINE LOVE, WHOSE MEASURE
WE CANNOT KNOW

O Love so far beyond imagining or telling!
Your very absence of a sense of measure

JACOPONE DA TODI

Makes Measure complain and lament;
Such love, she argues, is torment.

Measurelessness intervenes and restrains Measure,
Afraid that love might be smothered,
Stripped of its wildness,
And placed beyond the experience of man.

Wisdom, in the meantime, has silenced Affection;
See how quickly and resolutely she acts:
She takes Affection and imprisons him,
Makes him subject to Reason!

Disconsolate, Affection makes loud lament
And will not be consoled:
He is drunk with the world of the senses
And curses the hand that stripped him of hope.

O corrupt love, violently shaken by unruly desires,
Much inclined to protest and complain—
You have taken time as your own,
Time, which belongs to God!

Justice is ready to condemn you
And strip you of every function
Because you lead others
To erroneous judgments.

Divine Wisdom takes Justice into its service
And assigns her a task,
Insisting that it be accomplished
Without compromise:

Human wisdom must be silenced, and the senses
Must no longer be allowed to distract the soul,
So that virtues may flower freely
And man may be united with God.

O storm-tossed love, cut off from the world
Now that they have taken back

JACOPONE DA TODI

What was only loaned to you,
You seem to be shattered;

But the ardent longing of the Beloved
Has embraced the object of its desire;
He has totally humiliated Himself
Without feeling humiliation.

The ear no longer hears,
For no sound comes to it,
And intellect sees nothing,
For it has submerged its every power.

No longer able to possess,
You are not possessed by others;
Love has such a grip on you
That every faculty is returned to you.

Transformed into love by Love,
The senses no longer give pleasure.
Scent, though given back, no longer delights
And taste turns mute.

Silence has come on the scene—
No longer is there need for language;
The soul speaks without words,
And closed in silent intimacy, gathers strength.

Now the faculties of the soul, both old and new,
Rest firmly on *nichil*, formed without form,
With no limits set to time or space, fused with Truth.
Affection reigns, the intellect is at rest, one with Love.

JACOPONE DA TODI

88 HOW MAN IN A PERFECT STATE MIRRORS WITHIN HIM THE NINE CHOIRS OF ANGELS AND THEIR THREE HIERARCHIES

He who has mastery over his tongue
Has lordship over himself;
For man can scarcely open his mouth
Without running the risk of sin.

I think of speaking, and then think better of it:
Of what value are the words
That I feel compelled to utter?
Is there in me the wisdom for lasting utterance?

Still, stronger than reason
Is the will to speak out;
It leads me by the bridle,
And I follow along.

Silence may be wisdom,
But it is not the wisdom I possess.
Listen to my words, then, I pray you,
And correct me when you disagree.

In His wisdom God gave the power of speech
To Balaam's ass; may He inspire me as well
That I may utter words of praise
That will be to His honor and our good.

Man was created in the image and likeness of God,
And Heaven was given order by nine choirs of angels.
That blessed assembly in turn is composed of three hierarchies,
And their concordance, if I see rightly, can be mirrored in man.

The perfect man, too, has three hierarchies—
The first hierarchy is a good beginning;
The second is the continuation of his striving;
And the highest is his perseverance in the good until death.

JACOPONE DA TODI

No one who dwells in these three states
Is ever disillusioned; and I,
Who did not wish to rise to that first hierarchy,
Still feel the anguish of that refusal and hesitation.

Perfect man, I now see clearly,
Is like to a tree; the deeper the roots,
The greater the strength
To resist a violent onslaught.

Mantled with humble bark
That serves to protect it
And to conserve its moisture,
Adorned with branches, leaves, and fruit,

The tree labors without ceasing.
Once it has brought forth fruit
It continues to nourish that fruit
And bring it to perfection.

The hole in which the tree is planted
Is perfect humility,
Because if the delicate roots
Take firm hold there,

They can grow strong
And draw up the moisture
That makes the tree soar heavenward,
Fearing neither cold nor drought.

The tree harbors in its branches
Birds that announce the winter's end
With piercing sweetness, and so fashion their nests
That no enemy can discover them.

The base of the trunk is faith in action,
The twelve radiating roots are the articles of faith;
If all these are not bound together
Disease will hollow out and destroy the tree.

JACOPONE DA TODI

Cling to the whole and it will smile on you
And lead you to a fair country,
Delivering you from the place
Where those who hold it imperfectly are punished.

The soaring trunk of the tree is lofty hope,
Which separates you from this world and brings you close
To Heaven; make this your home for all seasons
And joy will be yours in abundance.

Visit every corner of the city
And you will hear songs of joy.
Viewed from there you will see that the world
Is a prison, full of lies and deceit.

Where the branches first shoot out from the trunk,
There, I believe, I see charity;
This is the beginning
Of the first hierarchy.

Three branches you will find, bound together,
But each with a beauty all its own.
The thickness is much greater at the point where they meet;
One without the others leads to error, never to perfect truth.

The first branch in this beginning corresponds
To the first order of the heavenly choirs—
Scripture calls them Angels.
An angel is "a messenger, most noble by nature."

This messenger, to be found in your soul,
Is there in the form of innocent thoughts,
Thoughts that are not of our own making
But are infused by the Holy Spirit.

After you have stood at length in contemplation
And grown accustomed to the presence of God,
His love will reveal to you the abundance of His gifts
And what you are, you for whom He died:

JACOPONE DA TODI

You the faithless sinner
For whom He suffered so many insults.
In your shame and inner turmoil
Where will you be able to hide?

Out of this shame and distress of heart
Is born a yearning which we can call the second branch,
The abode of Archangels, the most exalted of messengers;
Nothing now will check my tears.

"Where is my Lord, for whom I search in vain?
I am the one He sought to redeem.
Answer me, Lord, I beg of You!
May I die out of love of You!"

The intellect and the will offer me counsel
That if I would want to find my Lord
And have His love live and grow in me,
I must persevere to the end.

I turn to the third branch, which offers the Virtues as guides.
He who ascends to this height should hold on tightly
(Here he dwells in the presence of the exalted Emperor)
And learn a way of life that will allow him to grow in fervor.

*   *   *

The second hierarchy, too, has three branches
And unless you continue upward here
You will lose the ground you gained before.
Peace is to be won in battle!

On the first of these branches
You must confront and defeat all the senses,
Which have inflicted a death blow on the heart:
This holy lordship is called Dominion.

The second branch is that of the Principalities,
Who regulate the nonrational orders of creation.

JACOPONE DA TODI

There all that is seen and heard and thought
Brings consolation to all God's creatures,

Who praise the Lord for His goodness
And the delight He takes in them.
Each obeys the laws of his station
(A reproach to man, who does not).

Keep your heart, then,
In such a state
That it always finds
Its satisfaction in God.

Meanwhile, the Vices, in hiding,
Rally their forces, resisting expulsion.
But moving quickly against them,
The Powers summon the Virtues.

The two opposing forces
Line up against each other.
Once the Vices see the enemy approach
In fear they flee from the field of battle.

Humility hurtles Pride from her mountain fortress;
Envy witnesses that defeat and wounds herself in rage.
Then Charity sets her afire and burns her to ashes, while Anger,
Left to her own devices, kills herself, vanquished by Meekness.

Sloth, streaked red with whiplashes
At the hands of Justice, will never smile again.
At the same time Mercy flays Avarice,
Already murdered by her own offspring.

Trusting in her beauty, Lust hopes to survive;
But Chastity metes out a cruel death,
Puts a sword through her heart and buries her,
Where she will be devoured by worms.

JACOPONE DA TODI

Gluttony, hard-pressed and terrified,
Would like to put on the mantle of discretion;
But Temperance binds her
And casts her into prison.

*   *   *

The battle over, the Virtues move to assure peace and order.
They call for help to the third hierarchy, for they know
That without that aid the victory will be short-lived.
Searching the Scriptures the Virtues read

That on the seventh day God took His rest;
And in this spirit they call on Concord
To be designated queen of the Virtues,
To rule and watch over them.

The Virtues ask her what they are to do,
For each demands her own rights and statutes.
They come to the house of Concord
(Where they are to live with her)

And forthwith they imprison Discord,
The author of so much evil.
They demand justice at all times,
With no exceptions to be made.

Yet since Concord cannot rule
Without the help of Wisdom,
The Virtues call out for aid
To the second branch, to the Cherubim,

Who seek to embrace God with understanding,
Linger in His school and there deepen their knowledge.
Intellect, who loves to learn,
Wants to join the Virtues;

For the more his knowledge increases,
The more he experiences the limitlessness of God—

JACOPONE DA TODI

The understanding is annihilated,
Drowned in the depths.

But with the appearance of the order of Seraphim,
Succumbing to the fire of love, he gradually comes to life again,
Acquires new strength, and in the plenitude of love
Embraces the Lord forever, in the consummation of charity.

                    *   *   *

Let us pray to the Lord, then,
That out of His goodness and mercy He direct our thoughts
That we will follow the straight path
And always be of His company.

Those who dwell in Hell, in eternal fire,
They will make loud lament.
O Blessed Virgin Mary,
Help us to escape that end!

89   THE TREE OF DIVINE LOVE

There is a tree planted by God which we call Love.
You there, you I see up in its branches—
Show me where I can begin to climb,
That I might leave this darkness behind.

> I climb so slowly that if I stop to speak to you
> A puff of wind will blow me down.
> I have a long way to go;
> Indeed, there's a hard struggle ahead.

The glory of the ascent, I know, is God's, not yours,
But help me work free of this swamp—
If thanks to your aid I come to serve God
It will be you who has won me back for Him.

JACOPONE DA TODI

To the praise of God I tell you,
And as a friend,
That in fear of the Enemy
Was I led to this tree.

I looked at it in my mind's eye
Meditated on it at length,
And burned with the desire
To climb that measureless height.

I could not even guess
How high the branches reached;
The trunk was straight and smooth.
I saw no place where I could get a hold,

Except for one branch
That curved down to the ground;
A poor despised little bit of a branch,
It bore the mark of humility.

I was ready to climb when suddenly
I heard a voice: "Do not touch me
Unless you have first confessed,
Cleansed yourself of all mortal sin."

Contrition flooded my heart,
I cleansed myself with confession
And with the help of God
Made satisfaction.

Coming back to the tree I felt fear and misgivings,
In anticipation of the exhausting effort;
I devoutly prayed to God for help,
For without His aid I could not climb the tree.

"Sign yourself with the sign of the cross,"
Said a voice that came from Heaven,
"And take hold of the shining bough,
A branch that is pleasing to God."

JACOPONE DA TODI

I made the sign of the cross
And took hold of the luminous bough,
Surrendering myself to it,
And was raised on high.

Then, lifted to those heights,
I found such joy in righteousness
That it freed my heart
Of the temptation of fear.

As soon as I found myself there,
Without a moment's rest
I was made to climb still higher,
To the branch above.

Once on that branch
Which grew out to my right,
Light from the Spouse fell on me,
And I could not but sigh.

I looked toward the branch on the other side
And suddenly found myself there;
Love smiled on me:
It was he who had borne me there.

Peering up above me,
I saw two branches:
One was named Perseverance,
The other, Lasting Love.

When I had climbed up
I meant to rest;
But Love did not allow that,
He had me move to the branch above.

There I rested; from that branch
Hung fruit inscribed with the tale
Of the tears Love shed
For the Spouse who hid Himself.

JACOPONE DA TODI

My heart turned to the other side:
I saw the branch of ardor,
And once again Love's warmth
Spread all through me.

I could not rest; Love,
Which dwelt on the branch above, urged me on.
To rise to that level, I read, I was to hate myself
And give all of my love to the Lord, my Creator.

Love easily drew me
To the branch on the other side,
To the contemplation that separates the soul
From the experience of sin.

Lightly was I drawn up
To the next branch above,
Where one becomes faint with joy
And scents the nearness of Love.

On the other side I saw a branch
Pleasant to the eye;
The heat from that branch
Struck the heart and liquefied it.

Melted by that fire, my heart incapable of action,
I was gradually raised to the next level.
Here Love struck me with a mortal blow:
In ecstasy I saw my Spouse and embraced Him.

Led to that sacred branch I fainted,
Seeing so deeply into the plenitude of things
That my heart sank beneath the waves
And I drowned.

To the praise of the Lord I have told you
How the tree is ordered;
If you wish to climb it,
Let your heart follow my words.

JACOPONE DA TODI

He who would climb the tree of contemplation
Must never think of resting,
But continue to push on
With thoughts and words and deeds.

90 THE LAMENT OF THE SOUL
FOR THE INTENSITY OF INFUSED CHARITY

Why do you wound me, cruel charity,
Bind me and tie me tight?
My heart all trembling, in fragments,
Encircled by flames,
Like wax melts into death.
I ask for respite. None is granted.
My heart, cast into a blazing furnace,
Lives and dies in that fire.

Before my heart knew this, all unsuspecting
I asked for the grace to love you, O Christ,
Confident that love would be a gentle peace,
A soaring to a height and leaving pain behind.
Now I feel torment I could never have imagined
For that searing heat rends my heart.
This love is beyond image or similitude—
My heart beats no longer, and in joy I die.

Heart, mind, and will,
Pleasure, feeling—all are gone.
Beauty has turned into mud,
Rich delights have lost their savor;
A tree of love that grows in my heart
And nourishes me with its fruit
Effected this change without delay,
Destroying the old will and mind and strength.

For this Love I have renounced all,
Traded the world and myself;
Were I the lord of creation

257

JACOPONE DA TODI

I would give it all away for Love.
And yet Love still plays with me,
Makes me act as if out of my senses,
Destroys me and draws me I know not where—
But since I sold myself I have no power to resist.

Friends have urged me to change my ways,
To take another path. I cannot.
I have already given myself away
And have nothing left to give.
A slave cannot escape from his master;
Stone will liquefy before Love lets me go.
Intense desire flames high, fusing my will—
Oh, who could separate me from this Love?

Neither iron nor fire can pry us apart;
The soul now dwells in a sphere
Beyond the reach of death and suffering.
It looks down on all creation
And basks in its peace. My soul,
How did you come to possess this good?
It was Christ's dear embrace
That gave it to you.

My heart and will and feeling
Can no longer endure the created
But cry out in longing for the Creator.
The earth and the heavens have no sweetness;
Compared to Christ, all is stench.
His shining countenance makes sunlight seem dark;
The wisdom of the cherubim and ardor of the seraphim
Are but a faded memory to one who beholds the Lord.

Let no man mock me, then,
If that Love drives me to madness.
Once captured, no heart can shield itself,
Or escape Love's hold.
How can it withstand the searing flame
Without turning to ashes?

JACOPONE DA TODI

Where can I find someone who can understand,
Who can take pity on me in my agony?

For heaven and earth and all things created
Cry out insistently that I should love:
"Make haste to embrace the Love
That made us all, love with all your heart!
Because that Love so desires you
He uses all things to draw you to Himself."
I see all goodness and beauty and gentleness
Spilling out of this superabundance of holy light!

Oh, that my heart would not stumble and sag!
That I were able to love more intensely,
That I had more than myself to give
To that measureless light,
That sweet splendor.
I have given all that I have
To possess the Lover who constantly renews me,
That ancient Beauty forever new!

At the sight of such beauty I am swept up
Out of myself to who knows where;
My heart melts, like wax near fire.
Christ puts His mark on me, and stripped of myself
(O wondrous exchange!) I put on Christ.
Robed in this precious garment,
Crying out its love,
The soul drowns in ecstasy!

Surrendering all her powers and riches,
Bound ever so gently,
She stretches out her arms
To Christ—embraces Him
And gazes on His beauty.
No longer mistress of herself, even the memory
Of herself and her needs and desires is gone.

United with Christ she is almost Christ;
Fused with God she becomes divine.

JACOPONE DA TODI

Raised to this summit, possessing such riches,
The soul is queen of Christ and all His realm!
How can it ever again be sad
And in need of healing?
Gone the cesspool, the breeding place of sin,
Gone is the old world with all its stench.

A new creature is born in Christ:
I hasten to put on the new man,
And Love continues to rise in the veins,
A knife blade cutting into the heart,
A heat that sears all powers of thought.
Christ in His beauty draws me to Him,
Locks me in His embrace, and I cry out:
"Love for whom I hunger, let me die of love!

"For You, Love, I weaken and die;
I cry out to embrace You.
When You are gone, mine is a living death,
And I sigh and weep for Your return;
Once You are back my heart blossoms.
Come back, my Love, come back
And hasten to my aid! Come back,
Love that consumes and binds me tight!

"Sweet Love, consider my suffering!
I cannot endure the fire.
Love has captured me and I know not where I am
Or what I am doing or saying.
My weakness is anguish;
I go about like someone dazed.
How can I continue to endure such torment,
Which, as it nourishes me, steals my heart?

"My heart is no longer mine;
I cannot see what I should do
Or what I am doing. Some ask me, Lord,
Whether love without deeds is acceptable to You:
If it is not, of what worth am I?

JACOPONE DA TODI

Love without limits immobilizes my mind;
The Love that embraces me leaves me mute,
No longer conscious of willing or doing.

"Once I spoke, now I am mute;
I could see once, now I am blind.
Oh, the depths of the abyss in which,
Though silent, I speak; fleeing, I am bound;
Descending, I rise; holding, I am held;
Outside, I am within; I pursue and am pursued.
Love without limits, why do You drive me mad
And destroy me in this blazing furnace?"

"O you who love Me, put order into your love,
For without order there is no virtue!
Now that you love Me with fierce desire
(For it is virtue that renews the soul)
You need charity, well-ordered love.
A tree is judged by its fruits.
My creation is patterned in number and measure,
Each thing according to its purpose.

"Order maintains and sustains
Each particular function;
And this, by its very nature,
Is even more true of charity.
Why, then, has the burning intensity of love
Made you almost lose your senses?
Because you have passed the limits of order,
Because your fervor knows no restraint."

"Christ, You have pierced my heart,
And now You speak of orderly love.
How can I experience love of that sort
Once united with You?
Just as a red-hot iron
Or forms touched by burning colors of dawn
Lose their original contours,
So does the soul immersed in You, O Love.

"This new creation has no strength to act on its own;
When it had form it had power,
And could act and bring forth fruit.
Therefore, if I am truly transformed,
United with You, Christ, with such gentle love,
You, not I, are responsible for what I do.
If I displease You, then,
You are displeasing Yourself, Love.

"I know well, O Highest Wisdom,
That if I am mad, it is Your doing—
This dates from the day I surrendered myself to Love,
Laid aside my old self and put on You
And was drawn—I know not how—to new life.
Now, strong Love, You have undone me;
You have battered down the doors
And I lie with You, Love.

"If it was temperance You wanted,
Why did You lead me to this fiery furnace?
In giving Yourself, the Infinite,
You canceled all measure in me. To contemplate You
As a babe was as much as my heart could bear;
How can it ever endure Your love in its fullness?
If there is fault in my immoderate love it is Yours,
Not mine: it was You who led the way, Love.

"You did not defend Yourself against that Love
That made You come down from heaven to earth;
Love, in trodding this earth
You humbled and humiliated Yourself,
Demanding neither dwelling place nor possessions
Taking on such poverty so that we might be enriched!
In Your life and in Your death You revealed
The infinite love that burned in Your heart.

"You went about the world as if You were drunk,
Led by Love as if You were a slave;
In all things You let Love shine through You
Without thought of compensation. In the Temple

JACOPONE DA TODI

You spoke out and taught with a clear voice:
Let him who thirsts come to drink
And he will receive boundless Love,
Which will nourish him with sweetness.

"You, Wisdom, did not hold Yourself back,
But poured out your Love in abundance—born of Love,
Not of the flesh, out of love for man, to save him!
You rushed to the cross to embrace us;
I think that is why, Love, You did not answer Pilate,
Or defend Yourself before his judgment seat—
You wanted to pay the price of Love
By dying on the cross for us.

"Wisdom, I see, hid herself,
Only Love could be seen.
Nor did You make a show of Your power—
A great Love it was
That poured itself out,
Love and Love alone, in act and desire,
Binding itself to the cross
And embracing Man.

"Thus, Jesus, if I am enamored
And drunk with sweetness,
If I lose my senses and mastery of self,
How can You reproach me?
I see that Love has so bound You
As to almost strip You of Your greatness;
How, then, could I find the strength to resist,
To refuse to share in its madness?

"For the same Love that makes me lose my senses
Seems to have stripped You of wisdom;
The love that makes me weak
Is the love that made You renounce all power.
I cannot delay, nor seek to—
Love's captive, I make no resistance.
Let the sentence of death for love's sake be passed;
The only comfort for which I long, Love, is death.

JACOPONE DA TODI

"Love, Love, You have wounded me,
Your name only can I invoke;
Love, Love, I am one with You,
Let me embrace You alone.
Love, Love, You have swept me up violently,
My heart is beside itself with love;
I want to faint, Love; may I always be close to You:
Love, I beseech You, let me die of love.

"Love, Love-Jesus, I have come to port;
Love, Love-Jesus, You have led me there.
Love, Love-Jesus, comfort me;
Love, Love-Jesus, You have set me afire.
Love, Love-Jesus, consider my needs:
Keep me always in Your embrace,
United with You in true charity,
The supreme realization of unifying love.

" 'Love, Love,' the world cries out,
'Love, Love,' shouts all of creation.
Love, Love, so inexhaustible are You
That he who clasps You close desires You all the more!
Love, Love, perfect circle, he who enters into You
With his whole heart loves You forever. For You are warp and
     woof
Of the robe of him who loves You, filling him with such delight
That he calls out again and again, 'Love!'

"Love, Love, You are so dear;
Love, Love, no more!
Love, Love, You give Yourself to me;
Love, Love, I am close to dying.
Love, Love, so tightly You clasp me;
Love, Love, make me die in You!
Love, sweet languor, sweetest of deaths,
Healing Love, drown me in Love.

"Love, Love, my heart breaks;
Love, Love, so deep the wound!
Love, Love, Your beauty draws me to You;

JACOPONE DA TODI

Love, Love, I am swept up by You.
Love, Love, I have contempt for life;
Love, Love, may my soul be one with You!
Love, You are life—my soul cannot live without You;
Why do You make it faint, clasping it so tightly, Love?

"Love, Love-Jesus, full of desire,
Love, I want to die in Your embrace.
Love, Love-Jesus, my sweet Spouse, I ask You for death.
Love, Love-Jesus, my delight,
You surrender Yourself to me, make me one with You:
Consider that I am faint with love of You,
Love, and know not where I am.
Jesus, my hope, drown me in Love.

91 SELF-ANNIHILATION AND CHARITY LEAD THE SOUL TO WHAT LIES BEYOND KNOWLEDGE AND LANGUAGE

Love beyond all telling,
Goodness beyond imagining,
Light of infinite intensity
Glows in my heart.

I once thought that reason
Had led me to You,
And that through feeling
I sensed Your presence,
Caught a glimpse of You in similitudes,
Knew You in Your perfection.
I know now that I was wrong,
That that truth was flawed.

Light beyond metaphor,
Why did You deign to come into this darkness?
Your light does not illumine those who think they see You
And believe they sound Your depths.
Night, I know now, is day,
Virtue no more to be found.

JACOPONE DA TODI

He who witnesses Your splendor
Can never describe it.

On achieving their desired end
Human powers cease to function,
And the soul sees that what it thought was right
Was wrong. A new exchange occurs
At that point where all light disappears;
A new and unsought state is needed:
The soul has what it did not love,
And is stripped of all it possessed, no matter how dear.

In God the spiritual faculties
Come to their desired end,
Lose all sense of self and self-consciousness,
And are swept into infinity.
The soul, made new again,
Marveling to find itself
In that immensity, drowns.
How this comes about it does not know.

It is within and sees no exit;
It no longer knows how to think of itself
Or to speak of the wondrous change.
It knows only that it finds itself
Clothed in new garments.
Fused with God, it ventures forth
Onto a sea without a shore
And gazes on Beauty without color or hue.

Participating in the essence of all creatures
It can now say, "All things are mine."
The doors open wide, and entering within
The soul becomes one with God,
Possesses what He possesses. It hears
What it did not hear, sees what it did not know,
Possesses what it did not believe,
Savors that which has no taste.

JACOPONE DA TODI

In losing all, the soul has risen
To the pinnacle of the measureless;
Because it has renounced all
That is not divine,
It now holds in its grasp
The unimaginable Good
In all its abundance,
A loss and a gain impossible to describe.

To lose and to hold tightly,
To love and take delight in,
To gaze upon and contemplate,
To possess utterly,
To float in that immensity
And to rest therein—
That is the work of unceasing exchange
Of charity and truth.

There is no other action at those heights;
What the questing soul once was it has ceased to be.
Neither heat nor fiery love
Nor suffering has place here.
This is not light as the soul had imagined it.
All it had sought it must now forget,
And pass on to a new world,
Beyond its powers of perception.

The light of the intellect,
Which had seemed dazzling,
Now seems dark and feeble;
What it thought was strength
It now recognizes as weakness.
No longer can the intellect describe divinity
As it once did when it could speak;
For perfect Good no metaphor is adequate.

Once united with God it knows
That what you think is day is night,
What you think is light is darkness.

JACOPONE DA TODI

Until you reach this point, and the self is annihilated,
Everything you think is true is really false.
You do not yet have in you pure charity
While you can think of yourself
And the victory you are striving for.

Oh, the futility of seeking to convey
With images and feelings
That which surpasses all measure!
The futility of seeking
To make infinite power ours!
Thought cannot come to certainty of belief
And there is no likeness of God
That is not flawed.

Hence, if He should call you,
Let yourself be drawn to Him.
He may lead you to a great truth.
Do not dwell on yourself, nor should you—
A creature subject to multiplicity and change—seek Him;
Rest in tranquility, loftier than action or feeling,
And you will find that as you lose yourself
He will give you strength.

Be pleased to remain where it pleases Him to place you.
Straining to find Him is of no avail;
Be at peace with yourself. If He embraces you,
Return His embrace, but do not feel wronged
When He absents Himself. Give no thought to yourself;
If you love as you should, you will be filled with joy,
Because that love in itself
Glows with a light that does not fail.

You know that you can only possess
To the extent that He will give;
What He withholds you cannot acquire;
Nor can you hold onto what you have
Unless He grants you that grace.
Your path from beginning to end

JACOPONE DA TODI

Lies beyond your power;
The choice is not yours but the Lord's.

Hence, if you have found Him know in truth
That it was through no power of yours.
The good that is given you
Comes out of charity; it is a gift,
Not the fruit of your own efforts.
Let all your desire, then,
Be directed toward Him,
The Infinite One, Giver of all good.

Will nothing for yourself but what He wills for you;
Lose yourself, be united to Him,
Do His bidding. Shed your self
And put on the Lord;
You will ascend to a height
Surpassing all virtue
And Christ, who is there,
Will never let you slip and fall.

When you no longer love yourself
But love Goodness,
You and your Beloved will become one.
When you love Him, He must love you in return;
In His charity you are drawn to Him
And the two are made one.
This is a true union
That admits of no divisions.

If you have given to Him
All of yourself without reservation,
Loving Him and not yourself, He cannot leave you.
That Good you were given when He fused you with Himself,
Would it not be lost as well
Were He to allow you to fall into sin?
Therefore, as that Light cannot abandon itself,
Neither can it abandon you: Love has made you one.

JACOPONE DA TODI

O Deepest Truth that reigns over all,
You are the road and the end of the road
For the soul who has found You.
A sweet tranquility superior to all other states,
Not susceptible to change,
You are a light that is steady and strong,
That does not lose its radiance,
Even when it shines through that which is base.

The soul that possesses You
Remains forever pure,
Does not wound or sully itself with sin.
On a height and in peace it looks down
On the world below steeped in sin.
The sense of self disappears,
For it can never rise to this level,
Where the infinite charity of God engulfs all.

The war is over—
Virtue's struggle, anguish of soul;
All enemies have been vanquished.
The soul is reborn,
Clad in such mail as need fear no blow,
Fixed on the light, seeking no images,
For at those heights
One asks for no light from without.

Past the starry firmament
Adorned with the virtues,
Past the crystalline sky the soul has climbed;
It has been transformed and purified.
It has come to the third heaven,
To the ardor of the seraphim.
This holy light, forever freshly scented,
Cannot know stain of sin or degradation.

Faith at this point ceases, for the soul sees;
Hope ceases, for it clings to the One it once hoped in.
Gone is desire, the straining of the will, the fear of loss.
The soul has more than it knew how to yearn for.

JACOPONE DA TODI

What it had once thought was vision
Is now revealed as total blindness;
What it had hungered painfully for
Has now been proven an illusion.

The height and depth of this third heaven
Is beyond demonstration; the more do I marvel
(And no demonstration is possible)
That the soul, united to the immutable God,
Can be constantly renewed.
It can no longer err or fall into shadow:
Night has turned into day,
Pitiful inadequacy into perfect love.

As air becomes the medium for light when the sun rises,
And as wax melts from the heat of fire,
So the soul drawn to that light is resplendent,
Feels self melt away,
Its will and actions no longer its own.
So clear is the imprint of God
That the soul, conquered, is conqueror;
Annihilated, it lives in triumph.

What happens to the drop of wine
That you pour into the sea?
Does it remain itself, unchanged?
It is as if it never existed.
So it is with the soul: Love drinks it in,
It is united with Truth,
Its old nature fades away,
It is no longer master of itself.

The soul wills and yet does not will:
Its will belongs to Another.
It has eyes only for this beauty;
It no longer seeks to possess, as was its wont—
It lacks the strength to possess such sweetness.
The base of this highest of peaks
Is founded on *nichil*,
Shaped nothingness, made one with the Lord.

JACOPONE DA TODI

Lofty self-annihilation,
Your strength batters down all doors
And opens on infinity. You feed on Truth
And have no fear of death;
You straighten the crooked
And illumine the darkness. You bind the heart
So close to God in friendship that all differences
And obstacles to Love are banished

You pass lightly over all difficulties
And arrive at Truth,
Never looking back over your shoulder
To meditate on the sins of your past.
In harmony with God,
Yours is constant joy,
A dwelling on Truth
Without shadow of pain.

You have cast out both pleasure and displeasure;
Surrendering yourself to God,
You find joy in what pleases Him.
You have drowned both wanting and not wanting
And extinguished desire; yours is peace unending.
You are the flame that purifies
But does not destroy,
That overcomes both heat and cold.

You seek no recompense, but always find it;
You are bathed in light,
Given gifts you have not sought. Embracing God
So that you will never be separated from Him,
You experience unending joy, and flower in Him.
You run and stand still, you rise as you fall;
The more you give the more you receive:
You possess the Creator.

In being possessed you possess,
In seamless union;
As you drink you are being drunk—
Nothing can separate you

JACOPONE DA TODI

From this perfection.
There is no impediment,
For he will no longer close His hand to you,
To you, His Lady, His bride.

You have passed through death to true life,
Safe forever from attacks or violence;
Leaving yourself behind, you live in God,
In Infinity, without opposition.
No one can comprehend you,
Or know how you are fashioned,
Except the One who created you
And raised you up.

From humble station
You are raised on high,
Seated at the right hand of God,
As your wretchedness sinks from sight
In the depths of that divine abyss.
He who has no experience
Of this fusion of rise and fall
Can never understand.

The riches you possess
Now that you have lost all!
Never has there been such an exchange. O Light,
You who turn even human weakness to our advantage
If we strip ourselves of our powers,
This is the new covenant:
There where life ebbs and dies,
It finds new and lasting strength.

Self-annihilation, you transform every loss into gain;
Your light destroys all
That would keep us from God.
The good you bring is the one perfect good.
You heal the sick and raise the dead
Because you know how to counteract poison
With the proper antidote:
Desolation with strength, darkness with light.

JACOPONE DA TODI

You are a garden
Adorned with every flower,
The tree of life in the center.
You are pure light without shadow,
So firmly fixed in God
That you cannot be wounded;
And being one with Truth,
Fear cannot make you falter.

Without you, self-annihilation,
There can be no perfect union,
Nor can love, no matter how strong, reign.
Man without your help
Cannot possess or contemplate God.
Doors are never closed to you;
Great is your dignity
In the court of the Emperor.

The bride of Christ and of all His saints,
You reign with them in holy light.
We beseech you, Lady,
To shield us with your mantle
So that our song might rise to Him
And we might love with purity and see,
Without images, the deepest and highest Truth
Through the annihilation of our poor hearts.

92   HOW FIRM FAITH AND HOPE BRING ONE
TO THE THREEFOLD STATE OF SELF-ANNIHILATION

Faith and hope have estranged me from myself,
Struck at my heart, annihilated me.

Within and without I am shattered,
Reduced to nothingness:
This the fruit of centering my life on love.
I am no longer able to flee or to pursue;
Caught in the swell of the sea
I drown, and my words drown with me!

JACOPONE DA TODI

My speech is silence and shout.
I know where He is hidden, for though I see Him not
I recognize the signs of His presence
In every creature that is one with Him.
Being and nonbeing I have fused together,
And out of love banished my will with its "yes" and "no."

Once cut off from all things,
Nothing is lost and nothing is sought;
Without appetite, being, or desire to possess,
The soul possesses all and is beyond corruption.
Utter annihilation—that is the food
That truly leads me to despise myself!

I disown all things and share in their possession!
The man who is possessed
By the Possessor of All Things
No longer cares to possess.
In this, the first stage of self-annihilation,
The will of man drowns completely.

Submerged, it is made one with God;
It has given itself to divine folly
So as to learn reason.
The turbulent alternations of fortune,
The winds of yesteryear,
Are no more.

All turmoil has faded away,
Opened on the freshness of a new dawn.
Let us offer counsel to those who aspire
To the first realm, the second, and the highest of all;
And let us vow that Reason
Will hold sway at all times,

That it never be allowed to rest a moment,
But always be in action;
For the Intellect has yet to come to port
And the ocean is wide and deep.

JACOPONE DA TODI

Let him who knows not how to swim
Not plunge into these waters!

The sin of presumption can make man drown,
When he does not recognize his limits;
There lies the risk of this second stage,
For one who does not keep his feelings in check.
The intellect stilled, taking feeling as my guide,
The light that shines seems to me darkness.

O dark light shining within me,
What is it that I do not see in you?
Sin blinds me to what I ought to see,
And that which is not there I think I see;
[*Text illegible at this point*]
How then can I bear witness to the light?

In the depths of this sea I cry out,
"Help me, Lord, for I drown in this storm;
I know not how I have survived till now."
Let no man in folly
Launch out into that great sea
Without first stripping himself of all.

He must strip his soul of all thought
(In this, the second stage), hold on to nothing,
If he wants to be called to the next stage;
He must be purified by fire,
[*Text illegible at this point*]
That fire which tests us.

To come to the crystalline sphere
The will must drown itself.
(Nothing, I repeat, is to be possessed.)
This is a rule that is not subject to change:
Works have no place in the second heaven;
They belong, it seems to me, only on earth.

The cycle of the seasons is no longer,
The heavens are immobile, they spin no more.

JACOPONE DA TODI

Their harmonies are stilled, and the profound silence
Makes me cry out, "O unsoundable sea,
I am engulfed by your depths
And shall drown in the abyss!"

Intellect drowns
In this silence of frozen waters,
Far beyond exultation and suffering,
Beyond shame and honor.
Nothing grieves me, for perfect peace
Makes the soul reign in all places.

To find myself in the Kingdom,
In the heart of the sovereignty of God!
To sail under this banner,
With authority over Rome and its Curia,
Where God cures us of all our ills.
The Apostle points the way:

He will help you reach a heaven,
A hidden heaven where zeal has disappeared,
The heaven of the Throne and the Dominion
And of the Power of God,
Where you come to the heights as a soldier
In the hosts of Israel, the Promised Land.

God, the Patriarch, dwells in the hearts
Of those close to Him, and reigns in Israel
Where those He loves find refuge,
Having fled all other kingdoms
To be united with Him.
This is the land I seek in inheritance.

The land of promise is promised to them,
There where the perfect man once lived;
There will come all the perfect
Who have centered their love on Supreme Virtue,
If they put Intellect aside
And use Love as their guide.

Formed without form, the features of all faces
Blurred out of love, acquire once more
The traits of an original innocence;
And this is so because in the third Heaven
The soul, reborn in the new Adam,
No longer sins in thought or deed.

93   THE LAMENT OF THE VIRGIN

Lady, Queen of Heaven, they have taken your son;
Hurry, come and see—they're beating Him,
Whipping Him brutally; they will kill Him.

> How can this be? My son, who has done no wrong,
> My hope—how could they have taken Him?

Judas betrayed Him for thirty pieces of silver;
For him, a good business deal.

> Magdalene, help! Help me—Oh, the anguish!
> They have taken him prisoner, just as I was told.

Lady, Queen of Heaven, come rescue Him,
Quick, they're spitting on Him;
Now they're taking Him before Pilate.

> Pilate, I beseech you, do Him no harm;
> I can show you that those who accuse Him lie.

Crucify Him, crucify Him! According to our law
He who claims to be king must be punished.

> Listen to me, I beg of you, look at me.
> Have you ever seen any suffering like mine?
> Will you not be moved to pity?

Bring out two thieves to be His companions;
Crown the pretender, crown Him with thorns!

JACOPONE DA TODI

My Son, my Son, my Son, my loving lily,
Who can console me in my anguish?
Son whose gentle eyes once smiled on me,
Why do you not answer me?
Why hide from the mother who nursed You?

Lady, here is the cross
On which they will raise
The true Light of the world.

O cross, will you take my son from me?
And what will you accuse Him of,
Since he has done no wrong?

Hurry, O sorrowful one,
They're stripping your son;
They will nail Him to the cross.

If they have stripped Him of His garments,
Let me then see His bloody wounds!

Lady, they've taken one of His hands,
Pressed it against the cross,
And the nail has ripped through the flesh.
They've taken the other hand,
Stretched it out on the cross,
And the pain spreads and grows.
Lady, they've taken His feet
And nailed them to the tree;
They have broken all His bones and joints.

Oh, let me begin to chant the dirge,
My son has been taken from me.
O Son, my fair Son,
Who was it that killed You?
Oh, that they had ripped out my heart,
That I might not see Your torn flesh
Hanging from the cross!

JACOPONE DA TODI

Mother, why have you come?
Your agony and tears crush Me;
To see you suffer so will be My death.

> My anguish is not without cause;
> O my Son, Father and Spouse,
> Who was it wounded and stripped You?

Mother, weep no more; stay and help
Those dear to Me, the friends I leave behind.

> Son, do not ask this of me; let me die with You.
> Let me breathe my last here at Your side.
> A common grave for son and mother,
> Since ours is a common agony.

Mother, My heart in tears, I commend you into the hands
Of John, My chosen one; call him your son.
John, here is My mother, take her with love;
Have pity on her, they have pierced her heart.

> My Son, You have breathed Your last;
> Son of a mother frightened and dazed,
> Son of a mother destroyed by grief,
> Tortured, tormented Son!
> Son without peer, fair and rosy-cheeked,
> To whom shall I turn now that You have left me?
> Why did the world so despise You?
> Gentle and sweet Son, Son of a sorrowful mother,
> How cruelly You have been treated!
> John, my new son, your brother is dead:
> The sword they prophesied has pierced my heart.
> They have killed both mother and son,
> One cruel death for both,
> Embracing each other and their common cross!

Bibliography

Since most of the works on the life and poetry of Jacopone da Todi are in Italian and not translated, it has been thought best to limit the bibliography to essentials. Readers with a knowledge of Italian, French, and German will find an excellent and very up-to-date bibliography in George T. Peck's *The Fool of God—Jacopone da Todi* (University of Alabama Press, 1980).

EDITIONS OF THE LAUDS

Laude di Frate Jacopone da Todi impresse per me Ser Francesco Bonaccorsi in Firenze, 1490. (This is the text used by Giovanni Ferri in his edition of the *Laude*, Rome, Società Filologica Romana, 1910, and Bari, Laterza, 1915. The work was republished by Laterza in 1930 with revisions by Santino Caramella.)

Le laude del Beato frate Iacopone del sacro ordine di frati minori de observantia . . . stampate in la magnifica città de Bressa per Bernardino di Misinti de Pavia ad instantia de Magistro Angelo britannicho de Pallazolo citadino de Bressa adi 10 luio 1495.

Li cantici del beato Iacopone da Todi, con diligenza ristampati con la gionta di alcuni discorsi del padre Giambattista Modio *et con la vita sua, in Roma, appresso Ippolito Salviano, 1558.*

Li cantici del beato Iacopone da Todi alcuni canti cavati da un manoscritto antico non più stampato. Napoli: Lazzaro Scoriggio, 1615.

Le Poesie spirituali del B. Iacopone da Todi . . . con le scolie e le annotazioni di fra Francesco Tresatti da Lugnano . . . in Venetia, Appresso Nicolò Misserini, MDCXVII.

Laudi, Trattato e Detti, ed. Franca Ageno. Florence: Le Monnier, 1953.

Laude, ed. Franco Mancini. Bari: Laterza, 1974.

BIBLIOGRAPHY

Le Laudi, ed. Luigi Fallacara. Florence: Libreria Editrice Fiorentina, 1976.

LITERARY AND HISTORICAL STUDIES

Accademia Tudertina. *Jacopone e il suo tempo.* Todi, 1959.

Apollonio, Mario. *Iacopone da Todi e la poetica delle confraternite religiose nella cultura preumanistica.* Milan: Vita e Pensiero, 1946.

Battaglia, Salvatore. *La coscienza letteraria del Medioevo.* Naples: Liguori, 1965.

Bettarini, Rosanna. *Jacopone e il Laudario urbinate.* Florence: Sansoni, 1969.

Casella, Mario. "Iacopone da Todi," *Archivum Romanicum* IV (1920):281–329, 429–485.

Contini, Gianfranco. *"Esperienze d'un antologista del Duecento poetico italiano,"* in *Studi e problemi di critica testuale,* pp. 241–272. Bologna: Commissione per i testi di lingua, 1961.

Contini, Gianfranco. *Poeti del Duecento.* 2 vols. Milan and Naples: Ricciardi, 1960.

Cousins, Ewart. *St. Bonaventure.* New York: Paulist Press, 1979.

Croce, Benedetto. *Poesia d'arte e poesia popolare.* Bari: Laterza, 1946.

Croce, Benedetto. *La poesia di Dante.* Bari: Laterza, 1921.

D'Ancona, Alessandro. *Iacopone da Todi il Giullare di Dio del secolo XIII.* Todi: Atanòr, 1914.

De Sanctis, Francesco. *Storia della letteratura italiana,* 3rd ed. 2 vols. Milan: Feltrinelli, 1964.

Frugoni, Arsenio. *Incontri nel Medioevo.* Bologna: Il Mulino, 1980.

Fubini, Mario. *Metrica e poesia, I. Dal Duecento al Petrarca.* Milano: Feltrinelli, 1962.

Hatzfield, Helmut A. *Saggi di stilistica romanza.* Bari: Adriatica Editrice, 1967.

Hughes, Serge. *The Little Flowers of St. Francis and Other Franciscan Writings.* New York: New American Library, 1964.

Lambert, M. D. *Franciscan Poverty.* London: Society for Promoting Christian Knowledge, 1961.

Levasti, Arrigo, ed. *Mistici del Duecento e del Trecento.* Milan and Rome: Rizzoli, 1935.

Peck, George. *The Fool of God—Jacopone da Todi.* University of Alabama Press, 1980.

BIBLIOGRAPHY

Russo, Luigi. "Iacopone da Todi mistico-poeta," in *Ritratti e disegni storici*, 3rd series, *Studi sul Due e Trecento*. Bari: Laterza, 1951.

Sapegno, Natalino. *Frate Jacopone*. Torino: Baretti, 1926.

Underhill, Evelyn. *Jacopone da Todi—A Spiritual Biography*. London: J. Dent & Sons, Ltd., 1919.

Index to Preface, Foreword and Introduction

285

INDEX

D'Ancona, Alessandro, 13–15, 18, 21, 22, 24

Da Capestrano, Giovanni, 8

Dame Poverty, xiv

Da Marrone, Pier. *See* Celestine V, Pope

Dante, xvi, xvii, xix, 8, 11, 12, 17, 37, 45, 50, 63, 65

Da Todi, Jacopone. *See* Jacopone da Todi

De la Porée, Marguerite, xvi

De Montaigne, Michel Eyquem, 54

De Sanctis, Francesco, 10–19, 22, 23

Di Bernardino di Guidone, Vanna, xix, 24, 27

Di Bondone, Giotto, xiii

Deśa prajña, xi

Eckhart, Meister, xv

Ecstasy, experiences of, xv

Egidio of Assisi, xv, xvi

Elias, Brother, 48

Emotionalism, xii

England, xvii

Eucharist, the, 41, 63

Everyman, 26, 28

Fascism, 15

Faust, 1

Ferri, Giovanni, 21, 23

Fioretti, the, 9, 33

Flanders, xiv

Flora, Joachim of, 63

Franciscans, the; Cf. Conventuals, the; Francis of Assisi, St.; Spirituals, the; xi, 4, 13, 34, 38, 56; and the cardinal protector, 46; and the Conventuals, xix–xx, 12; and education, 8, 32–33; and holy poverty, xiv, xvii, xix, 32, 46, 60; and humility, 33–34; Jacopone and, 30–31, 37, 56–57, 60; and Messianism, xv; mysticism of, xiv–xv, xvii; and the papacy, xx, 46, 50; and the Spirituals, xix–xx, 12

France, xvii

Francis of Assisi, St. (also *Il Poverello*), 9, 12, 13, 30–31, 34, 38, 56, 57; the Calvary of, 47; and the cardinal protector, 46; and Christ, 37, 45; and the Church, 41; his experience of God, 41, his First Rule, 40; founding the Order, 42–43; and Gregory IX, 48; and holy poverty, xiv–xv, 29, 37, 39–48; influence on Jacopone, xx, 12, 33, 35, 39–40, 47, 48, 55, 61; and money,

44–45; mysticism of, 8; obedience of, 60; and the papacy, 40–43, 46, 48, 50; and the Sacraments, 41; his Second Rule, 44–46, 47–48; and the Sermon on the Mount, 42, 43; the spirituality of, 32; and the stigmata, 37; the Testament of, 44, 46, 47, 48; and the world, 41

Gaetani, Cardinal Benedetto. *See* Boniface VIII, Pope

Gaetani, Roffredo, 54

Ganfredi, 30

Giotto di Bondone, xiii

Giovanni da Capestrano, 8

God, 28; absence of, 25, 27, 59–60; as love, xvii; faith in, xvi; Jacopone's experience of, 19–20; Jacopone's search for, xix, 2, 4; Jacopone's visions of, 29; the Kingdom of, 2, 4, 16, 42, 43; love for, xvii; love of, 24, 28–29, 60; as playful, xvii; the soul and, xvi–xvii; the Spirituals and, 39

Goethe, Johann Wolfgang von, 17

Gospels, the, xv

Greccio, xi

Gregory VII, Pope, 50

Gregory IX, Pope, 48

Gubbio, xi

Guidone, Vanna di Bernardino di, xix, 24, 27

Handel, George Frederick, 29

Hegel, Georg Wilhelm Friedrich, 10, 14, 16, 17

Hell, xvi, 56

Holy poverty; benefits of, xv; betrothal to, xiv–xv, xvii; St. Bonaventure and, xx; Boniface VIII and, 54; the Church and, xv; the Franciscans and, xvii, 48; St. Francis and, xiv–xv, 29, 39–40; the Gospels and, xv; the Incarnation and, 36, and the inner life, xv; in Italy, xiv; Jacopone and, xiv–xv, xix, 25, 29, 32, 37, 39, 56, 58, 60; the Spirituals and, 32, 48, 48

Holy Roman Empire, the, 42

Honorius IV, Pope, 49

Icon, xi, xiii

Idealism, 16, 19

Illumination, 26

Il Poverello. See Francis of Assisi, St.

INDEX

Immanence, 16, 19
Incarnation, the, 34, 36
India, xi
Innocent III, Pope, 40, 41, 42, 44, 50, 53, 54
Innocent IV, Pope, 48
Inquisition, the, xv
Italian Renaissance, the, 10
Italy, the Church in, xiv; the culture of, xi, xix, 7, 10, 15; the literature of, xi, xix; the Spirituals in, xiv

Jacopone da Todi; and absence of God, 25, 27, 59–60; and anti-intellectualism, 33–34; and Benedict XI, xx, 14; as a *bizzocone*, xix, 14, 25, 30; in Bologna, xix; and Boniface VIII, xiii, xx, 14, 53, 55, 56, 58, 65; and Celestine V, xx, 50–52, 56; and compromise, 28, 30; and the Conventuals, 12, 30–32, 55; the conversion of, 27, 28–29; and corruption in the Church, xx, 25, 38–39; and the Cross, 36–37; and "divine madness," 36; and emotionalism, xii; his experience of God, 19–20, 35, 63; and fear, xvi; and Franciscanism, xii, xiv–xv, 35, 39, 57; and St. Francis of Assisi, xx, 12, 33, 35, 39–40, 47, 48, 49, 56, 57, 60; and freedom, xv; as a Friar Minor, xx, 14, 24, 30, 32–33, 49; and God's love, 21, 60; and God as love, xvii; and holy poverty, xiv–xv, xvii, 25, 29, 32, 35, 36, 38–39, 56, 58, 60; and hope, xvi; and human condition, xvi; and human nature, 29; his imprisonment, xx, 56–57; and the Incarnation, 34, 36; his journey into God, 33; and joy, 35, 61; and jubilation, xiii, xv; Lauds of, xii–xiii, xiv, xvi, xix, xx–xxi, 2–30, 63–65; and levels of consciousness, xiii; and liberation, xvi; and the Longhezza Manifesto, xx, 25, 55; and lordship, xvii; and love of God, 35–36, 39; the marriage of, xix, 24; his use of mantra, xiii; as master of incantation, xiii; and meditation, xii, xx; and melodrama, xii, xx; and Messianism, xv; and misfortune, xvi; and mysticism, xi, xv, xvii, 20, 21, 25; as a *notaio*, xix, 24; and nothingness, xv; and oneness, xvii; and the papacy, xix, xx, 38, 49, 60; and the Passion, xii; as a poet, xix, 2–5, 9; and the psychic world, xv, xvi; and quietude, xii, xv; his search for God, xix, 2, 4; and self-annihilation, 61; and self-surrender, 61; and sentimentality, xii; and sin, xvi, xvii, 28, 39; and the soul, xvi–xvii; and the Spanish Sufis, xiii–xiv; as a spiritual master, xii; and the Spirituals, xiv, xix–xx, 14, 24, 30, 55; and the stigmata of Francis, 37; and success, xvi; and the Virgin Mary, xvi; and women, xii

Jerome, St., 7
Joachim of Flora, 63
John of La Verna, 30, 59, 63
John of Parma, 30, 32, 33
Jubilation, xiii, xv
Julian, Dame, 61
Juniper, Brother, 20

Kant, Immanuel, 17

La Verna, John of, 30, 59, 63
La Verna, 13
Legalism, 38
Leopardi, Count Giacomo, 10
Longhezza Manifesto of 1297, the, xx, 25, 55
Lucifer, 55

Machiavelli, Niccolò, 10, 29, 43
Mancini, Franco, 22–23, 63–64, 65
Mangano, Lucia, xi
Mantra, xiii
Manzoni, Alessandro, xxi, 10, 26, 55
Marini, Marino, 5
Marguerite de la Porée, xvi
Marxism, 41
Messianism, xv
Michelangelo, 48
Middle Ages, the, xix, 10, 12, 16, 17–18, 52
Milton, John, 12
Modio, G. B., 8
Montaigne, Michel Eyquem de, 54
Morrone, Pier da. *See* Celestine V, Pope
Mysticism, 19, 26; Franciscan, xiv–xv; Jacopone and, xi, xv, xvii, 20, 21, 25; mystical visions, xv

Neri, St. Philip, 8
Nicholas III, Pope, 49
Nicholas IV, Pope, 48, 49
Nothingness, xv

INDEX

Index to Text

INDEX

Counsel, 155
Court, the Heavenly (Celestial), 131, 147, 148, 150, 203, 205; of love, 150; the papal, 173; the Roman, 176–77
Creation, 153
Creator. *See* God
Cross, of Christ, 143–44, 145–46, 200, 219, 240–41, 279; clinging to, 212; contemplation of, 225–27; St. Francis and, 187–89; the sign of, 254–55
Cruelty, 92
Curia, the Roman, 169, 277

Damned, the, 75
Da Morrone, Pier, 173
Da Todi, Jacopone. *See* Jacopone da Todi
Daughter-in-law, 105, 106
Death, 69, 72, 84, 87, 90, 95, 100, 102, 106, 109, 135, 241; contemplation of, 114–16; of deceptive woman, 83; evil thoughts and, 79; fear of, 69, 272; fruit of, 76; and sin, 88–89
Deception, 82–83
Demons, 95, 118
Detachment, 184
Devil, the, 72, 86, 89, 96, 118, 123, 157, 168, 214; accuses sinner before Christ, 103–105; arrows of, 119; his battles against St. Francis, 190–93; deceived man, 149; disguised as angel, 212, 213; disguised as Christ, 213; as Father of Lies, 161; and the flesh, 79–80; guarding against, 78; love of, 212; and man after the Fall, 146; and redeemed man, 69, 152, 154; the senses and, 78–80; sin delivers man into hands of, 75, 90, 207–208; terror of, 75, 254; vs. Truth and Reason, 80; wages war against man, 160–63; women and, 81, 192
Discord, 252
Discretion, 229–30
Divine Office, the, 73, 120
Doctors, the, 132, 170, 172

Elias, 234
Elizabeth, St., 149
Emperor, the, 250, 274
Enemy, the. *See* Devil, the
Envy, 90, 92–94, 251
Eternal Life, 71, 114, 209
Eternal pain, 101
Eternity, 77

Evil, 99; the desire to commit, 87; the Devil compounds, 80; the flesh (Body) as, 71; the hatred of, 135; praying against, 157; Sloth as the source of, 214
Evil One, the. *See* Devil, the
Excommunication, 178

Faith, 152, 155; act of, 231; the Articles of, 168, 219, 248; ceases in union with God, 270; leads the soul to the Realm of the Invisible, 158–60; living, 131; making one's way to the heaven of, 209, 211; points to true happiness, 218; and self-annihilation, 274–78
Faithfulness, 132
Fall, the, 146, 213
Family, 78, 81, 84
Fasting, 76, 85, 97, 136
Father, of the Church, 132, 171; God as, 148, 157–58, 221; human, 110; of Lies, 161; of Light, 159
Fathers, the Church, 132, 171
Fear, 95, 147; defeated 272, 274; of the Devil, 75, 254; drives away the Enemy, 75; of dying (death) 69, 272; of God, 98, 155, 182; God revealed in, 157; of Hell, 69, 185, 210; of loss, 270; temptation of, 255
Fermo, Brother John of, 193
Flesh, the, 118, 161, 229, 230; vs. Conscience, 79–80; as evil, 71; inclined to sin, 154; vs. Reason, 79–80; sins of, 94
Fools, 82, 83
Forgiveness, begging for after death, 102–105; through contrition, 75, 79, 86; praying for, 156
Fortitude, the endurance of, 155; of Virgin Mary, 71; the virtue of, 217–18, 219
Franciscan Order, The. *See* Order, The (Franciscan)
Francis of Assisi, St., 122, 179; the Enemy's battles against, 190–93; and founding the Franciscan Order, 192; and the order for married penitents, 192; and the order of sisters, 192; and the seven visions of the cross, 187–89; and the stigmata, 188–89
Freedom, 76, 127, 186
Friars, 175
Friends, 119
Fruit, of death, 76; of false delights, 81; of grace, 76; of love, 212
Futility, 268

INDEX

INDEX

Holy Spirit, the, 170, 249; being filled
with, 216; to come upon Mary, 149;
Gifts of, 150, 155, 169; the will of, 215
Holy Week, 182
Honor, of God, 98, 137, 138, 178, 213,
216, 217; human desire for, 121, 122,
242; lost through pride, 94; stripping
oneself of, 185
Hope, 132, 155; brings one close to
Heaven, 249; ceases in union with
God, 270; Christ redeems those who
have lost, 71; the friend of the
Heavenly Court, 131; gives confidence,
219; in the goodness of the Lord, 161;
those in Hell are beyond, 97; in
Heaven, 233; the heaven of, 209; leads
to true happiness, 218; of salvation,
135; and self-annihilation, 274–78; the
vermilion tree and, 211
Human, seed, 108; will, 129, 130, 154,
231–32, 275, 276
Humiliation, the Valley of, 144
Humility, 139, 248; of Christ, 70, 141,
246, 262; defeats pride, 251; of God,
128; the need for, 97–98, 121; in
prosperity, 219; replaces pride through
grace, 91, 254; of sinner, 69; the Valley
of Humiliation, 144
Hypocrisy, 120–21, 185, 228

Ignorance, 215
Illness, 164–65
Illuminated, the, 120
Impatience, 120
Incarnation, the, 168, 243
Infants, 110
Innocence, 167
Intellect, the, 130, 277; and Affection,
223–25; and contemplation, 224–25;
the ignorant, 231; the light of, 267;
man's, 212, 222; and reason, 275–76; at
rest, 246; and virtues, 252–53
Intelligence, 218
Invisible, the Realm of the, 158–60
Israel, 277

Jacopone da Todi, at the brink of Hell,
179; in prison, 174–82
Jesus Christ, 81, 96, 118, 186, 237, 240;
the absence of, 207–208; the angels
marvel at, 140–44; and the Antichrist,
166–67; His baptism, 152; became
man, 70, 71, 140; the birth of, 149,
194–203; the Body of, 153; the bride
of, 142–43, 199–203; as Creator, 201;
the cross of, 143–44, 145–46, 200, 219,
279; the Devil disguised as, 213; as
eternal life in swaddling clothes, 71; in
the Eucharist, 158; the example of,
210; and the Father, 148; the
forgiveness of, 102–105, 235; the
goodness of, 122; the humility of, 70,
141, 246, 262; the Incarnation of, 168,
169, 194; innocence reborn in, 167; as
Justice Incarnate, 103; the justice of,
119; the Kingdom of, 96, 117, 142; as
the Lamb, 194, 241; His lament for the
Church of Rome, 169–70; His lament
over the sinner, 116–18; at the Last
Judgment, 96; the life of, 137–40, 168;
as Love made flesh, 196–97; love of,
117, 143, 144, 207, 221, 242–44; love
for, 240–42, 257–65; the mercy of, 118;
as the Messiah, 150, 241; the Nativity
of, 194–203, 204; the Passion of, 168;
the peace of, 235; the people of 142–43,
166–67, 199–203; His pilgrimage to
earth, 140–41, 142–44; and poverty,
210; as Redeemer (Savior), 71, 144,
149–51, 201, 208; the Righteousness of,
103; the sacrifice of, 221–23; as the Son
of God, 96; the soul as the queen of,
260; as the source of all delight, 118; as
the Spouse (Bridegroom), 134, 202,
215, 218–20, 255–56, 265; the suffering
of, 134, 142–43, 204, 278–80; taught us
to pray, 156–57; in the Temple, 262;
the truth of, 103; union with, 186; the
Virgin Mary and, 70–71, 278–80; as
Wisdom, 148, 262–63; wisdom of, 170,
215; as the Word of God, 70, 194, 221
John, the Apostle, 280
John the Baptist, 121
John the Evangelist, St., 195
John of Fermo, Brother, 193
John of La Verna, Brother, 193–94
Jordan, the River, 166
Joseph, St., 196
Joy, 76, 212, 255; eternal, 77; fleshly
(ungodly) joy through lust, 72, 94,
101–102; in Heaven, 249, 260; through
penance, 71, 74, 75, 160; in sin, 75
Jubilation, 227–28, 233
Judas, 278
Judgment; the conscience and, 165;
escaping, 71, 87; the Last, 94, 164; and

292

INDEX

the sinner after death, 103–105; and the will, 129

Justice, 206; and Affection, 223; of Christ, 119; after death, 103, 139; hunger for, 155; Incarnate, 103; and mercy, 146–56; through penitence, 76; reborn through grace, 91; semblances of, 121–23; and Sloth, 251; the virtue of, 217, 219; and Wisdom, 245

Knowledge, 123, 128, 155, 265

La Verna, Brother John of, 193–94
La Verna, Italy, 188, 193
Law; of God, 74, 156, 232; of Grace, 168; of Moses, 168; the natural, 168
Lazarus, 180
Life, 241; of Christ, 137–40, 168; on earth, 113; eternal, 71, 114, 209
Living, 109–114
Lord, the. See God; Jesus Christ
Love, Cf. Charity; 95, 135, 265; carnal, 127; for Christ, 240–42, 257–65; of Christ, 117, 143, 144, 207, 221, 242–44; conjugal, 157–58; counterfeit, 125–26, 127–29; the court of, 150; divine, 129–31, 232–39, 244–46, 253–57; St. Francis' love for Christ, 187; the fruit of, 212; God as, 204–207; for God, 131, 204, 211, 217, 229, 241–42, 258; of God, 229, 241–42, 253–57; happiness in, 218; the healing of, 157–58; holy, 85, 155; infinite, 231; as the key to Heaven, 237; made flesh in Christ, 196; natural, 127; of neighbor, 91, 128, 131, 136, 137, 160, 162, 178, 187, 217–18, 220–21; self-, 75, 127; and silence, 228; spiritual, 127–28; suffering for the sake of, 75; true, 127–29, 229–30; union of lover and beloved in Christ, 186; united with Truth, 271; and wisdom, 225
Lucifer. See Devil, the
Lust, 214; and Chastity, 91, 251; the flesh (Body) and, 71–74, 94; guarding against, 78; routed by divine love, 238; smothers the soul, 91
Luxury, 99

Magdalene, Mary, 278
Man, condition of, 112; created for eternal life, 209; God and, 140, 152; Jesus Christ became, 70, 71, 140; his likeness to God, 75, 76, 127, 247; made

whole, 146–56; in perfect state, 247–53; wretchedness of, 108–109

Marriage, 154
Martyrs, the, 132
Martha, 180
Mary Magdalene, 278
Mary, sister of Martha, 180
Mary, the Blessed Virgin. See Virgin Mary, the Blessed
Mass, the, 102, 181
Matins, 73
Meekness, 91, 155, 251
Memory, 130, 212, 223
Mercy, defeats Avarice, 91, 251; of Christ, 118; of God, 87; and Justice, 146–56
Messiah, the, 150, 241
Misery, 108
Monaldo, Blessed Brother, 187
Money, 100, 105
Morrone, Pier da, 173
Moses, the Law of, 168
Mother; of Christ, 70–71, 278–80; the Church as, 159, 171; of men, 109–110

Nativity, the, 194–203, 204
Neighbor, love of, 91, 128, 131, 136, 137, 160, 162, 178, 187, 217–18, 220–21
Nonbeing, 186
Nothingness, 211, 271

Obedience, 120, 210
Offense of sin, 87
Office, the Divine, 73, 120
Old Age, 105–108, 113
Order, the (Franciscan), 122, 123, 179, 192, 210
Orders, religious, 166, 169
Ortolana, Donna, 192
Our Father, the, 156–57

Pacifico, Brother, 187
Pain, of Christ on cross, 278–80; eternal, 101; of living, 109–114; man born in, 108, 109; of sin, 119
Palestrina, 174
Papacy, the, 166, 180, 181, 182
Paradise, 91, 108, 131, 221
Paris, 99, 123, 241
Paris, University of, 241
Passion, the, 168
Peace, 135, 155, 270; of Christ, 235; lost because of sin, 80, 93; the secret of, 166; won in battle, 250

293

INDEX

INDEX

103–105; the penitent, 101; redemption of, 69; the Virgin Mary and, 69; the wretchedness of, 118

Sloth, 90–91; born in proud heart, 92; defeated by Justice, 251; possesses the soul, 92–94; the source of all evil, 214

Sodom, 127

Solomon's Portico, 179

Sons, of the Church, 171–72; desire for, 112; ungrateful, 101, 105

Sorrow, 209

Soul, the, 79, 81, 115, 132, 143, 161, 163; and the Body, 71–74; cries for help, 118–20; desires to die with Christ, 240–41; and divine love, 129–31; evil thoughts and, 79; faith and, 131, 158–60; finds God, 239–40; grace transforms, 90–91; infused with will of God, 223; laments absence of God, 203–208; laments for grace, 203–204; laments over intensity of infused charity, 257–65; lost through pride, 102; the mirror of, 137–40; as the Queen of Christ, 260; reborn, 270; renewed by virtue, 261; repose of, 100; rests in God, 220; returns to body for judgment, 94–96; seeks Christ, 144–46; sin kills, 88; sloth and, 92–93; the turmoil of, 135–36; the vice-ridden, 90; the virtuous, 218–20; the wolf and, 124–25; women as destroyers of, 81

Spirit, the Holy. *See* Holy Spirit, the

Spirit, Gifts of the, 150, 155, 169

Stephen, St., 195

Stigmata, the, 188–89

Suffering, 114, 135; of the body through penance, 71–74, 75; the damned flee, 75; enduring, 154, 177, 193–94; eternal, 101; in Hell, 98; mastered by self-hatred, 75, 176; in penance for love's sake, 75; and sin, 69, 75, 88, 101, 119; of Christ, 134, 142–43, 204, 278–80; sweetness of, 212

Syria, 111

Temperance, 132, 133, 155, 262; and gluttony, 91, 252; mastery of body through, 218; the virtue of, 217–18, 219

Temptation, 157

Theologians, 123

Time, 232, 245

Todi, Italy, 177

Todi, Jacopone da. *See* Jacopone da Todi

Tomb, 114–16

Tongue, the, 162, 247

Tranquility, 137, 270

Tribulation, 166–67

Trinity, the, 128, 133, 156, 216, 231

Truth, 99, 186, 246, 267, 270; of Christ, 103; and the Flesh, 79; the mirror of, 137; possessed in soul, 220; and self-annihilation, 272–74; united with love, 271; weeps over the death of Goodness, 167–69

Understanding, 155

Union, in Christ, 186; with God, 219, 259, 266–75; of truth and love, 271

University of Bologna, 242

University of Paris, 241

Uriah, 204

Usury, 103

Vainglory, 214

Valley of Humiliation, the, 144

Vanity, 69, 82–83

Vermilion tree, the, 211

Vice, 90, 215, 251–52

Virgin Mary, the Blessed, 116, 150, 220, 253; and the Apostle John, 280; and the birth of Christ, 196; her conception of Christ, 70, 149; her fortitude, 71; Gabriel's announcement to, 149; her lament over her Son, 278–80, her motherhood of Christ, 70–71; as restorer of our ruined estate, 149; her sinlessness, 70, 148; and sinner, 69, 102

Virginity, 70, 96

Virtue(s), 121, 155, 270, 277; abandons man after the Fall, 146; adorning oneself with, 134; attaining to, 135–37; the four cardinal, 216–18; is made strong in trial, 128; man defeats vices with, 215; offended by counterfeit love, 125–26; renews the soul, 261; the Vices defeated by, 251–52; from virtue to glory, 131–33; as guide, 250

Voluptuousness, 215

Weak, the, 92

Wealth, 100, 109

Wife, 93, 111

Will, the, 229, 270; of God, 156, 223; human, 129, 130, 154, 231–32, 275, 276; of the Spirit, 215